THE ALL NEW *Ball*® BOOK OF
CANNING
AND PRESERVING

THE ALL NEW *Ball*® BOOK OF
CANNING
AND PRESERVING

Over 350 of the Best Canned, Jammed, Pickled, and Preserved Recipes

Oxmoor House®

Editor: Meredith L. Butcher
**Senior Manager, Business Development +
    Partnerships:** Nina Reed
Project Editor: Lacie Pinyan
Senior Designers: Teresa Cole, Maribeth Jones,
    Shay McNamee
Photographers: Iain Bagwell, Caitlin Bensel,
    Hélène Dujardin, Victor Protasio
Prop Stylists: Cindy Barr, Kay E. Clarke,
    Katelyn Hardwick, Mindi Shapiro Levine,
    Lindsey Lower
Food Stylists: Nathan Carrabba, Victoria E. Cox,
    Margaret Monroe Dickey, Catherine Crowell Steele
Recipe Testers: Julia Levy, Callie Nash, Karen Rankin
Assistant Production Manager: Diane Rose Keener
Assistant Production Director: Sue Chodakiewicz
Copy Editors: Donna Baldone, Rebecca Brennan
Indexer: Mary Ann Laurens
Recipe Editor: Julie Christopher
Fellows: Jessica Baude, Dree Deacon,
    Rishon Hanners, Olivia Pierce, Natalie Schumann,
    Mallory Short

Photo Credits: Matt Armendariz (OFFSET):
129; Thomas Barwick (Getty): 8-9; Kimberly
Davis (OFFSET): 115; Chris Gramly (Getty): 21,
210-211; Johner Images (Getty): 6, 248, 270;
Kelli Kroneberger (Getty): 341; Ladid Levy
(OFFSET): 19; Joann Pai (OFFSET): 196-197;
Marketa Pavleye (OFFSET): 22; Scott Payne: 17;
Westend61 (Getty): 279; Jeremy Woodhouse
(Getty): 162

Culinary Marketing Manager: Sarah Green Page
Copy Writer and Recipe Developer: Tamika Adjemian
Recipe Developers: Grady L. Best, Sarah Green Page,
    Michael B. Ruoss, Mariann Sauvion, Dave Watson
Recipe Testers: Cheryl Crowder, Debbie Foster,
    Renee Stine, Brian Toomer
Quality Assurance Engineers: Matt Cheever,
    Brandon Shrock, Hank Vores
Proofreaders: Tamika Adjemian, Judy Harrold

Special Thanks: Marguerite Bolte, Melissa Burns,
    Chris Carlisle, Brian Cunningham, Sara L. Green,
    Steve Hungsberg, Janine Moore, John H. Page,
    Jessica L. Piper, Sony Yadav

ISBN-13: 978-0-8487-4678-0
ISBN-10: 0-8487-4678-3
Library of Congress Control Number: 2015958285

Printed in the United States of America

10 9 8 7 6 5 4 3 2

First Edition 2016

Contents

THE RECIPES IN THIS
BOOK ARE A ROBUST
BALANCE OF CLASSIC
AND NEW, AS WELL
AS HEALTHIER AND
GLOBALLY INSPIRED
OPTIONS, TO INVIGORATE
THE MODERN PALATE

Welcome to the All New Ball® Book of Canning and Preserving!

Who we are as a culture is intimately tied to how we feed ourselves. Our diet and cuisine are a direct reflection of our identity, our values, and our history, both personal and cultural. In turn, how and what we eat also shapes who we are. Although the necessity to preserve our own food is, in most cases, no longer physical, there is still a strong emotional pull to return to traditional foodways and seasonal cuisine.

Whether motivated by a practical need to preserve the bounty of a late summer garden or a simple desire to create something delicious and wholesome from the local farmers' market, preserving our own food puts us in touch with who we are. It fosters a sense of being rooted, self-sufficient, and part of the natural world. It creates lasting connections with family and friends that can endure beyond our lifetime to future generations. We're not only preserving the flavors of a harvest, we're preserving memories, connections, and an ever-changing, shared culinary heritage.

Since 1884, the Ball® name has been recognized as the most reliable authority in home food preservation and is associated with the science, tools, knowledge, and tried, true, and safe recipes that help home cooks preserve and savor the fresh goodness of their kitchen gardens year after year. At the Fresh Preserving Test Kitchen, we take our trusted role very seriously and have developed precise and documentable testing standards for all of our recipes to ensure the safety of each and every one. We've worked closely with the engineers on The Jarden Home Brands Quality Assurance Team in Muncie, Indiana, to ensure every recipe is not only wholesome and delicious but also as safe as possible. We offer guidance to demystify, simplify, enhance knowledge, and increase confidence every step of the way. It's our mission to keep Ball at the center of American tables for generations to come.

In this book, you'll discover more than 350 new and inspired recipes for the modern home preserver, designed to excite the creative spirit as well as the palate. They represent over a year of dedicated research, flavor refinement, and safety testing and are built upon years of technical expertise and garden-to-table recipes.

This work is the result of inspired collaboration between seasoned home canners and chefs and represents a fresh, new focus on flavor—both subtle and bold—on the stovetop as well as inside the jar. Classic techniques for building flavor, such as caramelization and slow roasting, showcase and maximize the goodness of each fresh ingredient.

The recipes in this book are a robust balance of classic and new, as well as healthier and globally inspired options, to invigorate the modern palate. In addition, many low- or no-sugar options are provided, along with a few gut-healthy home fermentations.

As much of the modern pantry is targeted towards convenience, you'll find recipe solutions to address this need in the form of heat-and-eat soups, recipes in a jar, plus marinades and simmer sauces to fit a busy lifestyle.

In the spirit of creating something delicious and enduring, we share these recipes with you and hope they inspire creativity and renewed connections with family, friends, and the planet. These recipes are specially made here—in Indiana—for you. We hope you enjoy them!

Sarah Green Page
Chef and Culinary Marketing Manager
Jarden Home Brands

FOOD IS SO CENTRAL TO OUR HUMAN EXISTENCE THAT WE INSTINCTIVELY LEARNED WAYS TO PRESERVE IT.

For thousands of years, food has been dried, brined, salted, soaked in honey, and fermented in an effort to keep it safe for eating for months at a time. Human cultures developed the skills to raise livestock, cultivate grains, vegetables, and fruits, and then out of necessity, developed techniques to preserve these foods for long-term survival and nourishment, safe from spoilage-causing enzymes, bacteria, yeasts, and molds.

The modern food preservation recipes and techniques in this book marry these practical age-old traditions with up-to-date science to offer safe and delicious ways to enjoy and share your personalized creations for months, whether it be for pleasure or sustenance or both. These techniques include water bath canning, pressure canning, fermenting, freezing, dehydrating, curing, and smoking. The pages that follow will provide you with a brief but necessary grounding in the science of each method and explain the tools and steps to make each experience a success!

The Importance of Acidity in Foods

The most important factor in determining which canning method must be used to safely preserve foods for storage at room temperature is acidity—the pH level of the food (or recipe). The chart on the next page lists common foods and their relative acidity.

HIGH-ACID FOODS AND ACIDIFIED FOODS

Foods having naturally high levels of acid, or those with a sufficient amount of acid added to decrease the pH level to 4.6 or lower, may be processed in a boiling-water canner. Generally, fruits, jams, and jellies are classified as high-acid foods, although some fruits, such as figs, rhubarb, and tomatoes require the addition of extra acid. This will ensure that a safe pH is maintained throughout and after processing.

LOW-ACID FOODS

Foods and recipes having very little natural acid (pH higher than 4.6), such as vegetables, meats, poultry, and seafood, as well as soups, stews, and meat sauces, must be processed in a pressure canner to ensure a high enough temperature is reached to kill any harmful bacterial spores and their toxins. Before one can fully understand how food is safely preserved for pantry storage during the home-canning process, it is helpful to become familiar with how and why food spoils in the first place and how spoilage can be prevented.

MOLDS AND YEAST

Molds are visible and nonvisible fungi that grow in food. Although some mold is relatively harmless, certain molds can produce mycotoxins that are toxic. Yeasts are also a form of fungi that cause fermentation. Both can make for inedible food that may even be harmful to eat. Foods of low pH are largely protected from bacterial growth; however, molds and yeasts are ever-present and, if left untreated, continue to grow. That said, they are easily destroyed when exposed to high temperatures (between 140° and 190°F/60°C and 88°C). Since boiling-water canners heat food to 212°F (100°C), high-acid foods can safely be preserved using this method.

BACTERIA

Bacteria are not easily destroyed by heat; in fact, certain bacteria actually thrive at temperatures that destroy molds and yeasts and will continue to survive in the absence of oxygen within a moist environment—exactly the conditions inside a sealed jar of food. Toxin-producing spores of both the bacterium Clostridium botulinum and staph bacteria must be destroyed by heating food in a sealed jar to 240°F (116°C). This high temperature can only be reached using a pressure canner, since the steam it creates can achieve temperatures hotter than the boiling water in a water bath canner.

INDICATIONS THAT THE FOOD HAS SPOILED INCLUDE:

- Broken seal
- Mold
- Gassiness
- Cloudiness
- Spurting liquid
- Bubbles rising in jar
- Seepage
- Yeast growth
- Fermentation
- Slime
- Disagreeable odor

ENZYMES

Enzymes are proteins that are present in all living things and are the catalysts that promote organic changes and reactions in our bodies and in food. They promote spoilage if not inactivated. Luckily, enzymes are easily inactivated by temperatures starting at 140°F (60°C). Therefore, they are easily inactivated in a boiling-water process.

SIGNS OF SPOILAGE

Do not taste food from a jar that came unsealed or shows signs of spoilage. Examine each jar of food carefully before using it to ensure a vacuum seal is present. Lids that are concave indicate the jar is sealed. Do not use any jar of food that is unsealed, has a bulged lid, or does not require a can opener for the lid to be removed.

Food spoilage produces gases that cause the lids to swell and/or break their seals. Visually examine jars of food for other signs of spoilage that might be present. Jars that are suspected of containing spoiled low-acid or tomato products must be handled carefully. They may exhibit different signs of spoilage or no signs of spoilage. Thus, suspect jars should be treated as having produced botulinum toxin and handled carefully, following these guidelines:

- Place jars of sealed home-canned food showing signs of spoilage in a garbage bag. Secure the bag closed and place it in the regular trash container or dispose of it at a landfill.
- Unsealed, open, or leaking jars of spoiled home-canned food should be detoxified before disposal.

Home-canned food that shows signs of spoilage must be discarded in a manner that no human or animal will come in contact with the product. Contact with botulinum toxin can be fatal whether it is ingested or enters the body through the skin. Avoid contact with suspect food.

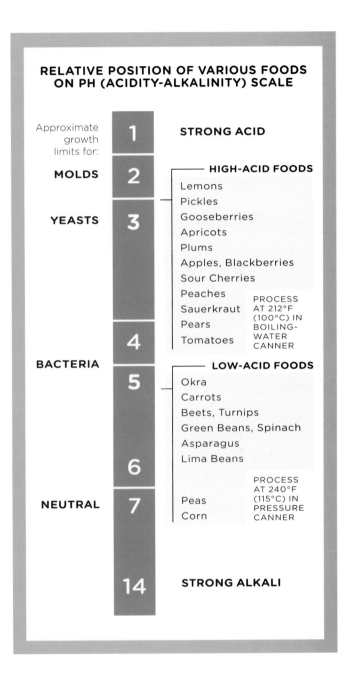

RELATIVE POSITION OF VARIOUS FOODS ON PH (ACIDITY-ALKALINITY) SCALE

Approximate growth limits for:

1 STRONG ACID

MOLDS

2 — HIGH-ACID FOODS

Lemons
Pickles

YEASTS

3 Gooseberries
Apricots
Plums
Apples, Blackberries
Sour Cherries
Peaches — PROCESS AT 212°F (100°C) IN BOILING-WATER CANNER
Sauerkraut
Pears

4 Tomatoes

BACTERIA — LOW-ACID FOODS

5 Okra
Carrots
Beets, Turnips
Green Beans, Spinach
Asparagus
Lima Beans

6

PROCESS AT 240°F (115°C) IN PRESSURE CANNER

NEUTRAL **7** Peas
Corn

14 STRONG ALKALI

Basic Gear

1. Rack to hold jars off bottom of the pot

2. Jar lifter to maneuver jars in and out of the pot. Be sure to hold lifter by its black handle

3. Jar funnel to keep jar rims clean

4. Kitchen timer to time the boil

5. Nonreactive saucepan, enameled or stainless steel-clad metal, but not aluminum

6. Labels for processed jars

7. Liquid and **dry measuring cups** and **measuring spoons**

8. Utensils, wood or stainless steel spoon, ladle, and slotted spoon/skimmer to avoid chemical reactions with brines and other acidic mixtures that can cause a metallic taste

9. Canning lids, the flat metal discs with the rubber ring, and **jars** specifically designed for canning, free of chips, bubbles, or cracks

10. Bands, the screw-top rings that secure the lids until they are sealed

11. Bubble Remover & Headspace Measuring Tool to remove air bubbles and measure proper headspace

12. Clean towels on which to rest the hot jars, and **paper towels** to wipe rims

13. Sure Tight Band Tool to ensure that the band is tightened properly

Choose the Right Jar

		IDEAL FOR	FREEZER SAFE
REGULAR MOUTH	Jelly Jars (4 oz)	Jams, jellies, mustards, ketchups, dipping sauces, flavored vinegars, and small portion sizes	❄
	Jelly Jars (8 oz)	Jams, jellies, conserves, and preserves	❄
	Jelly Jars (12 oz)	Jams, jellies, conserves, and marmalades	❄
	Half Pint (8 oz)	Fruit syrups, chutneys, and pizza sauces	❄
	Pint (16 oz)	Salsas, sauces, relishes, and pie fillings	
	Quart (32 oz)	Sliced fruits and vegetables, pickles, tomato-based juices, and sauces	

		IDEAL FOR	
WIDE MOUTH	Pint (16 oz)	Salsas, sauces, relishes, and fruit butters	❄
	Pint & Half (24 oz)	Asparagus, pickles, sauces, soups, and stews	❄
	Quart (32 oz)	Pickles, tomatoes, and whole or halved fruits and vegetables	
	Half Gallon (64 oz)	Apple and grape juices	

NOTE: When filling freezer-safe jars, leave / -inch headspace to allow for food expansion during freezing.

JAR SIZE

Choose from over six jar sizes. Some jars have shoulders while others have straight sides that work best for freezing. Your recipe will guide you on the recommended jar sizes. See the chart above for some suggestions to get you started.

MOUTH SIZE

The diameter of the jar opening determines the mouth size. Choose from either regular or Wide Mouth sizes. All jelly jars have a regular mouth.

- **Regular mouth** works best with pourable foods, such as jams, jellies, salsas, sauces, and pie fillings, or chopped fruits and vegetables.
- **Wide Mouth** works best with whole fruits and vegetables or when you need a large mouth for filling.

Know Your Altitude

BOILING-WATER METHOD

The processing times given in this book for high-acid foods are based on canning at or below 1,000 feet above sea level using the boiling-water method. When processing at altitudes higher than 1,000 feet above sea level, adjust the processing time according to this boiling-water canner chart.

BOILING-WATER CANNER ALTITUDE ADJUSTMENTS

ALTITUDE IN FEET	INCREASE PROCESSING TIME
1,001 to 3,000	5 minutes
3,001 to 6,000	10 minutes
6,001 to 8,000	15 minutes
8,001 to 10,000	20 minutes

PRESSURE METHOD

The pressure method is used for low-acid foods. There are two types of pressure canners currently available, weighted gauge and dial gauge. Refer to your canner's user manual for specifics. When processing at altitudes higher than 1,000 feet above sea level, adjust pounds pressure according to this pressure canner chart.

PRESSURE CANNER ALTITUDE ADJUSTMENTS

ALTITUDE IN FEET	WEIGHTED GAUGE	DIAL GAUGE
0 to 1,000	10	11
1,001 to 2,000	15	11
2,001 to 4,000	15	12
4,001 to 6,000	15	13
6,001 to 8,000	15	14
8,001 to 10,000	15	15

Barometric pressure is reduced at high altitudes, affecting the temperature at which water boils. This means boiling-water and pressure processing methods must be adjusted to ensure the safety of home-canned food. Additional processing time must be added when using the boiling-water method. Increased temperature is required when using the pressure method. The altitude charts above give adjustments for both methods at various elevations.

Processing times and temperatures for recipes in this book are based on canning at an elevation of 1,000 feet above sea level or lower. If you are processing at a higher elevation, refer to the altitude chart for adjustments.

Contact your Natural Resources Conservation Service, Cooperative Extension Service, or Public Library Service for the altitude in your area.

Canning and Preserving 101

WATER BATH CANNING

Water bath canning is a preservation method used only for high-acid or acidulated foods, fruits to pickles, that creates an anaerobic environment in a vacuum-sealed jar. This high-acid environment is inhospitable to molds, yeasts, bacteria, and enzymes (the spoilers).

HERE'S HOW IT WORKS

A packed and loosely sealed jar is placed in a bath of boiling water long enough to bring the food inside to 212°F (100°C). The heat expands the food, pushing out all the air. When the jar is removed from the water bath, it begins to cool and contract, which forms the vacuum seal (and the famous "pinging" sound Ball canning lids make). This newly created sealed environment keeps all microorganisms out while killing off any remaining in the food. The acid level of the food is an important consideration here. As the chart on page 11 shows, fruits are naturally high in acid, while vegetables are not. Mixing high-acid foods with low-acid foods in a recipe still requires acidulation. As with salsas and chutneys, the low-acid foods can raise the pH level and cause dangerous conditions once canned, which is why it's necessary to follow thoroughly tested recipes.

FRUIT-BASED JAMS, JELLIES, AND PRESERVES

These are generally high enough in acid to safely water bath can (with the exception of tomatoes, melons, papaya, and figs, which require additional acid). Sugar has preserving properties as it replaces some of the water in the fruit, but the amount used in canning is just enough to help delay spoiling by microorganisms and enzymes once jars are opened. Low-sugar/no-sugar fruit jams and jellies preserve just as safely but need to be consumed quickly once opened.

MARMALADE

The addition of pieces of fruit and cooked-down peel is what differentiates marmalades from jellies and jams. Citrus fruits have great quantities of natural pectin that is contained in the albedo, or pith, part of the peel (the white flesh between the peel and the fruit itself). This is also the source of the bitter flavor in citrus. When making marmalade, the traditional long method of soaking, then cooking the citrus, as with British-style marmalade, mellows the bitter taste of the pith. **Long-method (Traditional)** marmalades usually require a 2- to 3-day process during which time the fruit sections are boiled, then soaked and left to drain before being mixed together and cooked down with sugars. **Quick-cook** marmalades call for peels, separated from the pith; juiced or segmented fruits; and added pectin to quickly bind the juices and fruits together.

PECTIN

Pectin is a natural substance found in fruits, vegetables, and plants that is responsible for cell structure. It is also one of the four key ingredients allowing for thickening in jams, jellies, preserves, and marmalades, along with fruit, acid, and sugar. A balance of all four of these ingredients is necessary to achieve a successful set (or gel). Commercial pectin, such as Ball® RealFruit™Classic Pectin, Ball® RealFruit® Low or No-Sugar Needed Pectin, Ball® RealFruit® Instant Pectin, and Ball® RealFruit® Liquid Pectin, is extracted from apples and citrus fruits, as both have very naturally high levels of pectin. The recipes give complete instructions for the type of pectin to be used, as well as the correct balance of acid, fruit, and sugar needed to achieve a satisfactory set. Each type of pectin has unique attributes and therefore are not interchangeable.

TESTING THE SET OR GEL

Jams, jellies, and marmalades are all about the gelling action. Getting your preserves to "set" when using added pectin is easy, but achieving the perfect gel point when making traditional no-pectin-added preserves can be a challenge. Follow these easy tests designed to let you know when your spread is perfect. Remove your preserve pot from the burner while testing. If you find your preserve isn't ready, replace your pot to high heat and boil only for a few minutes more before retesting.

TEMPERATURE TEST

The temperature test is used for jam, jelly, and marmalade. Set a candy thermometer on the edge of your jam pot making sure it does not touch the sides or bottom. Once the preserve is at a rolling boil start monitoring the temperature. Gel is achieved once thermometer reads 220°F (104°C) (at 1,000 feet) or 8°F above boiling point for your elevation.

FROZEN PLATE OR SPOON TEST

The frozen plate or spoon test is used for jams and marmalades: Place several small plates or several spoons in the freezer. As your preserve begins to boil down and thicken take a plate or spoon out, use your jam stirring spoon to scoop a small amount onto the frozen plate. Return plate to freezer for a few minutes. The jam is set if it wrinkles when pushed with your finger and does not have a pool of syrup around it.

SPOON TEST

The sheet test or "sheeting" is used primarily for jelly and marmalades along with the temperature test: Dip a large metal spoon into the boiling jelly, lift it out, and hold it horizontally over the pot letting the jelly slide off. When drops come together along the edge of the spoon forming a thick sheet, the preserve is ready. If the drops are light and syrupy, it's not ready. Continue to boil for a few minutes more and retest.

You'll also find recipes in this book that do not contain added pectin. These recipes feature traditional long-cook methods. To know when your long-cook recipe is done, refer to the chart entitled Testing the Set or Gel, and use one of the tried-and-true methods outlined. As a general rule, the riper the fruit the less natural occurring pectin.

PICKLES

Pickling is so much more than just cucumbers in a salty vinegar brine. It's the process of preserving vegetables and fruits in vinegar or with salt by fermentation (which we discuss later). Both vinegar and salt have preserving qualities: Salt draws out water from produce, helping it stay crunchy, while vinegar adds the acid needed to help keep preserved vegetables safe to eat. Together with herbs and spices, vinegar and salt create that distinctly tangy "pickled" flavor that can be sweet, spicy, or full of garlic and dill.

When pickling, for best results use only granulated salt with no additives, such as Ball® Salt for Pickling and Preserving. Different vinegars offer unique flavoring options; just be sure the one you're using has 5% acidity. Anything less than 5% acidity can cause the pH of your pickle to be thrown out of balance, making the pickle potentially unsafe. Pickle brine contains water. Avoid using hard water since it has minerals that can have an adverse effect on your final pickle. Instead, use soft, spring, or distilled water. A great way to ensure extra crispiness when making fresh-pack pickles is to use a crisping agent, such as Ball® Pickle Crisp™ (calcium chloride, a naturally occurring salt found in some mineral deposits).

In this book, we include recipes for fresh and refrigerator pickles, relishes, and chutneys. Fresh and refrigerator pickles are fresh-packed, meaning the produce is put into jars either raw or quickly heated, usually along with the spices, then a hot vinegar brine is poured over the pickles, which then can be either preserved in a water bath canner for shelf storage in the pantry, or put in the refrigerator for convenient quick eating. Relish is basically a pickle with ingredients that have been diced or chopped. It's usually cooked in its brine, which will be thick, before ladling into jars. Chutney refers to a type of relish that usually contains a combination of fruit, vinegar, sugar, and spices, originating from South Asia.

As a general rule, keep freshly harvested vegetables very cold and use them within 24 hours.

TOMATOES

Tomatoes are the eagerly awaited and glorious fruit we use as a vegetable. They are in the danger range on the pH scale, as some varieties are sweet and contain less acid. Some, notably heirloom, tomatoes are 4.6 pH or higher, and as they ripen their pH level rises even higher, which makes it necessary to add acid during canning to ensure a safe pH is maintained. Citric acid, lemon or lime juice, and vinegar have low pH and bring different flavors to tomato recipes. A pinch of sugar can offset the tartness.

Despite the acidity level of the tomatoes used, some recipes featuring other low-acid ingredients may still need to be processed in a pressure canner.

Canning tomatoes whole, halved, or quartered can be done by either of two methods: raw pack or hot pack. Raw pack refers to raw, peeled tomatoes packed into jars, then topped off with hot water. With the hot-pack method, the tomatoes are heated through then packed into jars and topped off with the hot cooking liquid. Citric acid or lemon juice is always added, along with desired dry seasonings. The recipes in this book give you the option to use either Ball® Citric Acid or lemon juice to ensure a safe pH.

Finally, our exciting new collection of tomato-based salsas are loaded with fresh vegetables like onions and chiles and have plenty of added acid, making them safe for water bath preservation.

TO GUARANTEE THE MOST
DELICIOUS PRESERVED
FOODS, ALWAYS BEGIN
WITH THE BEST-QUALITY
PRODUCE AT ITS PEAK OF
RIPENESS.

PRESSURE CANNING

Pressure canning is the preservation method necessary for safely preserving low-acid foods, such as nonpickled vegetables, meats, seafood, and recipes containing a combination of low- and high-acid foods, like soups, stews, and meat sauces. Because these foods have a cumulative pH higher than 4.6, they must be processed at a temperature of 240°F (116°C) to destroy all bacteria, spores, and the toxins they produce. This high temperature can be achieved only in a pressurized environment, such as in a pressure canner. Like water bath canning, it creates an anaerobic environment in a vacuum-sealed jar. The difference between pressure canning and water bath canning is the method and temperature in which the jars are heated.

HERE'S HOW IT WORKS

Pressure canners create a pressurized vacuum inside the pot. By adding a few inches of water, securing the lid, and bringing the water to a boil, steam is released through a steam-vent pipe which is then capped with a pressure regulator or a weighted gauge, creating pressure and intense 240°F (116°C) heat (at 1,000 feet elevation). This must be maintained throughout the entire processing time. This crucial combination of temperature and time kills all potential food spoilers—bacteria and their spores and toxins—creating a safe, shelf-stable, preserved food. (See our how-to steps for pressure canning on page 272.)

Recipes designed for pressure canning are very specific in quantities of low-acid ingredients, liquids, seasonings, and pre-canning preparation. Our recipes have been thoroughly heat tested during processing to ensure that all food safely reaches proper temperatures for the correct time period. For safe and successful results, always follow the recipes and guidelines exactly.

Similar to tomatoes, pressure-canned foods are made by one of two methods: raw pack or hot pack, which describes the state of the ingredients going into the jar. Both types of recipes are included here.

FERMENTATION

Fermenting vegetables and fruits, also known as lacto-fermentation, is the craft of preserving by methods that attract naturally occurring good bacteria. These probiotics transform the foods' sugars into lactic acid that creates the delicious, tangy ferments we love and plays a powerful role in keeping the food safe from harmful toxins and other food spoilers. There are three techniques used for fermenting vegetables and fruits: dry salted (sauerkraut method), brined, and kimchi style, which utilizes both methods. All methods draw moisture out of the vegetables and fruits, creating brine in which the foods will then safely ferment. It's this brine that attracts the good bacterias and produces the acids that create an anaerobic environment that is key to safe and healthy fermented foods. An important rule to remember in fermenting is to keep the food at least one inch beneath the brine at all times.

Salt: The balance of salt to vegetable or fruit matter is important. If there is too little salt, the good bacteria won't develop; with too much salt, food may ferment too quickly, creating a mushy ferment (a common occurrence in brined pickles). Basic guidelines are 2% to 5% salt to vegetables/fruits; the lower end (2%) for softer fruits and vegetables and the higher end (5%) for harder vegetables such as cucumbers. The basic safety range for everything is 3.5%. Use only additive-free pickling or sea salts.

Temperature and location: Vegetables and fruits ferment best at temperatures between 65° to 75°F (18° to 24°C). With colder temperatures, foods take longer to ferment or may not ferment at all. With warmer temperatures, fermentation will speed up, causing yeast and molds to ruin the food. Store your ferments in a dark, undisturbed place such as a kitchen cabinet or pantry.

Signs of health: There are different stages of smell—from mild and sweet to pungent and sour—all depending on what you're fermenting. This smell, along with visual clues, will let you know where you are in the fermenting process.

Foods kept at proper temperatures and well beneath their brine will still attract naturally occurring yeasts. The most common is Kahm yeast, a white film which is completely safe and can be scraped off from time to time. Exposure to air may also cause mold growth. Small amounts of mold growth along the rim of your jar are normal and can be cleaned off as soon as you see it. If your ferment is not weighted beneath the brine, it will attract other yeasts and molds that are not safe for consumption. In this case, visual clues and a rotting smell will let you know to start over.

Taste is the final step in checking for a healthy ferment. If the food has been safely beneath the brine and looks and smells good, go ahead and taste it. Everyone's preferences are different. Some like sauerkraut and kimchi fresh with a short ferment, others prefer very pungent, long ferments. Ultimately, taste dictates how long you let the process go. Sauerkraut can be ready in as little as two weeks, while kimchi can be ready in just a few days. Brined pickles are best depending on how you like them, whether it's half sour at four days or full sour at 10, for example. Once you are happy with the taste, seal your jar with a lid and store it in the refrigerator. The fermenting process will continue but at a very slow rate.

FREEZING

Freezing is one of the simplest and most convenient ways to preserve both raw and freshly prepared foods. Freezing works on the principle that microorganism growth is delayed by extreme cold. While 32°F (0°C) and below is considered freezing, food is best frozen at 0°F (-18°C) or colder to ensure bacteria, yeasts, and molds are halted in their tracks. Once food is thawed, some of these natural food spoilers and enzymes will reactivate. That's why it's important to prepare foods properly for freezing and use correct freezer-safe packaging, which limits the decaying action. Freezer burn, ice crystal formation, and oxidation (discoloring) are signs of improperly frozen foods or foods not maintained at 0°F (-18°C) or below.

DEHYDRATION

Dehydration is an ancient preservation method that uses dry air to remove all the moisture from food. It also offers the added benefit of concentrating flavors. Since microorganisms need water to survive, this process halts their growth and essentially kills them. In some locations, people can rely on hot, dry sun to dehydrate food. Fortunately for the rest of us, we can use dehydrators.

HERE'S HOW IT WORKS

Food is prepared and placed on trays that are placed into the dehydrator. Some recipes, such as fruit leather, may require flexible sheets that are sold specifically for dehydrator use. A fan circulates warm air, set at a specific temperature, throughout the dehydrator. Occasionally, it may be necessary to rotate the trays to ensure even drying of all the food. Each dehydrator is different, so follow your unit's instruction manual.

CURING AND SMOKING

The unmistakable allure of salt-cured and smoked meats has kept this primitive and ancient preserving method a part of every cultural heritage in the world. Curing (and brining) preserves by using salt to draw out moisture; in the case of meats and seafood, however, it must be combined with another preservation method to make the proteins safe to eat. The techniques we use here—salt brining, curing, and hot smoking—offer robust flavors and some modicum of preservation, so these foods must be refrigerated or frozen to store.

Home curing of meats that will not be heat treated (as with our Pancetta, page 356) requires a curing salt with nitrites in it to prevent harmful toxins and bacteria from taking hold. Environmental elements are difficult to control during home curing; for example, a spike in temperature could spoil meats quickly by allowing molds and yeasts to spread. It's quite common for curing salts, known as "pink salt," to be used with heat-smoked meats as an added measure of safety during the curing and drying process, as temperatures and conditions fluctuate. Curing salts are dangerous in large quantities, therefore the salt is dyed pink so it isn't confused with regular salt in your kitchen. You can purchase pink curing salts (known by various commercial names) online or try a local butcher who cures his own meats.

When smoking meats, heat the smoker according to the manufacturer's directions and use a good-quality smoking wood. Try applewood, cherrywood, oak, cedar, or other aromatic wood chips to impart a subtle flavor. Soak wood chips in a bowl of water at least 20 minutes before placing on hot coals or starter wood. Most meats must reach 145°F (63°C) internal temperature before they can be considered safely smoked. Depending on the size and cut of meat, and whether there are bones in or not, this may take anywhere from 2 to 6 hours. Always let meat cool before wrapping and storing.

Chapter 1

WATER BATH CANNING

When a profusion of newly picked fruits and vegetables are offered up by local farms, farmers' markets, and home gardens, it's the prime time to stock your pantry with an appetizing array of goodness. Water bath canning, the most popular method of preserving for generations, offers the sheer joy and satisfaction of transforming a bounty of seasonal produce into delectable creations with a multitude of uses. From simple berry jams to more complex pickles, chutneys, and tomato-based sauces, or long-method marmalade to low-sugar preserves, a true culinary experience awaits.

STEP-BY-STEP FRESH PRESERVING OF HIGH-ACID FOODS THROUGH WATER BATH CANNING

Getting started: Visually examine jars for defects. Fill a large saucepan or stockpot halfway with water. Place jars in water to warm. (Filling jars with water from the saucepan will prevent flotation.) Bring almost to a simmer over medium heat. Keeping jars hot until ready for use is important as it will prevent jar breakage due to an abrupt change in temperature (also known as thermal shock). You may also use a dishwasher to wash and heat jars. Wash lids in warm soapy water and set aside. Leave bands at room temperature for easy handling.

YOU WILL NEED:

- Tested preserving recipe

- Fresh produce and other quality ingredients

- Boiling-water canner or a large, deep stockpot with a lid, and a rack (when preserving high-acid foods such as soft spreads like jams and jellies, fruit juice, fruits, pickles, and salsas

- Glass preserving jars with lids and bands (always start with new lids)

- Common kitchen utensils, such as a wooden spoon, ladle, kitchen towel, and rubber spatula

- Jar Lifter

- Bubble Remover & Headspace Measuring Tool

STEP 1: Fill hot jars one at a time with hot prepared food using a jar funnel.

STEP 2: Measure headspace of jar with designated Ball Bubble Remover & Headspace Measuring Tool, leaving ¼ inch for soft spreads, such as jams, jellies, and syrups, and ½ inch for fruits, pickles, salsas, sauces, and tomatoes.

STEP 3: Remove air bubbles if necessary by sliding a bubble remover or rubber spatula between the jar and food to release trapped air and ensure proper headspace during processing. Repeat around jar 2 or 3 times.

STEP 4: Clean rim and threads of jar using a clean, damp cloth or paper towel to remove any food residue.

STEP 5: Adjust lid on jar allowing sealing compound to come in contact with the jar rim. Apply band and adjust until fit is fingertip-tight.

STEP 6: Place filled jar in canner. Repeat until all jars are used or canner is full. Lower rack with jars into water. Make sure water covers jars by 1 to 2 inches.

STEP 7: Place lid on canner and bring water to a full rolling boil. Begin timing and maintain a rolling boil throughout the entire processing period. Turn off heat and remove lid. Let canner cool 5 minutes before removing jars.

STEP 8: Remove jars from canner to cool and set upright on a towel to prevent jar breakage that can occur from temperature differences (thermal shock). Leave jars undisturbed for 12 to 24 hours. Bands should not be retightened as this may interfere with the sealing process.

STEP 9: Check lids for seals after stand time. Lids should not flex up and down when center is pressed. Remove bands. Try to lift lids off with your fingertips. If the lid cannot be lifted off, the lid has a good seal.

STEP 10: Remove bands and wash jars and lids using a clean, damp cloth to remove residue that may have siphoned from the jar during processing. Add labels, and store in a cool, dry, dark place up to 1 year.

Jam in 5 Easy Steps

Refer to water bath canning procedures on pages 26-27
and follow recipe guidelines in steps and chart below.

Makes 4 (½-pt./250-mL) jars

STEP 1: Prepare 2⅔ cups (650 mL) chosen fruit according to Fruit Preparation for Jams chart below.

STEP 2: Combine prepared fruit and 3 Tbsp. (45 mL) Ball® Classic Pectin in large saucepan. Bring mixture to a rolling boil that cannot be stirred down, over high heat, stirring constantly.

STEP 3: Add 3⅓ cups (835 mL) sugar*, stirring to dissolve. Return to a full rolling boil. Boil hard 1 minute, stirring constantly. Remove from heat. Skim foam.

STEP 4: Ladle hot jam into a hot jar, leaving ¼-inch (.5-cm) headspace. Place jar in boiling-water canner. Repeat until all jars are filled.

STEP 5: Process jars 10 minutes, adjusting for altitude.

Fruit Preparation for Jams

FRUIT	PREPARATION
Apples	Peel, core, and chop.
Apricots	Pit and finely chop.
Berries	Wash; crush 1 layer at a time with a potato masher.
Blueberries	Wash; crush 1 layer at a time with a potato masher. Stir in 2 Tbsp. (30 mL) lemon juice.
Cherries Dark Sweet	Remove stems; pit and chop. Stir in 2 Tbsp. (30 mL) lemon juice.
Cherries Tart Red	Remove stems; pit and chop.
Peaches	Peel, halve, and pit; finely chop. Stir in 2 Tbsp. (30 mL) lemon juice.
Pears	Peel, core, and finely chop. Stir in 2 Tbsp. (30 mL) lemon juice.
Plums	Pit and finely chop.

*For a lower-sugar version, reduce sugar to 2 cups (500 mL). Set will not be as firm.

STRAWBERRY-RHUBARB JAM

MAKES ABOUT 6 (½-PT./250-ML) JARS

Did you know rhubarb is actually a vegetable? It is a perennial plant similar to celery but is cooked as if it were a fruit.

4½ cups (1.1 L) ¼-inch (.5-cm)-thick sliced fresh rhubarb

½ cup (125 mL) fresh orange juice (about 2 to 3 large oranges)

4 cups (1 L) ripe fresh strawberries

5 cups (1.25 L) sugar

1 (3-oz./88.5-mL) pouch Ball® Liquid Pectin

★

Peak of Freshness

Choose rhubarb stalks that are ½ to 1 inch in diameter when they are the most tender. If picking your own, make sure to cut off all portions of the leaves because they are poisonous.

---

1. Combine rhubarb and orange juice in a 3-qt. (3-L) stainless steel saucepan. Cover and bring to a boil over medium-high heat. Uncover, reduce heat, and simmer, stirring often, 5 minutes or until rhubarb is tender.

2. Wash strawberries; remove and discard stems and hulls. Mash strawberries with a potato masher until evenly crushed.

3. Measure 2 cups (500 mL) cooked rhubarb and 1¾ cups (425 mL) mashed strawberries into a 6-qt. (6-L) stainless steel or enameled Dutch oven. Stir in sugar. Bring mixture to a full rolling boil that cannot be stirred down, over high heat, stirring frequently.

4. Add pectin, immediately squeezing entire contents from pouch. Continue hard boil for 1 minute, stirring constantly. Remove from heat. Skim foam, if necessary.

5. Ladle hot jam into a hot jar, leaving ¼-inch (.5-cm) headspace. Remove air bubbles. Wipe jar rim. Center lid on jar. Apply band, and adjust to fingertip-tight. Place jar in boiling-water canner. Repeat until all jars are filled.

6. Process jars 10 minutes, adjusting for altitude. Turn off heat; remove lid, and let jars stand 5 minutes. Remove jars and cool.

NECTARINE-AND-SOUR CHERRY JAM

MAKES ABOUT 7 (½-PT./250-ML) JARS

Sour cherries are harvested in July, just in time for nectarine season to begin! The tart acidic flavor of the cherries is terrific with this sweet stone fruit.

- 1½ lb. (750 g) nectarines, pitted and finely chopped
- 2 cups (500 mL) chopped pitted tart cherries*
- 6 Tbsp. (90 mL) Ball® Classic Pectin
- 2 Tbsp. (30 mL) bottled lemon juice
- 6 cups (1.5 L) sugar

--------- ★ ---------

Peak of Freshness

Choose firm, ripe, unblemished fruits and keep them at a cool room temperature before canning.

1. Combine first 4 ingredients in a 4-qt. (4-L) stainless steel or enameled Dutch oven. Bring mixture to a full rolling boil that cannot be stirred down, over high heat, stirring constantly.

2. Add sugar, stirring to dissolve. Return mixture to a full rolling boil. Boil hard 1 minute, stirring constantly. Remove from heat. Skim foam, if necessary.

3. Ladle hot jam into a hot jar, leaving ¼-inch (.5-cm) headspace. Remove air bubbles. Wipe jar rim. Center lid on jar. Apply band, and adjust to fingertip-tight. Place jar in boiling-water canner. Repeat until all jars are filled.

4. Process jars 10 minutes, adjusting for altitude. Turn off heat; remove lid, and let jars stand 5 minutes. Remove jars and cool.

*Blackberries, raspberries, blueberries, or chopped strawberries may be substituted.

LOW-SUGAR STRAWBERRY-TEQUILA AGAVE JAM

MAKES ABOUT 4 (½-PT./250 ML) JARS

Agave syrup is a low-glycemic sweetener derived from the agave plant, the same plant tequila is made from, so they naturally go together in this lightly sweetened strawberry jam.

5 cups (1.25 L) chopped fresh strawberries

½ cup (125 mL) tequila

5 Tbsp. (75 mL) Ball® Low or No-Sugar Pectin

1 cup (250 mL) agave syrup

★

Peak of Freshness
Look for strawberries that are dark red and juicy ripe. Since this jam is cooked quickly with added pectin and low sugar, ripe berries will release the most flavor.

1. Combine first 2 ingredients in a 4-qt. (4-L) stainless steel or enameled Dutch oven. Crush berries with a potato masher.

2. Stir in pectin. Bring mixture to a full rolling boil that cannot be stirred down, over high heat, stirring constantly.

3. Stir in agave syrup. Return mixture to a full rolling boil. Boil hard 1 minute, stirring constantly. Remove from heat. Skim foam, if necessary.

4. Ladle hot jam into a hot jar, leaving ¼-inch (.5-cm) headspace. Remove air bubbles. Wipe jar rim. Center lid on jar. Apply band, and adjust to fingertip-tight. Place jar in boiling-water canner. Repeat until all jars are filled.

5. Process jars 10 minutes, adjusting for altitude. Turn off heat; remove lid, and let jars stand 5 minutes. Remove jars and cool.

CHOCOLATE-CHERRY JAM

MAKES ABOUT 6 (½-PT./250-ML) JARS

Cherries and chocolate are a decadent pairing in this luscious jam that will have you eating it off the spoon. Top ice cream or cheesecake, or stir into morning yogurt for a real treat!

6 cups (1.5 L) fresh or frozen pitted dark, sweet cherries, coarsely chopped

6 Tbsp. (90 mL) Ball® Classic Pectin

¼ cup (60 mL) bottled lemon juice

6 cups (1.5 L) sugar

⅔ cup (150 mL) unsweetened cocoa

★

Tricks of the Trade
Look for high-quality cocoa that is between 22% and 24% milk fat.

1. Combine first 3 ingredients in a 4-qt. (4-L) stainless steel or enameled Dutch oven. Bring mixture to a full rolling boil that cannot be stirred down, over high heat, stirring constantly.

2. Meanwhile, stir together sugar and cocoa until blended; add all at once to boiling cherry mixture. Return mixture to a full rolling boil. Boil hard 1 minute, stirring constantly. Remove from heat. Skim foam, if necessary.

3. Ladle hot jam into a hot jar, leaving ¼-inch (.5-cm) headspace. Remove air bubbles. Wipe jar rim. Center lid on jar. Apply band, and adjust to fingertip-tight. Place jar in boiling-water canner. Repeat until all jars are filled.

4. Process jars 10 minutes, adjusting for altitude. Turn off heat; remove lid, and let jars stand 5 minutes. Remove jars and cool.

ORANGE-BANANA JAM

MAKES ABOUT 5 (¹/₂-PT./250-ML) JARS

Very ripe bananas contain natural pectin that dissolves in water to thicken this jam.

- 2 cups (500 mL) fresh orange juice with pulp (about 8 oranges)
- 1 cup (250 mL) honey
- 3 Tbsp. (45 mL) bottled lemon juice
- 2 lb. (1 kg) very ripe bananas, peeled and chopped
- 1 vanilla bean, split

--- ★ ---

Tricks of the Trade

Use fresh bananas and cut them into chunks directly into the orange juice in the jam pot. The acid will keep them from browning until you're ready to cook.

1. Combine first 4 ingredients in a 4-qt. (4-L) stainless steel or enameled Dutch oven. Scrape seeds from vanilla bean; add to banana mixture. Cook, stirring often, over medium heat for about 25 minutes to gelling point (page 17).

2. Ladle hot jam into a hot jar, leaving ¼-inch (.5-cm) headspace. Remove air bubbles. Wipe jar rim. Center lid on jar. Apply band, and adjust to fingertip-tight. Place jar in boiling-water canner. Repeat until all jars are filled.

3. Process jars 15 minutes, adjusting for altitude. Turn off heat; remove lid, and let jars stand 5 minutes. Remove jars and cool.

NOTE: Because the sweetener in this jam is reduced, it will be softer when ready to process than jams with higher sugar content. However, it becomes more firm after processing.

APRICOT-LAVENDER JAM

MAKES ABOUT 6 (¹/₂-PT./250-ML) JARS

Since the Middle Ages, people have used lavender to infuse flavor. Lavender adds an aromatic and floral note to this apricot jam.

4 tsp. (20 mL) dried lavender buds

Cheesecloth

Kitchen string

3 lb. (1.5 kg) apricots, pitted and chopped (about 6 cups/1.5 L)

4 cups (1 L) sugar

3 Tbsp. (45 mL) bottled lemon juice

★

Tricks of the Trade

Make lavender sugar before making jam! In a quart jar place 6 lavender flower buds and fill with sugar; place the lid on and let it infuse. Remove lavender buds before using. May be used in place of loose lavender in this jam, or use it to sweeten iced tea and lemonade.

1. Place lavender buds on a 4-inch (10-cm) square of cheesecloth; tie with kitchen string.

2. Place apricots in a large bowl; mash with a potato masher until crushed. Stir in sugar and lemon juice; add cheesecloth bag, stirring until moistened. Cover and chill 4 hours or overnight.

3. Pour apricot mixture into a 6-qt. (6-L) stainless steel or enameled Dutch oven. Bring to a boil over medium heat, stirring until sugar dissolves. Increase heat to medium-high. Cook, stirring constantly, 45 minutes or until mixture is thickened and a candy thermometer registers 220°F (104°C). Remove from heat. Remove and discard cheesecloth bag.

4. Ladle hot jam into a hot jar, leaving ¼-inch (.5-cm) headspace. Remove air bubbles. Wipe jar rim. Center lid on jar. Apply band, and adjust to fingertip-tight. Place jar in boiling-water canner. Repeat until all jars are filled.

5. Process jars 10 minutes, adjusting for altitude. Turn off heat; remove lid, and let jars stand 5 minutes. Remove jars and cool.

FIG-AND-PEAR JAM

MAKES ABOUT 4 (½-PT./250-ML) JARS

This unique combination creates a rich and sweet fall-inspired jam.

- 2 cups (500 mL) chopped pears
- 2 cups (500 mL) chopped fresh figs
- 4 Tbsp. (60 mL) Ball® Classic Pectin
- 2 Tbsp. (30 mL) bottled lemon juice
- 1 Tbsp. (15 mL) water
- 3 cups (750 mL) sugar

————— ★ —————

Perfect Pairing
Serve on crostini with a nice hard cheese, such as Manchego, and fresh thyme leaves.

1. Combine all ingredients, except sugar, in a 4-qt. (4-L) stainless steel or enameled Dutch oven. Bring mixture to a full rolling boil that cannot be stirred down, over high heat, stirring constantly.

2. Add sugar, stirring to dissolve. Return mixture to a full rolling boil. Boil hard 1 minute, stirring constantly. Remove from heat. Skim foam, if necessary.

3. Ladle hot jam into a hot jar, leaving ¼-inch (.5-cm) headspace. Wipe jar rim. Center lid on jar. Apply band, and adjust to fingertip-tight. Place jar in boiling-water canner. Repeat until all jars are filled.

4. Process jars 10 minutes, adjusting for altitude. Turn off heat; remove lid, and let jars stand 5 minutes. Remove jars and cool.

FIG, ROSEMARY, AND RED WINE JAM

MAKES ABOUT 4 (½-PT./250-ML) JARS

Red wine, rosemary, and figs meld into this jam reminiscent of the South of France. Serve with a big blue cheese, which stands up in flavor.

1½ cups (375 mL) Merlot or other fruity red wine

2 Tbsp. (30 mL) fresh rosemary leaves

2 cups (500 mL) finely chopped fresh figs

3 Tbsp. (45 mL) Ball® Classic Pectin

2 Tbsp. (30 mL) bottled lemon juice

2½ cups (625 mL) sugar

★

Tricks of the Trade

Since the wine really stands out, use a good-quality Merlot or Pinot Noir with this jam.

1. Bring wine and rosemary to a simmer in a small stainless steel or enameled saucepan. Turn off heat; cover and steep 30 minutes.

2. Pour wine through a fine wire-mesh strainer into a 4-qt. (4-L) stainless steel or enameled saucepan. Discard rosemary. Stir in figs, pectin, and lemon juice. Bring mixture to a full rolling boil that cannot be stirred down, over high heat, stirring constantly.

3. Add sugar, stirring to dissolve. Return mixture to a full rolling boil. Boil hard 1 minute, stirring constantly. Remove from heat. Skim foam, if necessary.

4. Ladle hot jam into a hot jar, leaving ¼-inch (.5-cm) headspace. Remove air bubbles. Wipe jar rim. Center lid on jar. Apply band, and adjust to fingertip-tight. Place jar in boiling-water canner. Repeat until all jars are filled.

5. Process jars 10 minutes, adjusting for altitude. Turn off heat; remove lid, and let jars stand 5 minutes. Remove jars and cool.

MELON JAM

MAKES ABOUT 5 (¹/₂-PT./250-ML) JARS

Cantaloupe as you've never tasted it! Melon jam is a truly spectacular treat commonly seen in France. Serve with floral soft and hard cheeses and water crackers.

---

14   cups (3.5 L) 1-inch (1-cm) cantaloupe or other orange-fleshed melon cubes (about 2 large melons)

¹/₄   cup (60 mL) kosher salt

4   cups (1 L) sugar

³/₄   cup (175 mL) bottled lemon juice

1   Tbsp. (15 mL) crushed pink peppercorns (optional)

—————— ★ ——————

Tricks of the Trade
Choose a perfect ripe and juicy orange-fleshed melon for this jam. It will cook down into a rich, deep orange.

1. Toss together melon and salt in a large bowl. Cover and let stand 2 hours. Drain; rinse with cold water. Drain.

2. Stir together melon, sugar, and lemon juice in a 6-qt. (6-L) stainless steel or enameled Dutch oven. Bring to a boil; reduce heat, and simmer, uncovered, 20 minutes or until melon is soft. Mash melon pieces with a potato masher. Simmer, uncovered, stirring often, about 1 hour to gelling point (page 17). (Melons release a lot of water, so cooking time may vary.) Skim foam, if necessary, and, if desired, stir in peppercorns.

3. Ladle hot jam into a hot jar, leaving ¹/₄-inch (.5-cm) headspace. Remove air bubbles. Wipe jar rim. Center lid on jar. Apply band, and adjust to fingertip-tight. Place jar in boiling-water canner. Repeat until all jars are filled.

4. Process jars 15 minutes, adjusting for altitude. Turn off heat; remove lid, and let jars stand 5 minutes. Remove jars and cool.

PEACH-ROSEMARY JAM

MAKES ABOUT 6 (½-PT./250 ML) JARS

Sweet peaches play nicely off the tang of lime and herbal notes of rosemary in this jam.
Tie fresh garden rosemary in a bit of cheesecloth to make removing it easier.

2½   lb. (1.25 kg) fresh peaches (5 large)

1   tsp. (5 mL) lime zest

6   Tbsp. (90 mL) Ball® Classic Pectin

¼   cup (60 mL) fresh lime juice (about 3 limes)

2   (4-inch/10-cm) rosemary sprigs

5   cups (1.25 L) sugar

★

Perfect Pairing

This jam makes a delectable dip for bacon-wrapped shrimp.

---

1. Peel peaches with a vegetable peeler. Remove pits, and coarsely chop. Mash with a potato masher until evenly crushed. Measure 4 cups (1 L) crushed peaches into a 6-qt. (6-L) stainless steel or enameled Dutch oven. Stir in lime zest and next 3 ingredients.

2. Bring mixture to a full rolling boil that cannot be stirred down, over high heat, stirring constantly. Boil 1 minute, stirring constantly.

3. Add sugar, stirring to dissolve. Return mixture to a full rolling boil. Boil hard 1 minute, stirring constantly. Remove from heat. Remove and discard rosemary. Skim foam, if necessary.

4. Ladle hot jam into a hot jar, leaving ¼-inch (.5-cm) headspace. Remove air bubbles. Wipe jar rim. Center lid on jar. Apply band, and adjust to fingertip-tight. Place jar in boiling-water canner. Repeat until all jars are filled.

5. Process jars 10 minutes, adjusting for altitude. Turn off heat; remove lid, and let jars stand 5 minutes. Remove jars and cool.

HONEY-PEAR JAM

MAKES ABOUT 5 (½-PT./250-ML) JARS

A bit of apple juice and a little honey offer light sweetness to this delicious gingery pear jam.

3¼ lb. (1.5 kg) firm, ripe pears

½ cup (125 mL) apple juice

1 Tbsp. (15 mL) bottled lemon juice

½ tsp. (2.5 mL) ground cinnamon

1 (1-inch/2.5-cm) piece fresh ginger, peeled and finely grated*

6 Tbsp. (90 mL) Ball® Low or No-Sugar Pectin

½ cup (125 mL) honey

★

Simple Switch

Try mixing pear varieties, such as d'Anjou, Bosc, and Red Bartlett, for different flavor and texture. All are delicious!

1. Combine first 5 ingredients in a 6-qt. (6-L) stainless steel or enameled Dutch oven. Cook, uncovered, over medium heat 15 minutes or until pear is tender, stirring occasionally. Mash pear mixture slightly with a potato masher, breaking up large chunks.

2. Stir in pectin. Bring mixture to a full rolling boil that cannot be stirred down, over high heat, stirring constantly.

3. Stir in honey. Return mixture to a full rolling boil. Boil hard 1 minute, stirring constantly. Remove from heat. Skim foam, if necessary.

4. Ladle hot jam into a hot jar, leaving ¼-inch (.5-cm) headspace. Remove air bubbles. Wipe jar rim. Center lid on jar. Apply band, and adjust to fingertip-tight. Place jar in boiling-water canner. Repeat until all jars are filled.

5. Process jars 10 minutes, adjusting for altitude. Turn off heat; remove lid, and let jars stand 5 minutes. Remove jars and cool.

*1 tsp. (5 mL) ground ginger may be substituted.

APPLE PIE JAM

MAKES ABOUT 5 ($\frac{1}{2}$-PT./250-ML) JARS

Every day is apple pie day with this in the pantry! Toast and oatmeal will never be the same. Extra yummy served over ice cream.

- 6 cups (1.5 L) diced peeled Granny Smith apple (about 6 apples)
- 2 cups (500 mL) apple juice or apple cider
- 2 Tbsp. (30 mL) bottled lemon juice
- 3 Tbsp. (45 mL) Ball® Classic Pectin
- 1 tsp. (5 mL) ground cinnamon
- $\frac{1}{2}$ tsp. (2 mL) ground allspice
- $\frac{1}{4}$ tsp. (1 mL) ground nutmeg
- 2 cups (500 mL) sugar

★

Simple Switch

Just as all apple pies are not the same, why not make your jam unique? Swap out allspice and nutmeg for cardamom and ginger, or add a star anise to the cooking apples (and remove before canning).

---

1. Bring first 3 ingredients to a boil in a 6-qt. (6-L) stainless steel or enameled Dutch oven; reduce heat, and simmer, uncovered, 10 minutes or until apple is soft, stirring occasionally.

2. Whisk in pectin and next 3 ingredients. Bring mixture to a full rolling boil that cannot be stirred down, over high heat, stirring constantly.

3. Add sugar, stirring to dissolve. Return mixture to a full rolling boil. Boil hard 1 minute, stirring constantly. Remove from heat. Skim foam, if necessary.

4. Ladle hot jam into a hot jar, leaving $\frac{1}{4}$-inch (.5-cm) headspace. Remove air bubbles. Wipe jar rim. Center lid on jar. Apply band, and adjust to fingertip-tight. Place jar in boiling-water canner. Repeat until all jars are filled.

5. Process jars 10 minutes, adjusting for altitude. Turn off heat; remove lid, and let jars stand 5 minutes. Remove jars and cool.

PEACH-BOURBON JAM

MAKES ABOUT 6 (¹/₂-PT./250-ML) JARS

Bourbon and peaches together with a little ginger conjure up the flavors of the South in this sumptuous jam.

4   lb. (2 kg) fresh peaches, peeled*

6   Tbsp. (90 mL) Ball® Classic Pectin

¹/₄ cup (60 mL) bottled lemon juice

¹/₄ cup (60 mL) bourbon

2   Tbsp. (30 mL) finely chopped crystallized ginger

7   cups (1.75 L) sugar

★

Perfect Pairing

Peach bourbon is a flavor combination that goes well with everything! Spread on banana bread, use as a glaze for grilled ribs, or try it as an excellent sweet counterpart to sharp Cheddar on grilled cheese sandwiches.

1. Pit and coarsely chop peaches. Measure 4¹/₂ cups (1.1 L) chopped peaches into a 6-qt. (6-L) stainless steel or enameled Dutch oven, and mash with a potato masher until evenly crushed. Stir in pectin and next 3 ingredients.

2. Bring mixture to a full rolling boil that cannot be stirred down, over high heat, stirring constantly.

3. Add sugar, stirring to dissolve. Return mixture to a full rolling boil. Boil hard 1 minute, stirring constantly. Remove from heat. Skim foam, if necessary.

4. Ladle hot jam into a hot jar, leaving ¹/₄-inch (.5-cm) headspace. Remove air bubbles. Wipe jar rim. Center lid on jar. Apply band, and adjust to fingertip-tight. Place jar in boiling-water canner. Repeat until all jars are filled.

5. Process jars 10 minutes, adjusting for altitude. Turn off heat; remove lid, and let jars stand 5 minutes. Remove jars and cool.

*Frozen sliced peaches (4¹/₂ cups/1.1 L), coarsely chopped, may be substituted.

LOW-SUGAR RASPBERRY "LEMONADE" JAM

MAKES ABOUT 6 (1/2-PT./250-ML) JARS

Perfect for toast and crêpes, this jam is also remarkable blended into lemonade for ice pops!

3½ lb. (1.6 kg) fresh raspberries

½ cup (125 mL) fresh lemon juice (about 5 lemons)

4 Tbsp. (60 mL) Ball® Low or No-Sugar Pectin

1½ cups (375 mL) honey

1. Place raspberries in a 6-qt. (6-L) stainless steel or enameled Dutch oven. Crush raspberries with a potato masher.

2. Stir in lemon juice and pectin. Bring mixture to a full rolling boil that cannot be stirred down, over high heat, stirring constantly.

3. Stir in honey. Return mixture to a full rolling boil. Boil hard 1 minute, stirring constantly. Remove from heat. Skim foam, if necessary.

4. Ladle hot jam into a hot jar, leaving ¼-inch (.5-mL) headspace. Remove air bubbles. Wipe jar rim. Center lid on jar. Apply band, and adjust to fingertip-tight. Place jar in boiling-water canner. Repeat until all jars are filled.

5. Process jars 10 minutes, adjusting for altitude. Turn off heat; remove lid, and let jars stand 5 minutes. Remove jars and cool.

TOMATO-HERB JAM

MAKES ABOUT 4 (½-PT./250-ML) JARS

Tomatoes make superb jam, whether sweet or savory. We call this grown-up ketchup!

- 6 lb. (3 kg) plum tomatoes, cored and chopped
- 1 tsp. (5 mL) salt
- ½ tsp. (2 mL) freshly ground black pepper
- 3 garlic cloves, minced
- 2 bay leaves
- 1½ cups (375 mL) sugar
- ½ cup (125 mL) balsamic vinegar
- ¼ cup (60 mL) Pinot Grigio or other dry white wine
- 2 tsp. (10 mL) herbes de Provence*

--- ★ ---

Tricks of the Trade

Using an immersion blender makes quick work of the seeds and skins if you desire a smoother, thicker jam.

1. Combine first 5 ingredients in a 6-qt. (6-L) stainless steel or enameled Dutch oven. Cook, uncovered, over medium-high heat 1 hour or until reduced by half, stirring often.

2. Stir in sugar and next 3 ingredients. Cook, uncovered, over medium heat 45 minutes or until very thick, stirring occasionally. Remove and discard bay leaves.

3. Ladle hot jam into a hot jar, leaving ¼-inch (.5 mL) headspace. Remove air bubbles. Wipe jar rim. Center lid on jar. Apply band, and adjust to fingertip-tight. Place jar in boiling-water canner. Repeat until all jars are filled.

4. Process jars 10 minutes, adjusting for altitude. Turn off heat; remove lid, and let jars stand 5 minutes. Remove jars and cool.

*Equal amounts of dried thyme, crushed dried rosemary, dried marjoram, and dried oregano (or any combination of these) may be substituted.

MEATLOAF

MAKES 8 SERVINGS

This recipe serves eight, but leftovers make a great sandwich. When chilled, the meatloaf has a dense texture similar to pâté but without all the added fat. Great for a picnic meal accompanied with pickled veggies.

- ¾ cup (175 mL) soft, fresh breadcrumbs
- ⅓ cup (75 mL) milk
- ½ cup (125 mL) minced onion (about ½ medium onion)
- ⅓ cup (75 mL) minced celery (about 1 celery rib)
- ⅓ cup (75 mL) minced carrots (about 1 medium carrot)
- 1 Tbsp. (15 mL) olive oil
- 1½ lb. (750 mL) ground pork
- 1½ lb. (750 mL) ground beef
- 2 Tbsp. (30 mL) chopped fresh parsley
- 1 tsp. (5 mL) herbes de Provence*
- 1 tsp. (5 mL) kosher salt
- ½ tsp. (2 mL) freshly ground black pepper
- 2 large eggs, lightly beaten
- 1 cup (250 mL) Tomato-Herb Jam (page 53), divided

Vegetable cooking spray

1. Combine breadcrumbs and milk in a large bowl. Let stand 5 minutes or until milk is absorbed.

2. Sauté onion and next 2 ingredients in hot oil 5 to 7 minutes or until tender but not brown. Remove from heat and cool completely.

3. Add cooked vegetables, pork, next 6 ingredients, and ½ cup (125 mL) jam to breadcrumb mixture, mixing with hands just until combined. Cover and chill for at least 30 minutes but no longer than 4 hours.

4. Preheat oven to 375°F (190°C). Shape mixture into a 9- x 5-inch/23- x 12.5-cm loaf; place on an aluminum foil–lined rimmed baking sheet coated with cooking spray. Cover loosely with foil coated with cooking spray.

5. Bake at 375°F (190°C) for 45 minutes. Uncover and spread remaining ½ cup (125 mL) jam over meatloaf. Bake 10 more minutes or until a meat thermometer inserted in center registers 165°F (75°C) and jam is beginning to caramelize. Let stand 15 minutes before slicing.

*Equal amounts of dried thyme, crushed dried rosemary, dried marjoram, and dried oregano (or any combination of these) may be substituted.

ZUCCHINI-BREAD JAM

MAKES ABOUT 4 (¹/₂-PT./250-ML) JARS

Spread this jam on toast and you'll swear you're eating fresh-baked zucchini bread!

- 4 cups (1 L) shredded zucchini
- 1 cup (250 mL) apple juice
- 6 Tbsp. (90 mL) Ball® Classic Pectin
- ¹/₄ cup (60 mL) golden raisins
- 1 Tbsp. (15 mL) bottled lemon juice
- 1 tsp. (5 mL) ground cinnamon
- ¹/₂ tsp. (2 mL) ground nutmeg
- 3 cups (750 mL) sugar

---- ★ ----

Simple Switch

Have more yellow summer squash than zucchini? Not to worry, it can be used the same way as zucchini in this recipe.

1. Combine all ingredients, except sugar, in a 6-qt. (6-L) stainless steel or enameled Dutch oven. Bring mixture to a full rolling boil that cannot be stirred down, over high heat, stirring constantly.

2. Add sugar, stirring to dissolve. Return mixture to a full rolling boil. Boil hard 1 minute, stirring constantly. Remove from heat. Skim foam, if necessary.

3. Ladle hot jam into a hot jar, leaving ¹/₄-inch (.5-cm) headspace. Remove air bubbles. Wipe jar rim. Center lid on jar. Apply band, and adjust to fingertip-tight. Place jar in boiling-water canner. Repeat until all jars are filled.

4. Process jars 15 minutes, adjusting for altitude. Turn off heat; remove lid, and let jars stand 5 minutes. Remove jars and cool.

BERRY-ALE JAM

MAKES ABOUT 6 (¹/₂-PT./250-ML) JARS

This sweet and hoppy jam will take your peanut butter and jam sandwich to the next level. Enjoy it with a cold IPA on a hot summer day.

2 cups (500 mL) raspberries, blueberries, or strawberries

2 (12-oz./355-mL) bottles flat pale ale

6 Tbsp. (90 mL) Ball® Classic Pectin

1 tsp. (5 mL) lemon zest

2 Tbsp. (30 mL) fresh lemon juice

4 cups (1 L) sugar

★

Simple Switch
Use any berry or all berries in this jam; mix it up by using different ale brews.

1. Place berries in a 6-qt. (6-L) stainless steel or enameled Dutch oven. Crush berries with a potato masher. Stir in ale and next 3 ingredients. Bring mixture to a full rolling boil that cannot be stirred down, over high heat, stirring constantly.

2. Add sugar, stirring to dissolve. Return mixture to a full rolling boil. Boil hard 1 minute, stirring constantly. Remove from heat. Skim foam, if necessary.

3. Ladle hot jam into a hot jar, leaving ¼-inch (.5-cm) headspace. Remove air bubbles. Wipe jar rim. Center lid on jar. Apply band, and adjust to fingertip-tight. Place jar in boiling-water canner. Repeat until all jars are filled.

4. Process jars 10 minutes, adjusting for altitude. Turn off heat; remove lid, and let jars stand 5 minutes. Remove jars and cool.

LOW-SUGAR APPLE-CHILE JAM

MAKES ABOUT 5 (½-PT./250-ML) JARS

2 large apples (about 8½ oz./480 g, each), peeled and grated

3 Tbsp. (45 mL) bottled lemon juice

4 cups (1 L) apple juice

3 Tbsp. (45 mL) Ball® Low or No-Sugar Pectin

1 Tbsp. (15 mL) crushed chile de árbol, or dried crushed red pepper

½ cup (125 mL) sugar

½ cup (125 mL) honey

1. Combine grated apple and lemon juice in a 4-qt. (4-L) stainless steel or enameled Dutch oven. Cook, stirring constantly, 10 minutes or until apple is tender.

2. Stir in apple juice, pectin, and crushed chile de árbol. Bring mixture to a full rolling boil that cannot be stirred down, over high heat, stirring constantly.

3. Add sugar and honey, stirring to dissolve sugar. Return mixture to a full rolling boil. Boil hard 1 minute, stirring constantly. Remove from heat. Skim foam, if necessary.

4. Ladle hot jam into a hot jar, leaving ¼-inch (.5-cm) headspace. Remove air bubbles. Wipe jar rim. Center lid on jar. Apply band, and adjust to fingertip-tight. Place jar in boiling-water canner. Repeat until all jars are filled.

5. Process jars 10 minutes, adjusting for altitude. Turn off heat; remove lid, and let jars stand 5 minutes. Remove jars and cool.

« BALSAMIC-ONION JAM

MAKES ABOUT 5 (½-PT./250-ML) JARS

2 lb. (1 kg) onions, diced

½ cup (125 mL) balsamic vinegar

½ cup (125 mL) maple syrup

1½ tsp. (7.5 mL) salt

2 tsp. (10 mL) ground white pepper

1 bay leaf

2 cups (500 mL) apple juice

3 Tbsp. (45 mL) Ball® Low or No-Sugar Pectin

½ cup (125 mL) sugar

1. Combine first 6 ingredients in a 6-qt. (6-L) stainless steel or enameled Dutch oven. Cook over medium heat 15 minutes or until onions are translucent, stirring occasionally.

2. Stir in apple juice and pectin. Bring mixture to a full rolling boil that cannot be stirred down, over high heat, stirring constantly.

3. Add sugar, stirring to dissolve. Return mixture to a full rolling boil. Boil hard 1 minute, stirring constantly. Remove from heat. Remove and discard bay leaf. Skim foam, if necessary.

4. Ladle hot jam into a hot jar, leaving ¼-inch (.5-cm) headspace. Remove air bubbles. Wipe jar rim. Center lid on jar. Apply band, and adjust to fingertip-tight. Place jar in boiling-water canner. Repeat until all jars are filled.

5. Process jars 15 minutes, adjusting for altitude. Turn off heat; remove lid, and let jars stand 5 minutes. Remove jars and cool.

BLUEBERRY-LEMON JAM

MAKES ABOUT 4 (½-PT./250-ML) JARS

This lickety-split jam is a great way to use up extra blueberries. You'll have it sealed in jars and cooling on the windowsill in less than an hour.

4	cups (1 L) fresh blueberries
3½	cups (1.6 L) sugar
1	tsp. (5 mL) lemon zest
1	Tbsp. (15 mL) fresh lemon juice
1	(3-oz./88.5-mL) pouch Ball® Liquid Pectin

——————— ★ ———————

Tricks of the Trade
Though you'll be tempted to use this jam sooner, let it stand—it's perfection about three weeks after canning.

1. Wash, drain, and lightly crush blueberries with a spoon (just enough to split the skins). Measure 2½ cups (625 mL) crushed blueberries into a 6-qt. (6-L) stainless steel or enameled Dutch oven.

2. Add sugar and next 2 ingredients. Bring mixture to a full rolling boil that cannot be stirred down, over high heat, stirring constantly.

3. Add pectin, immediately squeezing entire contents from pouch. Continue hard boil for 1 minute, stirring constantly. Remove from heat. Skim foam, if necessary.

4. Ladle hot mixture into a hot jar, leaving ¼-inch (.5-cm) headspace. Remove air bubbles. Wipe jar rim. Center lid on jar. Apply band, and adjust to fingertip-tight. Place jar in boiling-water canner. Repeat until all jars are filled.

5. Process jars 10 minutes, adjusting for altitude. Turn off heat; remove lid, and let jars stand 5 minutes. Remove jars and cool.

CRÊPE CAKE

MAKES 6 SERVINGS

Impress your guests at your next dinner party with this showstopper of a cake. It might not be traditional, but it will be memorable.

- 4 cups (1 L) milk
- 2 cups (500 mL) all-purpose flour
- 1 tsp. (5 mL) salt
- ½ cup (125 mL) unsalted butter, melted
- 6 large eggs, beaten
- 2 Tbsp. (30 mL) vegetable oil

Wax paper

- 3 cups Blueberry-Lemon Jam (page 60)
- 2 cups lemon curd

★

Simple Switch

You may substitute any desired jam for the Blueberry-Lemon Jam and your favorite pastry cream or vanilla pudding for the lemon curd.

---

1. Whisk together first 5 ingredients in a large bowl until smooth. Cover and chill 1 hour.

2. Place a crêpe pan or 8-inch nonstick skillet over medium-low heat until hot. Lightly oil pan.

3. Pour a scant ¼ cup (about 60 mL) batter into pan; quickly tilt in all directions so batter evenly covers bottom of pan. Cook 2 to 3 minutes or until light golden brown. Carefully lift edge of crêpe with a spatula to test for doneness. The crêpe is ready to turn when it can be shaken loose from skillet. Turn crêpe over, and cook about 20 seconds or until done. Place crêpe on a dish towel to cool. Repeat procedure with remaining batter, oiling pan between batches. Stack crêpes between sheets of wax paper until ready to fill.

4. Gently fold together jam and lemon curd in a medium bowl until blended. Beginning with a crêpe, layer crêpes and jam mixture on a serving plate, spreading 3 Tbsp. (45 mL) jam mixture between each layer and on top. Serve immediately or chill, uncovered, 30 minutes.

DRESSINGS

Jams, jellies, and preserves transform into marinades and dressings by adding a bit of sweetness and bursts of flavor to simple recipes. These recipes are an excellent way to use up an opened jar of jam.

BALSAMIC-ONION JAM DRESSING

MAKES ABOUT 1 CUP

- ½ cup (125 mL) Balsamic-Onion Jam (page 59)
- 2 Tbsp. (30 mL) balsamic vinegar
- 2 tsp. (10 mL) Dijon Mustard (page 190)
- ½ tsp. (2 mL) dried thyme
- ½ tsp. (2 mL) salt
- ½ tsp. (2 mL) freshly ground black pepper
- 1 garlic clove, minced
- ½ cup (125 mL) olive oil

Process all ingredients, except olive oil, in a blender until smooth. With blender on, gradually add olive oil, processing until thickened.

CRANBERRY-PORT VINAIGRETTE

MAKES ABOUT 1 CUP

- ½ cup (125 mL) Cranberry-Port Jelly (page 84)
- ¼ cup (60 mL) olive oil
- 3 Tbsp. (45 mL) red wine vinegar
- 1 tsp. (5 mL) salt
- ½ tsp. (2 mL) freshly ground black pepper
- 1 garlic clove, minced

Whisk together all ingredients in a small bowl. Store, covered, in refrigerator.

GUAVA-GRAPEFRUIT VINAIGRETTE

MAKES ABOUT 1 CUP

- 1 tsp. (5 mL) pink grapefruit zest
- 1 cup (250 mL) pink grapefruit sections (about 1 small grapefruit)
- ½ cup (125 mL) Guava-Vanilla Bean Jelly (page 83)
- ¼ cup (60 mL) olive oil
- 2 Tbsp. (30 mL) fresh lime juice
- 1 tsp. (5 mL) salt
- ½ tsp. (2 mL) freshly ground black pepper
- 1 shallot, minced

Combine all ingredients in a small stainless steel or enameled saucepan. Bring to a simmer, whisking constantly. Cool completely. Use to marinate meat or vegetables or as a dipping sauce for egg rolls or dumplings.

MARINADES

The acid in jam and preserves is the perfect tenderizing ingredient for any marinade. Experiment with your favorite preserve flavors or try one of these.

PEAR-ROASTED GARLIC MARINADE

MAKES ABOUT 1½ CUPS

- 1 cup (250 mL) Pear-Roasted Garlic Preserves (page 111)
- ½ cup (125 mL) olive oil
- 2 Tbsp. (30 mL) chopped fresh thyme
- 1 Tbsp. (15 mL) chopped fresh rosemary
- 2 tsp. (10 mL) kosher salt
- ½ tsp. (2 mL) freshly ground black pepper
- 2 garlic cloves, minced

Stir together all ingredients. Use to marinate chicken or lamb.

HERBED TOMATO MARINADE

MAKES 2 CUPS

- 1 cup (250 mL) Tomato-Herb Jam (page 53)
- ½ cup (125 mL) apple cider vinegar
- ¼ cup (60 mL) olive oil
- 3 Tbsp. (45 mL) Worcestershire Sauce (page 257)
- 1 tsp. (5 mL) smoked paprika
- 2 garlic cloves, minced

Combine all ingredients in a small stainless steel or enameled saucepan. Bring to a simmer, whisking constantly. Cool completely. Use to marinate meat or vegetables.

APRICOT-LAVENDER MARINADE

MAKES 1½ CUPS

- 1 cup (250 mL) Apricot-Lavender Jam (page 39)
- ¼ cup (60 mL) rice vinegar
- ¼ cup (60 mL) water
- 1 tsp. (5 mL) soy sauce
- 1 Tbsp. (15 mL) Asian hot chili sauce (such as Sriracha), or sambal oelek (chile paste with garlic)
- 2 garlic cloves, minced

Process all ingredients in a blender until smooth.

Jelly in 5 Easy Steps

Refer to water bath canning procedures on pages 26-27
and follow recipe guidelines in steps and chart below.

Makes 4 (½-pt./250-mL) jars

STEP 1: Prepare chosen fruit according to Fruit Preparation for Jellies chart below. Pour prepared fruit mixture through a wire-mesh sieve lined with 3 layers of damp cheesecloth into a bowl. Let drain 2 to 4 hours or until juice measures 3 cups. (To avoid cloudy jelly, do not press or squeeze fruit mixture.)

STEP 2: Combine fruit juice and 4 Tbsp. (60 mL) Ball® Classic Pectin in large stainless steel or enameled saucepan. Bring mixture to a rolling boil that cannot be stirred down, over high heat, stirring constantly.

STEP 3: Add 3⅓ cups (835 mL)* sugar, stirring to dissolve. Return to a full rolling boil. Boil hard 1 minute, stirring constantly. Remove from heat. Skim foam.

STEP 4: Ladle hot jelly into a hot jar, leaving ¼-inch (.5-cm) headspace. Place jar in boiling-water canner. Repeat until all jars are filled.

STEP 5: Process jars 10 minutes, adjusting for altitude.

Fruit Preparation for Jellies

FRUIT	PREPARATION
Apples (2½ lb./1.25 kg)	Wash, stem, and cut into chunks (do not core). Combine apples and 3 cups (750 mL) water in a stainless steel or enameled Dutch oven; cover and simmer 10 minutes. Crush and simmer 5 more minutes.
Berries (4 lb./2 kg)	Wash; crush 1 layer at a time with a potato masher in a stainless steel or enameled Dutch oven. Cover and bring to a simmer; simmer 5 minutes.
Cherries Dark, Sweet (3 lb./1.5 kg)	Remove stems; pit and chop. Cover and bring to a simmer in a stainless steel or enameled Dutch oven with 6 Tbsp. (90 mL) water and 2 Tbsp. (30 mL) lemon juice. Simmer 10 minutes.
Cherries Tart, Red (3 lb./1.5 kg)	Remove stems; pit and chop. Cover and bring to a simmer in a stainless steel or enameled Dutch oven with 6 Tbsp. (90 mL) water. Simmer 10 minutes.
Currants (3 lb./1.5 kg)	Wash; crush 1 layer at a time with a potato masher in a stainless steel or enameled Dutch oven. Cover and bring to a simmer with 10 Tbsp. (150 mL) water; simmer 10 minutes.
Grapes (2½ lb./1.25 kg)	Wash; crush 1 layer at a time with a potato masher in a stainless steel or enameled Dutch oven. Cover and bring to a simmer with 10 Tbsp. (150 mL) water; simmer 10 minutes.
Plums (2½ lb./1.25 kg)	Halve, pit, and finely chop. Cover and bring to a simmer with 10 Tbsp. (150 mL) water in a stainless steel or enameled Dutch oven; simmer 10 minutes.
Strawberries (8 lb./4 kg)	Wash; crush 1 layer at a time with a potato masher in a stainless steel or enameled Dutch oven. Cover and bring to a simmer; simmer 5 minutes.

*For a lower-sugar version, reduce sugar to 2 cups (500 mL). Set will not be as firm.

WHITE BALSAMIC ROSEMARY JELLY

MAKES ABOUT 5 (½-PT./250-ML) JARS

A classy sweet and tart jelly bursting with the unique flavor of white balsamic vinegar infused with rosemary. It is excellent on skillet-roasted pork chops.

2½   **cups (625 ml) 100% apple juice**

¾   **cup (175 ml) white balsamic vinegar**

4   **Tbsp. (60 mL) Ball® Classic Pectin**

1   **(4-inch/10-cm) fresh rosemary sprig**

3⅓   **cups (825 mL) sugar**

————— ★ —————

Simple Switch
Not a big rosemary fan? Try switching it out with thyme or tarragon.

1. Combine first 4 ingredients in a 4-qt. (4-L) stainless steel or enameled Dutch oven. Bring mixture to a full rolling boil that cannot be stirred down, over high heat, stirring constantly.

2. Add sugar, stirring to dissolve. Return mixture to a full rolling boil. Boil hard 1 minute, stirring constantly. Remove from heat. Discard rosemary. Skim foam, if necessary.

3. Ladle hot jelly into a hot jar, leaving ¼-inch (.5-cm) headspace. Wipe jar rim. Center lid on jar. Apply band, and adjust to fingertip-tight. Place jar in boiling-water canner. Repeat until all jars are filled.

4. Process jars 10 minutes, adjusting for altitude. Turn off heat; remove lid, and let jars stand 5 minutes. Remove jars and cool.

GLAZED APPLE TART

MAKES 6 SERVINGS

Buttery crust, tart apples, and a fruity glaze over it all bring traditional apple pie up to new standards. Any favorite flavor of jelly may be substituted for the Red Plum–Raspberry Jelly (page 76), and commercial applesauce may be substituted for the home-canned version.

---

1 Flaky Piecrust (page 315), thawed

3 large Golden Delicious apples, divided

1 cup (250 mL) Applesauce (page 139)

⅓ cup (75 mL) sugar

½ tsp. (2 mL) ground cinnamon

1 Tbsp. (15 mL) butter, cut into small pieces

½ cup (125 mL) Red Plum–Raspberry Jelly (page 76), melted

Vanilla ice cream (optional)

──────── ★ ────────

Tricks of the Trade
Keep a piecrust in the freezer to make things even easier.

1. Preheat oven to 400°F (200°C). Fit piecrust into a 9-inch (23-cm) tart pan with removable bottom; press into fluted edges.

2. Peel, core, and finely chop 1 apple. Combine chopped apple and applesauce in a medium bowl.

3. Peel, quarter, and cut remaining 2 apples into thin vertical slices. Spread applesauce mixture in bottom of piecrust. Beginning at outside edge, top with tightly overlapping apple slices arranged in 2 concentric circles, leaving the center open. Chop remaining apple slices and place in center of tart.

4. Combine sugar and cinnamon in a small bowl. Sprinkle over top of pie; dot with butter.

5. Bake on bottom oven rack at 400°F (200°C) for 50 to 60 minutes or until crust is deep golden brown and filling is beginning to bubble around the edge. Cool in pan on a wire rack for 30 minutes.

6. Gently brush apple slices with melted jelly to coat. Serve slightly warm or at room temperature with a small scoop of vanilla ice cream, if desired.

LOW-SUGAR ROASTED STRAWBERRY–CHAMOMILE JELLY

MAKES ABOUT 4 (½-PT./250-ML) JARS

This mild strawberry jelly uses roasted fruit, chamomile tea, and honey to add depth of flavor.

- 3 cups (750 mL) water
- 4 regular-size chamomile tea bags
- 3 lb. (1.5 kg) strawberries, hulled

Cheesecloth

- 4 Tbsp. (60 mL) Ball® Low or No-Sugar Pectin
- ½ cup (125 mL) sugar
- ½ cup (125 mL) honey
- ⅛ tsp. (.5 mL) Himalayan pink salt (optional)

★

Perfect Pairing

Pair this lovely jelly with simple baked goods, such as scones, biscuits, and thumbprint cookies. Or get wild and turn your favorite sugared doughnut into a jelly doughnut!

---

1. Preheat oven to 375°F (190°C). Bring water to a boil in a 3-qt. saucepan. Remove from heat; add tea bags, cover, and steep 30 minutes. Remove tea bags.

2. Place strawberries in a single layer on a large rimmed baking sheet. Bake at 375°F/190°C for 30 to 40 minutes (depending on size of berries) or until strawberries release juices and are slightly shriveled.

3. Add strawberries and accumulated juices to tea. Bring to a boil; reduce heat, and simmer, uncovered, 15 minutes or until strawberries fall apart.

4. Line a fine wire-mesh strainer with 3 layers of dampened cheesecloth. Place strainer over a bowl. Pour strawberry mixture into strainer. (Do not press mixture.) Cover and let stand 4 hours or overnight or until collected juice measures 4 cups (1 L) and mixture no longer drips.

5. Combine strawberry juice and pectin in a 6-qt. (6-L) stainless steel or enameled Dutch oven. Bring strawberry mixture to a full rolling boil that cannot be stirred down, over high heat, stirring constantly.

6. Stir in sugar, honey, and, if desired, salt. Return mixture to a full rolling boil. Boil hard 1 minute, stirring constantly. Remove from heat. Skim foam, if necessary.

7. Ladle hot jelly into a hot jar, leaving ¼-inch (.5-cm) headspace. Wipe jar rim. Center lid on jar. Apply band, and adjust to fingertip-tight. Place jar in boiling-water canner. Repeat until all jars are filled.

8. Process jars 10 minutes, adjusting for altitude. Turn off heat; remove lid, and let jars stand 5 minutes. Remove jars and cool.

HABANERO-APRICOT JELLY

MAKES ABOUT 6 (½-PT./250-ML) JARS

The buttery flavor of apricots gets a spicy kick from habanero in this gorgeous jelly.

1½ cups (375 mL) white vinegar (5% acidity)

⅔ cup (150 mL) finely chopped dried apricots

6 cups (1.25 L) sugar

½ cup (125 mL) finely chopped red bell pepper

½ cup (125 mL) finely chopped red onion

¼ cup (60 mL) finely chopped seeded habanero pepper

1 (3-oz./88.5-mL) pouch Ball® Liquid Pectin

1. Combine first 2 ingredients in a medium bowl. Cover and let stand at room temperature at least 4 hours or overnight.

2. Stir together apricot mixture, sugar, and next 3 ingredients in a 6-qt. (6-L) stainless steel or enameled Dutch oven. Bring mixture to a full rolling boil that cannot be stirred down, over high heat, stirring frequently.

3. Add pectin, immediately squeezing entire contents from pouch. Continue hard boil for 1 minute, stirring constantly. Remove from heat. Skim foam, if necessary.

4. Ladle hot jelly into a hot jar, leaving ¼-inch (.5-cm) headspace. Wipe jar rim. Center lid on jar. Apply band, and adjust to fingertip-tight. Place jar in boiling-water canner. Repeat until all jars are filled.

5. Process jars 10 minutes, adjusting for altitude. Turn off heat; remove lid, and let jars stand 5 minutes. Remove jars and cool.

SPICY THAI CHICKEN WINGS

MAKES 12 APPETIZER SERVINGS

These will disappear at your next party, guaranteed.

3 lb. (1.5 kg) chicken wings

Vegetable cooking spray

1 cup (250 mL) Habanero-Apricot Jelly

¼ cup (60 mL) chopped fresh cilantro

1 Tbsp. (15 mL) grated fresh ginger

1 Tbsp. (15 mL) butter, melted

Zest and juice of 1 lime

1. Preheat oven to 425°F (220°C). Cut off wing tips, and discard; cut wings in half at joint. Arrange wings on a large rimmed baking sheet coated with cooking spray.

2. Bake at 425°F (220°C) for 50 minutes or until wings are crisp and done.

3. Combine jelly and next 4 ingredients in a large bowl. Add wings, tossing to coat.

SPICY APPLE-JALAPEÑO JELLY

MAKES ABOUT 5 (½-PT./250-ML) JARS

- 1 qt. (1 L) water
- 3 lb. (1.5 kg) unpeeled McIntosh apples, washed and quartered

Cheesecloth

- 4 cups (1 L) sugar
- ½ cup (125 mL) thinly sliced red and green jalapeño peppers
- 1 Tbsp. (15 mL) bottled lemon juice

——— ★ ———

Perfect Pairing
Use this bright jelly in our Fresh Cherry Salsa to serve with grilled chicken breasts.

1. Combine water and apples in a 4-qt. (4-L) stainless steel or enameled Dutch oven. Bring to a boil over medium-high heat. Cook, uncovered, 15 to 20 minutes or until apples are very tender. Remove from heat.

2. Line a fine wire-mesh strainer with 3 layers of dampened cheesecloth. Place strainer over a bowl. Pour apple mixture into strainer. (Do not press mixture.) Cover and let stand 2 hours or until collected juice measures 4 cups (1 L) and mixture no longer drips.

3. Wash Dutch oven. Stir together apple juice, sugar, and next 2 ingredients in Dutch oven. Bring to a boil; reduce heat, and simmer, uncovered, 15 to 20 minutes or until a candy thermometer registers 220°F (104°C), stirring often and skimming any foam.

4. Ladle hot jelly into a hot jar, leaving ¼-inch (.5-cm) headspace. Wipe jar rim. Center lid on jar. Apply band, and adjust to fingertip-tight. Place jar in boiling-water canner. Repeat until all jars are filled.

5. Process jars 10 minutes, adjusting for altitude. Turn off heat; remove lid, and let jars stand 5 minutes. Remove jars and cool.

FRESH CHERRY SALSA

MAKES ABOUT 2½ CUPS

- ½ cup (125 mL) Spicy Apple-Jalapeño Jelly
- 3 limes
- ¼ tsp. (1 mL) dried crushed red pepper
- 2 cups (500 mL) coarsely chopped pitted fresh dark, sweet cherries
- ¾ cup (175 mL) diced pitted nectarines
- ⅓ cup (75 mL) chopped fresh cilantro
- ⅓ cup (75 mL) chopped fresh chives

Whisk together Spicy Apple-Jalapeño Jelly, 1 Tbsp. (15 mL) lime zest, ¼ cup (60 mL) fresh lime juice, and dried crushed red pepper in a medium bowl. Stir in cherries and remaining ingredients.

RED PLUM—RASPBERRY JELLY

MAKES ABOUT 4 (½-PT./250-ML) JARS

Sweet raspberries and plums come together in a jelly that is luscious and beautiful. From accompanying morning scones to glazing a tart base or spreading between cake layers, this jelly is a perfect staple to have on hand.

2 lb. (1 kg) firm, ripe red plums, halved

1 cup (250 mL) water

4 cups (1 L) raspberries (about 5 [6-oz./180 g] containers)

Cheesecloth

3 cups (750 mL) sugar

★

Tricks of the Trade

Plum pits are super high in pectin, so simmering them with the fruit really helps give this jelly its velvety smooth set.

1. Pit plums, reserving pits. Chop plums, and place in a 6-qt. (6-L) stainless steel or enameled Dutch oven. Lightly crush plums with a potato masher. Stir in water and reserved pits. Bring to a boil; reduce heat, cover, and simmer 10 minutes. Add raspberries, crushing with potato masher. Return to a boil; cover, reduce heat, and simmer 10 minutes.

2. Line a fine wire-mesh strainer with 3 layers of dampened cheesecloth. Place strainer over a bowl. Pour plum mixture into strainer. (Do not press mixture.) Cover and let stand 3 hours or until collected juice measures 3½ cups (875 mL) and mixture no longer drips. Wash and dry Dutch oven.

3. Pour juice into a Dutch oven. Stir in sugar and bring to a boil over high heat. Boil, stirring constantly, to gelling point (page 17).

4. Ladle hot jelly into a hot jar, leaving ¼-inch (.5-cm) headspace. Wipe jar rim. Center lid on jar. Apply band, and adjust to fingertip-tight. Place jar in boiling-water canner. Repeat until all jars are filled.

5. Process jars 10 minutes, adjusting for altitude. Turn off heat; remove lid, and let jars stand 5 minutes. Remove jars and cool.

TART LEMON JELLY

MAKES ABOUT 4 (½-PT./250-ML) JARS

Like the lemon candies we loved as kids, this jelly is tart and sweet and fun to eat.

---

6 large lemons
(1½ lb./750 g)

1½ cups (375 mL) water

Cheesecloth

3 Tbsp. (45 mL) Ball®
Classic Pectin

4 cups (1 L) sugar

——————— ★ ———————

Simple Switch

Make lime jelly! Follow the recipe exactly using lime juice and lime rind instead of lemon.

1. Scrub lemons thoroughly; rinse well, and pat dry. Carefully strip rind from lemons with a vegetable peeler to measure 1 cup (250 mL), avoiding bitter white pith.

2. Using a sharp, thin-bladed knife, cut a ¼-inch (.5-cm)-thick slice from each end of lemons. Place flat-end down on a cutting board, and remove and discard peel (bitter white pith) in strips, cutting from top to bottom, and following the curvature of the fruit. Coarsely chop lemons, reserving all juice, to measure 4 cups (1 L).

3. Combine lemon peel, chopped lemon with reserved juice, and water in a 4-qt. (4-L) stainless steel or enameled Dutch oven. Bring to a boil; reduce heat, cover, and simmer 15 minutes.

4. Line a large wire-mesh strainer with 3 layers of dampened cheesecloth. Place over a large bowl. Pour lemon mixture into strainer, and let drain at least 3 hours or overnight to measure 2 cups (500 mL) juice. Discard solids.

5. Combine lemon juice and pectin in a 4-qt. (4-L) stainless steel or enameled Dutch oven. Bring mixture to a full rolling boil that cannot be stirred down, over high heat, stirring constantly.

6. Add sugar, stirring to dissolve. Return mixture to a full rolling boil. Boil hard 1 minute, stirring constantly. Remove from heat. Skim foam, if necessary.

7. Ladle hot jelly into a hot jar, leaving ¼-inch (.5-cm) headspace. Wipe jar rim. Center lid on jar. Apply band, and adjust to fingertip-tight. Place jar in boiling-water canner. Repeat until all jars are filled.

8. Process jars 10 minutes, adjusting for altitude. Turn off heat; remove lid, and let jars stand 5 minutes. Remove jars and cool.

CITRUS-WHEAT BEER JELLY

MAKES ABOUT 5 (¹/₂-PT./250-ML) JARS

This recipe combines the smooth texture of jelly and the bold citrus flavor of marmalade with a subtle beer background. Feel free to use whatever citrus juice strikes your fancy.

- 2 (12-oz./355 mL) bottles flat wheat beer
- 1 cup (250 mL) bottled orange or grapefruit juice
- 6 Tbsp. (90 mL) Ball® Classic Pectin
- 4 cups (1 L) sugar

——— ★ ———

Tricks of the Trade
Using beer that is flat is key to preventing vigorous bubbles and foam from forming.

1. Combine first 3 ingredients in a 6-qt. (6-L) stainless steel or enameled Dutch oven. Bring mixture to a full rolling boil that cannot be stirred down, over high heat, stirring constantly.

2. Add sugar, stirring to dissolve. Return mixture to a full rolling boil. Boil hard 1 minute, stirring constantly. Remove from heat. Skim foam, if necessary.

3. Ladle hot jelly into a hot jar, leaving ¼-inch (.5-cm) headspace. Wipe jar rim. Center lid on jar. Apply band, and adjust to fingertip-tight. Place jar in boiling-water canner. Repeat until all jars are filled.

4. Process jars 10 minutes, adjusting for altitude. Turn off heat; remove lid, and let jars stand 5 minutes. Remove jars and cool.

TART MINT OR BASIL JELLY

MAKES ABOUT 7 (½-PT./250 ML) JARS

This herb jelly is an ideal complement to both sweet and savory dishes, like the lamb chops below.

6¼ cups (1.5 L) sugar

2 cups (500 mL) water

1 cup (250 mL) white vinegar (5% acidity)

1 cup (250 mL) loosely packed fresh mint leaves, or 1½ cups (375 mL) loosely packed fresh basil leaves, rinsed, dried, bruised slightly, and tied in cheesecloth

6 drops green liquid food coloring (optional)

2 (3-oz./88.5-mL) pouches Ball® Liquid Pectin

1. Combine first 4 ingredients and, if desired, food coloring, in 6-qt. (6-L) stainless steel or enameled Dutch oven. Bring mixture to a full rolling boil that cannot be stirred down, over high heat, stirring frequently.

2. Add pectin, immediately squeezing entire contents from pouches. Continue hard boil for 1 minute, stirring constantly. Remove from heat; remove and discard mint and cheesecloth. Skim foam, if necessary.

3. Ladle hot jelly into a hot jar, leaving ¼-inch (.5-cm) headspace. Wipe jar rim. Center lid on jar. Apply band, and adjust to fingertip-tight. Place jar in boiling-water canner. Repeat until all jars are filled.

4. Process jars 10 minutes, adjusting for altitude. Turn off heat; remove lid, and let jars stand 5 minutes. Remove jars and cool.

GRILLED ROSEMARY AND MINT LAMB CHOPS

MAKES 6 SERVINGS

12 (4-oz./125 g) lamb loin chops

2¼ tsp. (11 mL) salt, divided

1⅛ tsp. (5.5 mL) ground black pepper, divided

¼ cup (60 mL) chopped fresh rosemary

2 Tbsp. (30 mL) butter

¼ cup (60 mL) finely chopped shallots

2 Tbsp. (30 mL) dry sherry

¼ cup (60 mL) Tart Mint or Basil Jelly

1. Preheat grill to medium-high (350°F to 400°F/180°C to 200°C) heat. Rub surface of lamb chops with 2 tsp. (10 mL) salt, 1 tsp. (5 mL) pepper, and rosemary. Cover and let stand at room temperature 20 minutes.

2. Meanwhile, melt butter in a small saucepan. Add shallots, remaining ¼ tsp. (1 mL) salt, and remaining ⅛ tsp. (.5 mL) pepper; cook, stirring often, 5 minutes or until shallots are tender and golden. Add sherry, and cook until liquid almost evaporates, stirring to loosen browned bits from bottom of skillet. Stir in jelly; bring to a simmer. Remove from heat; keep warm.

3. Add lamb chops to grill rack. Grill 5 minutes on each side or to desired degree of doneness. Place lamb chops on a serving platter; let stand 5 minutes.

4. Drizzle a small amount of sauce over lamb chops. Serve immediately with additional sauce.

GUAVA-VANILLA BEAN JELLY

MAKES ABOUT 6 (¹/₂-PT./250-ML) JARS

If you come across fresh ripe guavas, buy them right away and make this amazing traditional Caribbean jelly. You will not be disappointed!

4 lb. (2 kg) guavas

5¹/₂ (1.3 L) cups water

Cheesecloth

2 vanilla beans, split lengthwise

4 cups (1 L) sugar

1 Tbsp. (15 mL) fresh lemon juice

1 Tbsp. (15 mL) fresh lime juice

—— ★ ——

Perfect Pairing

Guava jelly is quite versatile and can be used on everything from toast to cheese plates, but try it as a glaze for roast or grilled pork and chicken. Thin it with a little warm water and spread it on intermittently during cooking.

1. Remove ends of guavas. Cut lengthwise into quarters, and then crosswise into thin slices. Combine guava slices and water in a 4-qt. (4-L) stainless steel or enameled Dutch oven. Bring to a boil; reduce heat, cover, and simmer 20 minutes, stirring occasionally.

2. Line a fine wire-mesh strainer with 3 layers of dampened cheesecloth. Place strainer over a bowl. Pour guava mixture into strainer. (Do not press mixture.) Cover and let stand 2 hours or until collected juice measures 4¹/₂ cups (1.1 L) and mixture no longer drips.

3. Scrape seeds from vanilla beans. Combine vanilla bean seeds, vanilla beans, guava juice, sugar, and citrus juices in same Dutch oven. Bring to a boil over medium-high heat, stirring until sugar dissolves. Reduce heat to medium, and simmer 25 to 30 minutes or until gelling point (page 17). Remove from heat. Remove and discard vanilla beans. Skim foam, if necessary.

4. Ladle hot jelly into a hot jar, leaving ¹/₄-inch (.5-cm) headspace. Wipe jar rim. Center lid on jar. Apply band, and adjust to fingertip-tight. Place jar in boiling-water canner. Repeat until all jars are filled.

5. Process jars 10 minutes, adjusting for altitude. Turn off heat; remove lid, and let jars stand 5 minutes. Remove jars and cool.

CRANBERRY-PORT JELLY

MAKES ABOUT 4 (½-PT./250-ML) JARS

Take cranberries back from the holidays with this one! Sour, tart berries are a perfect match with luscious port wine in this spectacular jelly. From cheese plates to sandwiches, there are so many uses.

2½ cups (625 mL) port wine

2½ cups (625 mL) sugar

5 whole cloves

1 tsp. (5 mL) black peppercorns

10 cups (2.4 L) fresh or frozen cranberries (about 3¼ lb./1.6 kg)

--- ★ ---

Peak of Freshness

Though you can use frozen cranberries, sometimes their pectin diminishes during processing. Fresh cranberries, however, are very high in natural pectin and have consistent gelling qualities.

1. Bring first 4 ingredients to a boil in a 6-qt. (6-L) stainless steel or enameled Dutch oven, stirring until sugar dissolves. Add cranberries, and return to a boil; reduce heat, and simmer, uncovered, 15 minutes or until cranberry skins begin to split.

2. Pour cranberry mixture through a fine wire-mesh strainer into a large bowl, pressing berries with back of a wooden spoon to release as much juice as possible. Pour juice into a large stainless steel saucepan. Bring to a boil; boil 2 minutes. Remove from heat.

3. Ladle hot jelly into a hot jar, leaving ¼-inch (.5-cm) headspace. Wipe jar rim. Center lid on jar. Apply band, and adjust to fingertip-tight. Place jar in boiling-water canner. Repeat until all jars are filled.

4. Process jars 10 minutes, adjusting for altitude. Turn off heat; remove lid, and let jars stand 5 minutes. Remove jars and cool.

SWEDISH MEATBALL STROGANOFF

MAKES 8 SERVINGS

Turn this party hors d'oeuvre into your family's favorite dinner.

5 Tbsp. (75 mL) unsalted butter, divided

2 cups (500 mL) finely chopped onion, divided

1 tsp. (5 mL) ground allspice

2 large eggs, beaten

1/4 cup (60 mL) half-and-half

2 Tbsp. (30 mL) Worcestershire Sauce (page 257)

1 cup (250 mL) soft, fresh breadcrumbs

1 lb. (450 g) ground pork

1 lb. (450 g) ground turkey

1/4 cup (60 mL) finely chopped fresh parsley, divided

1 1/2 tsp. (7.5 mL) salt, divided

1 tsp. (5 mL) freshly ground black pepper, divided

1 cup (250 mL) thinly sliced fresh mushrooms

1/2 cup (125 mL) Pinot Grigio or other dry white wine

1/2 cup (125 mL) Cranberry-Port Jelly (page 84)

1 cup (250 mL) Beef Bone Broth (page 289)

1/2 cup (125 mL) sour cream

Hot cooked egg noodles

1. Melt 1 Tbsp. (15 mL) butter in a large skillet. Add 1 cup (250 mL) onion and allspice; sauté 8 minutes or until onion is very tender. Remove from heat. Set aside to cool.

2. Combine eggs, half-and-half, and Worcestershire Sauce in a large bowl; stir in breadcrumbs. Stir in cooled onion, pork, next 2 ingredients, 1 tsp. (5 mL) salt, and 1/2 tsp. (2 mL) pepper. Shape meat mixture into 36 (1-oz./30-g) balls. Place on a rimmed baking sheet. Cover and freeze 30 minutes.

3. Melt 2 Tbsp. (30 mL) butter in a large nonstick skillet over medium heat. Cook meatballs, in batches, 8 minutes, turning to brown on all sides; drain. Wipe skillet clean with paper towels.

4. Melt remaining 2 Tbsp. butter in same skillet over medium heat. Add mushrooms and remaining 1 cup (250 mL) onion. Increase heat to medium-high, and cook, stirring often, 5 minutes or until golden brown.

5. Add wine to mushroom mixture, and cook 3 minutes, stirring to loosen browned bits from bottom of skillet. Add jelly, stirring until melted. Stir in Beef Bone Broth, remaining 1/2 tsp. (2 mL) salt, and remaining 1/2 tsp. (2 mL) pepper. Return meatballs to skillet. Bring to a boil; cover, reduce heat, and simmer 20 minutes or until meatballs are done.

6. Remove skillet from heat, and gently stir in sour cream. Serve over hot cooked egg noodles.

RHUBARB JELLY

MAKES ABOUT 5 ($^1/_2$-PT./250-ML) JARS

This beautiful pink jelly showcases the tart-sweet flavor of rhubarb.

- 1 qt. (960 mL) water
- 3$^1/_2$ lb. (1.6 kg) rhubarb, trimmed and cut into $^1/_2$-inch (1-cm) pieces (10 cups/2.5 L)

Cheesecloth

- 6 Tbsp. (90 mL) Ball® Classic Pectin
- 6 cups (1.5 L) sugar

--- ★ ---

Perfect Pairing

Rhubarb is a vegetable we traditionally use as a fruit. That doesn't mean we should keep it relegated to sweets! Rhubarb pairs well with pork roast and roasted vegetables.

1. Combine water and rhubarb in a 6-qt. (6-L) stainless steel or enameled Dutch oven. Bring to a boil; reduce heat, and simmer, uncovered, 20 minutes. Remove from heat. Skim foam, if necessary.

2. Line a fine wire-mesh strainer with 3 layers of dampened cheesecloth. Place strainer over a bowl. Pour rhubarb mixture into strainer. (Do not press mixture.) Cover and let stand 2 hours or until collected juice measures 4$^1/_2$ cups (1.13 L) and mixture no longer drips.

3. Wash Dutch oven. Stir together juice and pectin in same Dutch oven. Bring mixture to a full rolling boil that cannot be stirred down, over high heat, stirring constantly.

4. Add sugar, stirring to dissolve. Return mixture to a full rolling boil. Boil hard 1 minute, stirring constantly. Remove from heat. Skim foam, if necessary.

5. Ladle hot jelly into a hot jar, leaving $^1/_4$-inch (.5-cm) headspace. Wipe jar rim. Center lid on jar. Apply band, and adjust to fingertip-tight. Place jar in boiling-water canner. Repeat until all jars are filled.

6. Process jars 10 minutes, adjusting for altitude. Turn off heat; remove lid, and let jars stand 5 minutes. Remove jars and cool.

JELLY-ROLL CAKE

MAKES 10 SERVINGS

This cake is a treat in the summer but has endless possibilities any time of year. Roll cakes are a most gratifying baking experience; they're fun to make and always "wow" at serving time.

Wax paper

Shortening

- ³/₄ cup (175 mL) cake flour, sifted
- ³/₄ tsp. (3 mL) baking powder
- ¹/₄ tsp. (1 mL) salt
- 4 large eggs
- ³/₄ cup (175 mL) granulated sugar
- 1 tsp. (5 mL) vanilla extract

Powdered sugar

- ³/₄ cup (175 mL) Rhubarb Jelly (page 86)
- 1¹/₂ cups (375 mL) whipped cream, divided
- 1¹/₂ cups (375 mL) assorted fresh berries

1. Preheat oven to 400°F (200°C). Grease bottom and sides of a 15- x 10-inch (38- x 25-cm) jelly-roll pan; line with wax paper. Grease (with shortening) and flour wax paper.

2. Combine flour, baking powder, and salt, stirring well.

3. Beat eggs at high speed with an electric mixer until foamy. Gradually add granulated sugar, 1 Tbsp. (15 mL) at a time, beating 5 minutes or until thick and pale. Beat in vanilla. Gently fold in flour mixture, in 2 additions, just until blended. Spread batter evenly into prepared pan.

4. Bake at 400°F (200°C) for 12 minutes or until cake springs back when lightly touched.

5. While cake bakes, sift powdered sugar in a 15- x 10-inch (38- x 25-cm) rectangle on a cloth towel; set aside. When cake is done, immediately loosen from sides of pan, and turn out onto sugared towel. Peel off wax paper. Starting at narrow end, roll up cake and towel together; cool completely on a wire rack, seam side down.

6. Unroll cake and remove towel. Stir jelly. Spread on cake; top with 1¹/₂ cups (375 mL) whipped cream and 1¹/₂ cups (375 mL) berries. Carefully reroll cake. Place cake roll on a rectangular serving platter, seam side down; sprinkle cake with powdered sugar. Chill 1 hour before serving.

SCUPPERNONG GRAPE JELLY

MAKES ABOUT 6 (½-PT./250-ML) JARS

Elevate your PB&J to the next level with this classic grape jelly redo. Or serve with homemade sugared doughnut holes.

4 (1-qt./1-L) containers ripe Scuppernong grapes (about 5¼ lb./2.5 kg)

1 cup (250 mL) water

Cheesecloth

5½ cups (1.3 L) sugar

2 Tbsp. fresh lemon juice

1 (3-oz./88.5-mL) pouch Ball® Liquid Pectin

──────── ★ ────────

Simple Switch

If Scuppernong grapes are not available, feel free to swap them for Concord grapes.

1. Wash grapes; remove and discard stems. Bring grapes and water to a boil in a 6-qt. (6-L) stainless steel or enameled Dutch oven, stirring often. Boil, stirring often, 20 minutes or until most of seeds have been released from pulp. Mash grapes with a potato masher to slip skins from pulp.

2. Line a large wire-mesh strainer with 3 layers of dampened cheesecloth. Place over a large bowl. Pour grape mixture into strainer, and let drain at least 1 hour to measure 3⅔ cups (900 mL) juice. Discard solids.

3. Combine grape juice, sugar, and lemon juice in same Dutch oven. Bring mixture to a full rolling boil that cannot be stirred down, over high heat, stirring frequently.

4. Add pectin, immediately squeezing entire contents from pouch. Continue hard boil for 1 minute, stirring constantly. Remove from heat. Skim foam, if necessary.

5. Ladle hot jelly into a hot jar, leaving ¼-inch (.5-cm) headspace. Wipe jar rim. Center lid on jar. Apply band, and adjust to fingertip-tight. Place jar in boiling-water canner. Repeat until all jars are filled.

6. Process jars 10 minutes, adjusting for altitude. Turn off heat; remove lid, and let jars stand 5 minutes. Remove jars and cool.

POMEGRANATE-CHERRY JELLY

MAKES ABOUT 6 (¹/₂-PT./250-ML) JARS

Tart pomegranate and sweet cherry blend together in a jelly that is luscious and beautiful.

3¹/₂ cups (875 mL) bottled pomegranate-cherry juice

6 Tbsp. (90 mL) Ball® Classic Pectin

1 Tbsp. (15 mL) orange zest

5 cups (1.25 L) sugar

★

Perfect Pairing

Slather on morning scones or English muffins, glaze a tart base, or spread between cake layers. You'll find a multitude of reasons to keep this jelly on hand.

---

1. Whisk together first 3 ingredients in a 6-qt. (6-L) stainless steel or enameled Dutch oven. Bring mixture to a full rolling boil that cannot be stirred down, over high heat, stirring constantly.

2. Add sugar, stirring to dissolve. Return mixture to a full rolling boil. Boil hard 1 minute, stirring constantly. Remove from heat. Skim foam, if necessary.

3. Ladle hot jelly into a hot jar, leaving ¹/₄-inch (.5-cm) headspace. Wipe jar rim. Center lid on jar. Apply band, and adjust to fingertip-tight. Place jar in boiling-water canner. Repeat until all jars are filled.

4. Process jars 10 minutes, adjusting for altitude. Turn off heat; remove lid, and let jars stand 5 minutes. Remove jars and cool.

PEACH-ORANGE MARMALADE

MAKES ABOUT 6 (½-PT./250-ML) JARS

The end of winter meets early spring in this sweet, tart, and beautifully hued marmalade.

---

4 or 5 large navel oranges (about 3¾ lb/1.75 kg)

8 cups (2 L) chopped peeled peaches (about 6 lb./2.75 kg whole peaches)

5 cups (1.25 L) sugar

2 Tbsp. (30 mL) bottled lemon juice

--- ★ ---

Tricks of the Trade

When citrus rinds will be incorporated into a recipe, it's a good idea to wash them under hot running water to remove any food-grade wax first.

1. Scrub oranges thoroughly; rinse well, and pat dry. Strip rind from oranges with a vegetable peeler, avoiding bitter white pith. Thinly slice rind to measure ¾ cup (175 mL). Using a sharp, thin-bladed knife, cut a ¼-inch (.5-cm)-thick slice from each end of oranges. Place flat-end down on a cutting board, and remove and discard peel (bitter white pith and any remaining rind) in strips, cutting from top to bottom, and following the curvature of the fruit. Holding peeled fruit in the palm of your hand and working over bowl to collect juices, slice between membranes, and gently remove whole segments. Discard membranes and seeds. Chop sections to measure 1½ cups (350 mL) chopped fruit and juice.

2. Combine chopped orange sections and juice, sliced rind, peaches, and next 2 ingredients in a 6-qt. (6-L) stainless steel or enameled Dutch oven. Bring to a boil over medium heat, stirring occasionally until sugar dissolves. Boil 45 to 50 minutes or until thickened, stirring frequently to prevent sticking.

3. Remove marmalade from heat. Skim off foam, if necessary.

4. Ladle hot marmalade into a hot jar, leaving ¼-inch (.5-cm) headspace. Remove air bubbles. Wipe jar rim. Center lid on jar. Apply band, and adjust to fingertip-tight. Place jar in boiling-water canner. Repeat until all jars are filled.

5. Process jars 10 minutes, adjusting for altitude. Turn off heat; remove lid, and let jars stand 5 minutes. Remove jars and cool.

RHUBARB-ORANGE MARMALADE

MAKES ABOUT 8 (¹⁄₂-PT./250-ML) JARS

Using all green rhubarb will produce a golden-color marmalade. Using some red rhubarb will add a rosy tint.

- **2** oranges, halved crosswise and seeded
- **6** cups (1.5 L) 1-inch (2.5-cm) fresh or frozen rhubarb slices
- **6** cups (1.5 L) sugar

★

Tricks of the Trade

Beginning with orange pieces that are the same size will ensure that they are more evenly chopped in the food processor.

---

1. Cut each orange half into quarters. Pulse orange pieces in a food processor until coarsely chopped.

2. Combine chopped orange, rhubarb, and sugar in a 6-qt. (6-L) stainless steel or enameled Dutch oven. Bring to a boil; reduce heat, and simmer 1 hour or until gelling point (page 17).

3. Ladle hot marmalade into a hot jar, leaving ¼-inch (.5-cm) headspace. Remove air bubbles. Wipe jar rim. Center lid on jar. Apply band, and adjust to fingertip-tight. Place jar in boiling-water canner. Repeat until all jars are filled.

4. Process jars 10 minutes, adjusting for altitude. Turn off heat; remove lid, and let jars stand 5 minutes. Remove jars and cool.

ORANGE-SHANDY MARMALADE

MAKES ABOUT 8 (1/2-PT./250-ML) JARS

Shandy is a traditional British take on a summer drink, usually a mix of beer and lemonade, and it makes for a unique and dazzling marmalade when mixed with blood orange segments.

2½ lb. (1.25 kg) oranges (about 6 oranges)

2 (12-oz./355-mL) bottles flat shandy beer

6 Tbsp. (90 mL) Ball® Classic Pectin

6 cups (1.5 L) sugar

★

Perfect Pairing
On hot summer days, add a few tablespoons of marmalade to lemonade and ice in a blender to make a Shandy Slushy.

---

1. Scrub oranges thoroughly; rinse well, and pat dry. Carefully strip rind from oranges with a vegetable peeler, avoiding bitter white pith. Finely chop rind.

2. Using a sharp, thin-bladed knife, cut a ¼-inch (.5-cm)-thick slice from each end of oranges. Place flat-end down on a cutting board, and remove and discard peel (bitter white pith and any remaining rind) in strips, cutting from top to bottom, and following the curvature of the fruit. Holding peeled fruit in the palm of your hand and working over bowl to collect juices, slice between membranes, and gently remove whole segments. Discard membranes and seeds. Coarsely chop fruit.

3. Combine beer, pectin, chopped orange, accumulated juices, and chopped rind in a 6-qt. (6-L) stainless steel or enameled Dutch oven. Bring mixture to a full rolling boil that cannot be stirred down, over high heat, stirring constantly.

4. Add sugar, stirring to dissolve. Return mixture to a full rolling boil. Boil hard 1 minute, stirring constantly. Remove from heat. Skim foam, if necessary.

5. Ladle hot marmalade into a hot jar, leaving ¼-inch (.5-cm) headspace. Remove air bubbles. Wipe jar rim. Center lid on jar. Apply band, and adjust to fingertip-tight. Place jar in boiling-water canner. Repeat until all jars are filled.

6. Process jars 10 minutes, adjusting for altitude. Turn off heat; remove lid, and let jars stand 5 minutes. Remove jars and cool.

CITRUS-VANILLA BEAN MARMALADE

MAKES ABOUT 5 (½-PT./250-ML) JARS

Vanilla turns this trio of citrus fruits into a warm and aromatic winter treat.

---

4 large navel oranges (about 1½ lb./750 g)

4 large red grapefruit (about 3¾ lb./1.7 kg)

2 large lemons (about ½ lb./250 g)

4 cups (1 L) sugar

3½ cups (875 mL) water

¼ tsp. (1 mL) kosher salt

2 vanilla beans, split lengthwise

★

Peak of Freshness

Though any navel oranges will work here, try some heirloom varieties such as Sky Valley, Cara Cara, or Vintage Sweets. All offer unique and subtle differences to marmalade.

1. Scrub fruit thoroughly; rinse well, and pat dry. Grate zest from oranges to equal 2 Tbsp. (30 mL). Grate zest from grapefruit to equal 2 Tbsp. (30 mL). Grate zest from lemons to equal 2 tsp. (10 mL). Using a sharp, thin-bladed knife, cut a ¼-inch (.5-cm)-thick slice from each end of oranges, grapefruit, and lemons. Working with 1 piece of fruit at a time, place 1 flat-end down on a cutting board, and remove peel (bitter white pith and any remaining zest) in strips, cutting from top to bottom and following the curvature of the fruit. Holding peeled fruit in the palm of your hand and working over a bowl to collect juices, slice between membranes, and gently remove whole segments. Reserve 4½ cups (1.1 L) whole segments and ½ cup (125 mL) juice. Discard membranes and seeds.

2. Stir together sugar, next 2 ingredients, citrus zests, reserved citrus segments, and reserved citrus juice in a 6-qt. (6-L) stainless steel or enameled Dutch oven. Scrape seeds from vanilla beans; add seeds and beans to citrus mixture.

3. Bring to a boil; reduce heat, and simmer 1 hour or until gelling point (page 17). Remove mixture from heat. Remove and discard vanilla beans. Skim foam, if necessary.

4. Ladle hot marmalade into a hot jar, leaving ¼-inch (.5-cm) headspace. Remove air bubbles. Wipe jar rim. Center lid on jar. Apply band, and adjust to fingertip-tight. Place jar in boiling-water canner. Repeat until all jars are filled.

5. Process jars 10 minutes, adjusting for altitude. Turn off heat; remove lid, and let jars stand 5 minutes. Remove jars and cool.

GRAPEFRUIT MARMALADE

MAKES ABOUT 4 (½-PT./250-ML) JARS

This sunny pink marmalade has more perk and less bite than its traditional English cousin.

3   large red grapefruit
    (about 2¾ lb./1.6 kg)

1   lemon (5 oz./150 g)

2½ cups (625 mL) water

⅛   tsp. (.5 mL) baking soda

6   Tbsp. (90 mL) Ball®
    Classic Pectin

4   cups (1 L) sugar

★

Tricks of the Trade
The small amount of baking soda helps soften the rind.

1. Scrub fruit thoroughly; rinse well, and pat dry. Carefully strip rind from grapefruit and lemon with a vegetable peeler, avoiding bitter white pith. Coarsely chop rind to measure 1 cup (250 mL). Place rind, water, and baking soda in a 6-qt. (6-L) stainless steel or enameled Dutch oven. Bring to a boil over high heat; cover, reduce heat, and simmer, stirring occasionally, 20 minutes.

2. Using a sharp, thin-bladed knife, cut a ¼-inch (.5-cm)-thick slice from each end of grapefruit and lemon. Place flat-end down on a cutting board, and remove and discard peel (bitter white pith and any remaining rind) in strips, cutting from top to bottom, and following the curvature of the fruit. Holding peeled fruit in the palm of your hand and working over bowl to collect juices, slice between membranes, and gently remove whole segments. Discard membranes and seeds. Coarsely chop fruit to measure 2¼ cups (550 mL) fruit and juices.

3. Add fruit and juices to rind. Bring to a boil; reduce heat, and simmer, uncovered, stirring often, 10 minutes.

4. Stir in pectin. Bring mixture to a full rolling boil that cannot be stirred down, over high heat, stirring constantly.

5. Add sugar, stirring to dissolve. Return mixture to a full rolling boil. Boil hard 1 minute, stirring constantly. Remove from heat. Skim foam, if necessary.

6. Ladle hot marmalade into a hot jar, leaving ¼-inch (.5-cm) headspace. Remove air bubbles. Wipe jar rim. Center lid on jar. Apply band, and adjust to fingertip-tight. Place jar in boiling-water canner. Repeat until all jars are filled.

7. Process jars 10 minutes, adjusting for altitude. Turn off heat; remove lid, and let jars stand 5 minutes. Remove jars and cool.

MARMALADE TEA CAKES

MAKES 2 DOZEN

These quick and simple buttery little cakes are filled with your favorite marmalade and baked in muffin cups. Perfect for afternoon tea or lunch box treats.

24 (1-inch/2.5-cm) paper muffin cup liners

½ cup (125 mL) butter, softened

½ cup (125 mL) granulated sugar

1 large egg

½ cup (125 mL) plain Greek yogurt

½ cup (125 mL) marmalade*

1 tsp. (5 mL) vanilla extract

1½ cups (375 mL) all-purpose flour

½ tsp. (2 mL) baking powder

½ tsp. (2 mL) baking soda

⅛ tsp. (.5 mL) salt

¼ cup (60 mL) powdered sugar

★

Tricks of the Trade
Use a small ice-cream scoop to evenly divide batter among muffin cups.

---

1. Preheat oven to 350°F/180°C. Place paper muffin cup liners in 2 (12-cup) miniature muffin pans. Beat butter at medium speed with an electric mixer until creamy; gradually add granulated sugar, beating well. Add egg and next 3 ingredients, beating until blended.

2. Combine flour and next 3 ingredients; add to butter mixture. Beat at low speed just until blended.

3. Divide batter evenly among muffin cups. Bake at 350°F/180°C for 18 to 20 minutes or until golden brown and firm. Cool in pans 5 minutes. Transfer to wire racks, and cool completely (about 30 minutes). Dust with powdered sugar before serving.

*Blood Orange–Ginger Marmalade (page 104), Citrus–Vanilla Bean Marmalade (page 96), Peach-Orange Marmalade (page 93), Rhubarb-Orange Marmalade (page 94), or Orange–Shandy Marmalade (page 95) may be used.

MEYER LEMON MARMALADE

MAKES ABOUT 5 (¹/₂-PT./250-ML) JARS

Sunshine in a jar! Meyer lemons have a brief season and are worth finding just to make this marmalade. This recipe is a two-day process as it requires an overnight resting of fruit and juice.

- 2 lb. (1 kg) Meyer lemons, divided
- 2 regular lemons
- 6 cups (1.44 L) water, divided
- 5 cups (1.25 L) sugar
- ¹/₄ cup (60 mL) fresh lemon juice (about 2 lemons)

★

Perfect Pairing

A delicious addition to breakfast or afternoon tea, this is also a wonderful glaze for chicken or fish. Try stirring a spoonful into cold seltzer water for a bubbly lemonade.

1. Cut 1 lb. (450 g) Meyer lemons and regular lemons lengthwise into quarters, and place in a 6-qt. (6-mL) stainless steel or enameled Dutch oven. Add 3 cups (750 mL) water. Bring to a boil; reduce heat, and simmer, uncovered, 1 hour and 30 minutes or until lemons are very soft and liquid is syrupy, pressing lemons to release juice. Remove from heat, cover, and let stand at room temperature overnight.

2. While quartered lemons are simmering, quarter remaining Meyer lemons lengthwise; remove seeds, and cut crosswise into very thin slices. Place in a 6-qt. (6-L) stainless steel or enameled Dutch oven. Add remaining water (just enough to cover lemon slices). Bring to a boil; reduce heat, and simmer, uncovered, 30 minutes, stirring occasionally. Remove from heat; cover and let stand at room temperature overnight.

3. Pour lemon quarters mixture through a fine-mesh strainer into Dutch oven containing lemon slices, pressing with back of a wooden spoon to extract as much juice as possible. Discard solids. Add sugar and lemon juice to lemon slices. Bring to a rolling boil over high heat; reduce heat to medium, and cook, uncovered, stirring often, 45 minutes or to gelling point (page 17).

4. Ladle hot marmalade into a hot jar, leaving ¹/₄-inch (.5-cm) headspace. Remove air bubbles. Wipe jar rim. Center lid on jar. Apply band, and adjust to fingertip-tight. Place jar in boiling-water canner. Repeat until all jars are filled.

5. Process jars 10 minutes, adjusting for altitude. Turn off heat; remove lid, and let jars stand 5 minutes. Remove jars and cool.

DOUBLE-ONION MARMALADE

MAKES ABOUT 6 (½-PT./250-ML) JARS

A little dab of this sweet onion marmalade is all you need to jump-start an amazing appetizer or main dish.

1½ cups (375 mL) thinly sliced red onion

1½ cups (375 mL) thinly sliced Vidalia onion

¼ cup (60 mL) firmly packed light brown sugar

⅓ cup (75 mL) apple cider vinegar (5% acidity)

1 Tbsp. (15 mL) black peppercorns

2 bay leaves

Cheesecloth

Kitchen string

2½ cups (625 mL) unsweetened apple juice

½ cup (125 mL) raisins

6 Tbsp. (90 mL) Ball® Classic Pectin

4 cups (1 L) sugar

1. Combine first 4 ingredients in a 6-qt. (6-L) stainless steel or enameled Dutch oven. Cook, stirring often, over medium heat 13 minutes or until liquid evaporates.

2. Place peppercorns and bay leaves on a 5-inch (12.5-cm) square of cheesecloth; tie with kitchen string, and add to onion mixture. Add apple juice and raisins; stir in pectin. Bring mixture to a full rolling boil that cannot be stirred down, over high heat, stirring constantly. Hold spice bag to one side of Dutch oven with tongs. Add sugar, stirring until dissolved. Release spice bag. Return mixture to a full rolling boil. Boil hard 1 minute, stirring constantly. Remove from heat; remove and discard spice bag. Skim foam, if necessary.

3. Ladle hot marmalade into a hot jar, leaving ¼-inch (.5-cm) headspace. Remove air bubbles. Wipe jar rim. Center lid on jar. Apply band and adjust to fingertip-tight. Place jar in boiling-water canner. Repeat until all jars are filled.

4. Process jars 15 minutes, adjusting for altitude. Turn off heat; remove lid, and let jars stand 5 minutes. Remove jars and cool.

★

Perfect Pairing

Try this marmalade with roasted quail, pan-seared duck, grilled pork chops, or other dishes that pair well with caramelized onions.

ALSATIAN ONION MINI-TARTS

MAKES 30 TARTS

These delightful, rich-tasting northern French tarts are quick and easy. Add ¹/₂ cup crumbled cooked bacon to the filling for a true Alsatian experience.

- 1 large egg
- ½ cup (125 mL) heavy cream
- 1 tsp. (5 mL) chopped fresh thyme
- ½ tsp. (2 mL) salt
- ¼ tsp. (1 mL) ground black pepper
- 2 (1.9-oz./54-g) pkg. mini phyllo shells
- 1 (¹/₂-pint/250-mL) jar Double-Onion Marmalade (page 102)
- ½ cup (125 mL) crumbled crisp-cooked bacon
- 4 oz. (125 g) Gruyère cheese, shredded

1. Preheat oven to 425°F (220°C). Whisk egg in a 2-cup (500-mL) glass measuring cup. Whisk in cream and next 3 ingredients.

2. Place phyllo shells on a large baking sheet. Divide marmalade and crumbled bacon evenly among shells. Carefully spoon cream mixture evenly into shells, and top with cheese.

3. Bake at 425°F (220°C) for 12 minutes or until golden brown.

LARGE TART VARIATION: Preheat oven to 425°F (220°C). Fit 1 Flaky Piecrust (page 315), thawed, into a 9-inch (23-cm) tart pan with removable bottom; press into fluted edges. Fold any excess dough over outside of pan, and pinch to secure to pan. (This will keep piecrust from sliding down pan as it bakes.) Line dough with aluminum foil, and fill with pie weights or dried beans.

Bake at 425°F (220°C) for 8 minutes. Remove weights and foil, and bake 3 to 4 more minutes or until bottom is golden brown. Remove from oven to a wire rack, and cool completely (about 15 minutes). Gently tap excess crust from sides of pan, using a rolling pin.

Spread marmalade in bottom of crust; sprinkle crumbled bacon evenly over marmalade. Carefully pour cream mixture over bacon, and sprinkle with cheese. Bake at 425°F (220°C) for 25 minutes or until filling is set and cheese is golden brown.

BLOOD ORANGE-GINGER MARMALADE

MAKES ABOUT 6 (½-PT./250-ML) JARS

This traditional long-method marmalade meant for winter canning uses divine blood oranges infused with ginger to create one beautiful preserve.

4½ to 5 lb. (2 to 2.25 kg) blood oranges (about 12), well-scrubbed and divided

8 cups (2 L) sugar

¼ cup (60 mL) fresh lemon juice (about 2 lemons)

2 tsp. (10 mL) grated fresh ginger

★

Tricks of the Trade
This recipe takes two days to prepare. Boiling and soaking aids in the breakdown of tough citrus membranes and softens the rind so that sectioning isn't necessary.

1. Quarter 6 oranges lengthwise. Cut quarters crosswise into thin slices. Place orange slices in a large saucepan; add water to cover. Bring to a boil. Remove from heat, cover and let stand at room temperature 8 hours or overnight.

2. Next day, squeeze juice from remaining 6 blood oranges into a 1-qt. (1-L) glass measuring cup; discard rinds or reserve for another use.

3. Use a slotted spoon to transfer blood orange slices to a 6-qt. (6-L) stainless steel or enameled Dutch oven, reserving soaking liquid. Add enough soaking liquid to blood orange juice to measure 4 cups (1 L). Discard remaining soaking liquid.

4. Add blood orange juice mixture, sugar, and next 2 ingredients to orange slices. Bring to a rolling boil over high heat; reduce heat to medium and simmer, uncovered, stirring often to gelling point (page 17).

5. Ladle hot marmalade into a hot jar, leaving ¼-inch (.5-cm) headspace. Remove air bubbles. Wipe jar rim. Center lid on jar. Apply band, and adjust to fingertip-tight. Place jar in boiling-water canner. Repeat until all jars are filled.

6. Process jars 10 minutes, adjusting for altitude. Turn off heat; remove lid, and let jars stand 5 minutes. Remove jars and cool.

CITRUS-GLAZED ROAST CHICKEN

MAKES 4 SERVINGS

Juicy, tender roast chicken bursts with flavor from the first bite with this marinade and glaze.

- 1 cup (250 mL) thinly sliced onion
- ½ cup (125 mL) Blood Orange-Ginger Marmalade (page 104)
- 2 Tbsp. (30 mL) olive oil
- 1 Tbsp. (15 mL) Worcestershire sauce
- 1 Tbsp. (15 mL) fresh lemon juice
- 1 tsp. (5 mL) minced fresh garlic
- ½ tsp. (2 mL) dried oregano
- ½ tsp. (2 mL) dried thyme
- ½ tsp. (2 mL) kosher salt
- ¼ tsp. (1 mL) freshly ground black pepper
- 1 (3½- to 4-lb./1.75- to 2-kg) whole chicken, cut in half

★

Simple Switch
Feel free to substitute the Peach-Orange Marmalade (page 93) if blood oranges are not in season.

1. Stir together all ingredients, except chicken, in a 3½-qt. (3.5-L) casserole dish; add chicken, turning to coat. Cover and chill 2 to 3 hours, turning once. Drain, reserving marinade.

2. Preheat oven to 375°F (190°C). Pour two-thirds of reserved marinade into bottom of a large roasting pan. Place chicken, skin side up, in pan. Pour remaining one-third of marinade over chicken.

3. Bake at 375°F (190°C) for 1 hour and 15 minutes or until a meat thermometer registers 165°F (75°C) and juices run clear when thigh is pierced with a sharp knife, basting every 15 minutes during last 45 minutes of cooking.

4. Transfer chicken to a serving platter. Pour pan juices into a bowl; skim fat from juices. Serve pan juices with chicken.

ORANGE-DATE-CARDAMOM PRESERVES

MAKES ABOUT 6 (¹/₂-PT./250-ML) JARS

Mix lemon, honey, and cardamom for a Turkish-inspired preserve.

3½ to 4 lb. (1.75 to 2 kg) oranges, sectioned (6 cups/1.5 L, packed)

½ cup (125 mL) water

1 lemon (about 3 oz./90 g)

1 vanilla bean, split

2 cups (500 mL) dates, pitted and coarsely chopped

2 cups (500 mL) sugar

½ cup (125 mL) honey

1½ tsp. (7 mL) ground cardamom

½ tsp. (2 mL) ground cinnamon

1. Bring orange sections and water to a boil in a 4-qt. (4-L) stainless steel or enameled Dutch oven, crushing segments as they soften using a potato masher. Reduce heat, and simmer, uncovered, stirring often, 15 minutes or until most of sections are broken.

2. Grate zest and squeeze juice from lemon to measure 2 tsp. (10 mL) and 2 Tbsp. (30 mL), respectively; stir into orange mixture. Scrape seeds from vanilla bean; add vanilla bean seeds, bean pod, dates, and remaining ingredients to orange mixture. Cook over medium heat to gelling point (page 17). Remove and discard vanilla bean pod.

3. Ladle hot preserves into a hot jar, leaving ¼-inch (.5-cm) headspace. Remove air bubbles. Wipe jar rim. Center lid on jar. Apply band, and adjust to fingertip-tight. Place jar in boiling-water canner. Repeat until all jars are filled.

4. Process jars 10 minutes, adjusting for altitude. Turn off heat; remove lid, and let jars stand 5 minutes. Remove jars and cool.

«CURRIED TOMATO PRESERVES

MAKES ABOUT 6 (¹/₂-PT./250-ML) JARS

Make a delicious flatbread or grilled pita bread topped with roasted sweet potatoes and cilantro.

2½ cups (625 mL) sugar

½ cup (125 mL) diced onion

⅓ cup (75 mL) bottled lemon juice

6 lb. (2.7 kg) tomatoes, cored and coarsely chopped

2 Tbsp. (30 mL) curry powder

2 tsp. (10 mL) salt

¼ tsp. (1 mL) ground red pepper

1. Combine first 4 ingredients in a 6-qt. (6-L) stainless steel or enameled Dutch oven. Bring to a boil over medium heat. Cook, uncovered, 40 minutes, stirring often. Add curry powder and next 2 ingredients. Cook, stirring often, 20 minutes or until the consistency of jam.

2. Ladle hot preserves into a hot jar, leaving ¼-inch (.5-cm) headspace. Remove air bubbles. Wipe jar rim. Center lid on jar. Apply band, and adjust to fingertip-tight. Place jar in boiling-water canner. Repeat until all jars are filled.

3. Process jars 10 minutes, adjusting for altitude. Turn off heat; remove lid, and let jars stand 5 minutes. Remove jars and cool.

SPICY PINEAPPLE-AND-TART CHERRY PRESERVES

MAKES ABOUT 4 (¹/₂-PT./250 ML) JARS

Add a bit of heat to your morning with fresh pineapple and tart cherries. Serve with oatmeal date bread and cream cheese for a special weekend breakfast.

---

1 (2-lb./1-kg) fresh pineapple, peeled and cored

3³/₄ cups (925 mL) sugar

¹/₂ tsp. (2 mL) ground red pepper

1¹/₂ lb. (750 g) fresh tart red cherries, pitted and halved (about 5 cups/ 1.25 L)

2 Tbsp. (30 mL) bottled lemon juice

————— ★ —————

Simple Switch

To add a touch of smoky spice, substitute ground chipotle chili powder for the ground red pepper.

1. Finely chop pineapple to measure 4 cups (4 L). Spread chopped pineapple over bottom of a 6-qt. (6-L) stainless steel or enameled Dutch oven. Sprinkle half of sugar in an even layer over pineapple. Sprinkle with ground red pepper. Layer cherries over sugar, and sprinkle with lemon juice and remaining half of sugar; stir and cover with a clean towel. Let stand 2 hours, stirring occasionally until sugar dissolves.

2. Bring to a boil; boil, stirring often, over medium heat to gelling point (page 17).

3. Ladle hot preserves into a hot jar, leaving ¼-inch (.5-cm) headspace. Remove air bubbles. Wipe jar rim. Center lid on jar. Apply band, and adjust to fingertip-tight. Place jar in boiling-water canner. Repeat until all jars are filled.

4. Process jars 10 minutes, adjusting for altitude. Turn off heat; remove lid, and let jars stand 5 minutes. Remove jars and cool.

BRANDIED SHALLOT-FIG PRESERVES

MAKES ABOUT 4 (1-PT./500-ML) JARS

These sweet-and-sour roasted preserves accentuate the versatility of figs. A hint of brandy and fresh herbs rounds out the luscious flavor.

4 lb. (2 kg) fresh figs

2 cups (500 mL) thinly sliced shallots

Vegetable cooking spray

1½ cups (325 mL) sugar

¾ cup (175 mL) white vinegar (5% acidity)

½ cup (125 mL) brandy

1 Tbsp. (15 mL) fresh thyme leaves or 1 tsp. (5 mL) dried thyme

2 tsp. (2 mL) salt

1 bay leaf

★

Perfect Pairing
These preserves partner beautifully with crostini for a cheese plate, make a delicious spread on a hearty grilled Cheddar sandwich, or serve as an ideal side with roast chicken.

1. Preheat oven to 350°F (180°C). Place figs and shallots in a single layer on a large rimmed baking sheet coated with cooking spray. Bake at 350°F (180°C) for 25 minutes. Sprinkle sugar over fig mixture. Bake 15 more minutes.

2. Pour fig mixture into a 6-qt. (6-L) stainless steel or enameled Dutch oven. Stir in vinegar and next 4 ingredients. Cook, stirring often, over medium-high heat 20 minutes or until mixture thickens. Remove and discard bay leaf.

3. Ladle hot preserves into a hot jar, leaving ½-inch (1-cm) headspace. Remove air bubbles. Wipe jar rim. Center lid on jar. Apply band, and adjust to fingertip-tight. Place jar in boiling-water canner. Repeat until all jars are filled.

4. Process jars 15 minutes, adjusting for altitude. Turn off heat; remove lid, and let jars stand 5 minutes. Remove jars and cool.

PEAR-ROASTED GARLIC PRESERVES

MAKES ABOUT 4 (½-PT./250-ML) JARS

Roasting pears and garlic intensifies their flavor, creating a sumptuous savory fall treat.

- 1 garlic bulb (about 9½ oz./285 g)

Vegetable cooking spray

- 3½ to 4 lb. (1.6 to 4 kg) ripe pears, peeled, cored, and cut into eighths
- 1¼ cups (300 mL) sugar, divided
- ½ cup (125 mL) water
- ¼ cup (60 mL) apple cider vinegar (5% acidity)
- 4 Tbsp. (60 mL) Ball® Classic Pectin
- 1½ tsp. (7 mL) fresh thyme leaves
- ½ tsp. (2 mL) salt
- ½ tsp. (2 mL) ground black pepper

★

Perfect Pairing

To make a super-quick fall salad dressing, whisk together ¼ cup (60 mL) Pear-Roasted Garlic Preserves and 2 Tbsp. (30 mL) balsamic vinegar. Whisk in enough good-quality olive oil to thin to desired consistency.

1. Preheat oven to 400°F (200°C). Cut off pointed end of garlic; place garlic on a piece of aluminum foil. Fold foil to seal. Place in corner of a large rimmed baking sheet coated with cooking spray. Arrange pear wedges in a single layer on baking sheet. Bake at 400°F (200°C) for 25 minutes.

2. Turn pear wedges over; sprinkle with ¼ cup (60 mL) sugar. Bake 15 more minutes or until soft. Remove pan from oven. Transfer pear slices to a 6-qt. (6-L) stainless steel or enameled Dutch oven; add water. Place garlic in foil directly on oven rack. Bake 15 more minutes or until soft.

3. Squeeze pulp from garlic cloves into pear mixture. Mash pear mixture with a potato masher until coarsely chopped. Stir in vinegar, next 4 ingredients, and remaining 1 cup (250 mL) sugar. Bring to a boil, stirring often. Cook to gelling point (page 17).

4. Ladle hot preserves into a hot jar, leaving ¼-inch (.5-cm) headspace. Remove air bubbles. Wipe jar rim. Center lid on jar. Apply band, and adjust to fingertip-tight. Place jar in boiling-water canner. Repeat until all jars are filled.

5. Process jars 10 minutes, adjusting for altitude. Turn off heat; remove lid, and let jars stand 5 minutes. Remove jars and cool.

Canned Fruit in 3 Easy Steps

Refer to water bath canning procedures on pages 26-27
and follow recipe guidelines in steps and chart below.

STEP 1: Select fruit and packing method according to Canning Guidelines for Fruit chart (pages 113-114). Prepare syrup*, if using, according to Syrups for Canning Fruit chart below: Bring sugar, or alternate sweetener, and water to a boil in a saucepan, stirring to dissolve sugar. Reduce heat; cover and keep hot until needed. (Do not allow liquid to evaporate.)

STEP 2: Prepare fruit and pack jars according to Canning Guidelines for Fruit chart.

STEP 3: Process jars according to Canning Guidelines for Fruit chart, adjusting for altitude.

Syrups for Canning Fruit

SYRUP TYPE	SELECTION	% SUGAR	ALTERNATE SWEETENER	SUGAR	WATER	YIELD*
Super-Light	Approximates natural sugar level in most fruits.	10		½ cup (125 mL)	5 cups (1250 mL)	5¼ cups (1300 mL)
Extra-Light	Use with very sweet fruit.	20		1½ cups (300 mL)	5¾ cups (1375 mL)	6 cups (1500 mL)
Light	Use with sweet apples; dark, sweet cherries; berries; and grapes.	30		2¼ cups (550 mL)	5¼ cups (1300 mL)	6½ cups (1550 mL)
Medium	Use with tart apples; apricots; tart, red cherries; gooseberries; nectarines; peaches; pears; and plums.	40		3¼ cups (800 mL)	5 cups (1250 mL)	7 cups (1650 mL)
Heavy	Use with very sour fruit.	50		4¼ cups (1050 mL)	4¼ cups (1050 mL)	7 cups (1650 mL)
Honey			1 cup (250 mL)		4 cups (1000 mL)	5 cups (1250 mL)

*Each 1 (1-qt./1-L) jar of fruit requires about 1 to 1½ cups (250 to 375 mL) syrup.

Canning Guidelines for Fruit

Makes 2 (1-pt./500-mL) or 1 (1-qt./1-L) jars

FRUIT	PREPARATION	PACKING	SYRUP TYPE	PROCESSING TIME
Apples (2-3 lb./ 1-1.5 kg)	Wash, peel, and core. Halve, quarter, or cut into ¼-inch (.5-cm) slices. Treat with Ball® Fruit-Fresh®.	**Hot Pack:** Bring syrup to a boil; add apples, and boil gently 5 minutes. Pack hot apples in hot jar. Ladle hot syrup over apples, leaving ½-inch (1-cm) headspace.	Light or Medium	(1-pt./500-mL) or (1-qt./1-L) jars 20 minutes
Apricots (2½ lb./ 1.25 kg)	Wash; drain. Halve and pit.	**Raw Pack:** Pack halves, cavity side down, in overlapping layers in hot jar. Ladle hot syrup over fruit, leaving ½-inch (1-cm) headspace. **Hot Pack:** Simmer halves, 1 layer at a time, in hot syrup until thoroughly heated. Pack, cavity side down, in overlapping layers in hot jar. Ladle hot syrup over apricots, leaving ½-inch (1-cm) headspace.	Extra-Light, Light, or Medium syrup, juice, or water	(1-pt./500-mL) 20 minutes (1-qt./1-L) jars 25 minutes
Berries (1½-3 lb./ 750 g-1.5 kg)	Wash in cold water; drain.	**Raw Pack:** (Use with raspberries or other berries that don't hold their shape when heated): Pack berries gently into hot jar (do not crush). Ladle hot syrup over berries, leaving ½-inch (1-cm) headspace. **Hot Pack:** For each 1 qt. (1 L) berries, combine berries and ¼ to ½ cup (60 to 125 mL) sugar in a glass bowl. Cover and let stand in cool place 2 hours. Cook mixture over medium-low heat until thoroughly heated and sugar dissolves, stirring occasionally to prevent sticking. Ladle berry mixture into hot jar, leaving ½-inch (1-cm) headspace.	Extra-Light or Light	(1-pt./500-mL) or (1-qt./1-L) jars 15 minutes
Cherries, Sweet or Tart (2½ lb./ 1.25 kg)	Wash and remove stems; pit, if desired. (Prick skins of unpitted cherries on opposite sides with a needle to reduce splitting.)	**Raw Pack:** Pack cherries gently into hot jar (do not crush). Ladle hot syrup over cherries, leaving ½-inch (1-cm) headspace. **Hot Pack:** For each 1 qt. (1 L) cherries, combine cherries and ½ to ¾ cup (125 to 175 mL) sugar. Cook over medium-low heat until thoroughly heated, stirring until sugar dissolves. (Add just enough water to unpitted cherries to prevent sticking.) Ladle cherries and juice into hot jar leaving ½-inch (1-cm) headspace.	Light (sweet cherries) Medium or Heavy (tart cherries)	**Raw Pack:** (1-pt./500-mL) or (1-qt./1-L) jars 25 minutes **Hot Pack:** (1-pt./500-mL) jars 15 minutes (1-qt./1-L) jars 20 minutes
Cranberries (1½ lb./ 750 g)	Wash firm berries; remove stems.	**Hot Pack:** Simmer in syrup 3 minutes. Pack into hot jar and ladle hot syrup over cranberries, leaving ½-inch (1-cm) headspace.	Heavy	(1-pt./500-mL) or (1-qt./1-L) jars 15 minutes

Canning Guidelines for Fruit

Makes 2 (1-pt./500-mL) or 1 (1-qt./1-L) jars

FRUIT	PREPARATION	PACKING	SYRUP TYPE	PROCESSING TIME
Peaches/ Nectarines (2½ lb./ 1.25 kg)	Wash firm, ripe fruit; peel peaches. Leave nectarines unpeeled; halve and pit. Treat with Ball® Fruit-Fresh®. Cut into slices, if desired.	**Raw Pack:** Pack halves, cavity side down in overlapping layers, into hot jar. Ladle hot syrup over fruit, leaving ½-inch (1-cm) headspace. **Hot Pack:** Simmer halves, 1 layer at a time, in syrup until thoroughly heated. Pack halves, cavity side down, in overlapping layers in hot jar. Ladle hot syrup over fruit, leaving ½-inch (1-cm) headspace.	Light or Medium	**Raw Pack:** (1-pt./500-mL) jars 25 minutes (1-qt./1-L) jars 30 minutes **Hot Pack:** (1-pt./500-mL) jars 20 minutes (1-qt./1-L) jars 25 minutes
Pears (2½ lb./ 1.25 kg)	Wash firm, ripe pears; peel, halve, and core. Treat with Ball® Fruit-Fresh®.	**Hot Pack:** Simmer halves, 1 layer at a time, in syrup. Pack halves, cavity side down, in overlapping layers in hot jar. Ladle hot syrup over fruit, leaving ½-inch (1-cm) headspace.	Light or Medium	(1-pt./500-mL) jars 20 minutes (1-qt./1-L) jars 25 minutes
Pineapple (2½ lb./ 1.25 kg)	Wash, peel, core. Cut into ½-inch (1-cm) slices.	**Hot Pack:** Simmer slices, 1 layer at a time, in syrup until thoroughly heated; pack in hot jar. Ladle hot syrup over fruit, leaving ½-inch (1-cm) headspace.	Extra-Light or Light	(1-pt./500-mL) jars 15 minutes (1-qt./1-L) jars 20 minutes
Plums (2 lb./1 kg)	Wash firm, ripe plums; halve and pit.	**Hot Pack:** Simmer halves in syrup 5 minutes. Remove from heat and let stand 30 minutes. Transfer plums to a bowl; return syrup to a boil. Pack plums into hot jar, and ladle hot syrup over fruit, leaving ½-inch (1-cm) headspace.	Medium or Heavy	(1-pt./500-mL) jars 20 minutes (1-qt./1-L) jars 25 minutes
Rhubarb (2 lb./1 kg)	Wash young, tender, colorful stalks. Cut into 1-inch (2.5-cm) slices.	**Hot Pack:** For each 1 qt. (1 L) rhubarb, stir together rhubarb and ½ to 1 cup (125 to 250 mL) sugar in a glass bowl. Let stand in cool place for 4 hours, stirring occasionally until juice appears. Slowly bring to a boil, stirring to prevent sticking; boil 30 seconds. Pack hot rhubarb and juice into hot jar, leaving ½-inch (1-cm) headspace.	No syrup	(1-pt./500-mL) or (1-qt./1-L) jars 15 minutes
Strawberries (3 lb./1.5 kg)	Wash and hull firm, ripe strawberries.	**Hot Pack:** For each 1 qt. (1 L) strawberries, stir together berries and ½ to ¾ cup (125 to 175 mL) sugar in a glass bowl. Let stand in cool place for 5 hours. Slowly bring to a boil; reduce heat, and simmer, uncovered, just until thoroughly heated and sugar dissolves, stirring gently to prevent sticking. Ladle hot mixture into hot jar, leaving ½-inch (1-cm) headspace.	No Syrup	(1-pt./500-mL) jars 10 minutes (1-qt./1-L) jars 15 minutes

HONEYED APRICOTS »

MAKES ABOUT 5 (1-PT./500-ML) JARS

Light and easy canned apricot halves burst with flavor with a little help from honey.

3½ cups (875 mL) water

1 cup (250 mL) honey

¼ cup (60 mL) bottled lemon juice

1 (3-inch/7.5-cm) cinnamon stick

1 Tbsp. (15 mL) lemon zest

½ vanilla bean, split lengthwise

5 lb. (2.25 kg) firm ripe apricots, halved and pitted

1. Combine first 5 ingredients in a 6-qt. (6-L) stainless steel or enameled Dutch oven. Scrape seeds from vanilla bean; add seeds and vanilla bean to honey mixture. Bring to a boil; add apricot halves. Return to a boil; reduce heat and simmer 3 minutes. Remove and discard vanilla bean and cinnamon stick.

2. Pack hot apricot halves, cut side down, in a hot jar, leaving ½-inch (1-cm) headspace. Ladle hot syrup over apricots, leaving ½-inch (1-cm) headspace. Remove air bubbles. Wipe jar rim. Center lid on jar. Apply band, and adjust to fingertip-tight. Place jar in boiling-water canner. Repeat until all jars are filled.

3. Process jars 20 minutes, adjusting for altitude. Turn off heat; remove lid, and let jars stand 5 minutes. Remove jars and cool.

TART CHERRIES IN GINGER SYRUP

MAKES ABOUT 4 (1-PT./500-ML) JARS

Canning tart cherries in a slightly sweetened ginger syrup means delicious toppings for ice cream, cakes, and oatmeal with the pop of a lid.

6 cups (1.5 L) water

2 cups (500 mL) sugar

1 cup (250 mL) ⅛-inch (3-mm)-thick peeled fresh ginger slices

2½ lb. (1.25 kg) tart cherries (about 2 qt./2 L), pitted

1. Bring first 3 ingredients to a boil in a 6-qt. (6-L) stainless steel or enameled Dutch oven; reduce heat, and simmer, uncovered, 1 hour or until syrupy. Transfer ginger slices to a bowl, using a slotted spoon. Remaining syrup should measure 3 cups (750 mL).

2. Add cherries to syrup. Bring to a simmer; cook 5 minutes or until thoroughly heated.

3. Ladle hot cherries and syrup into a hot jar, adding several slices of reserved ginger and leaving ½-inch (1-cm) headspace. Remove air bubbles. Wipe jar rim. Center lid on jar. Apply band, and adjust to fingertip-tight. Place jar in boiling-water canner. Repeat until all jars are filled.

4. Process jars 10 minutes, adjusting for altitude. Turn off heat; remove lid, and let jars stand 5 minutes. Remove jars and cool.

DRUNKEN PEACHES

MAKES ABOUT 6 (1-PT./500-ML) WIDE MOUTH JARS

Bourbon and other fine spirits do double duty when it comes to fruit, acting as both preservative and flavor booster. Try these boozy babies straight up for dessert or blended into a cocktail.

- 1 lemon
- 5 lb. (2.3 kg) fresh freestone peaches
- 3 cups (750 mL) water
- 2½ cups (635 mL) sugar
- 3 vanilla beans, halved crosswise
- 6 (¼-inch/.5-cm)-thick orange slices (from 2 small navel oranges)
- ¾ cup (175 mL) bourbon

1. Bring a large pot of water to a boil. Fill a large bowl two-thirds full of ice water. Cut lemon in half, and squeeze juice into ice water. Working in batches, place peaches in a wire basket, lower into boiling water, and blanch 60 seconds. Place immediately in lemon juice mixture. When cool enough to handle, peel peaches, cut in half, and remove pits. Cut each half into 4 wedges; return to lemon juice mixture.

2. Stir together 3 cups (750 mL) water and sugar in a large saucepan. Split vanilla bean halves lengthwise; scrape out seeds. Add vanilla bean and seeds to sugar mixture; cook over medium-high heat, stirring until sugar dissolves. Bring to and maintain at a low simmer.

3. Place 1 orange slice and 1 vanilla bean half into a hot jar. Drain and tightly pack peach quarters into jar. Ladle hot syrup into jar, leaving 1½-inch (4-cm) headspace. Add 2 Tbsp. (30 mL) bourbon to jar. Add more hot syrup to jar, leaving ½-inch (1-cm) headspace. Remove air bubbles. Wipe jar rim. Center lid on jar. Apply band, and adjust to fingertip-tight. Repeat until all jars are filled.

4. Process jars 25 minutes, adjusting for altitude. Turn off heat; remove lid, and let jars stand 5 minutes. Remove jars and cool.

BOURBON-VANILLA SECKEL PEARS

MAKES ABOUT 5 (1-PT./500-ML) JARS

Seckel pears are a small golden-skinned heirloom variety with a sweet crunch, perfect for bathing in a bourbon-vanilla syrup. Serve with whipped cream and a sprinkle of cinnamon.

3½ cups (875 mL) water

1 cup (250 mL) honey

½ cup (125 mL) bourbon

1 Tbsp. (15 mL) lemon juice

1 vanilla bean, split

4 lb. (2 kg) unpeeled Seckel pears, halved and cored

★

Simple Switch
Pears may be peeled, if desired. Bartlett or d'Anjou pears may be substituted; core and quarter to fit jars.

1. Bring first 4 ingredients to a simmer in a 4-qt. (4-L) stainless steel or enameled Dutch oven over medium heat. Scrape seeds from vanilla bean, and add to syrup.

2. Add pear halves, and simmer 5 minutes or until thoroughly heated.

3. Fill a hot jar with hot pear halves, leaving ½-inch (1-cm) headspace. Ladle hot syrup over fruit, leaving ½-inch (1-cm) headspace. Remove air bubbles. Wipe jar rim. Center lid on jar. Apply band, and adjust to fingertip-tight. Place jar in boiling-water canner. Repeat until all jars are filled.

4. Process jars 15 minutes, adjusting for altitude. Turn off heat; remove lid, and let jars stand 5 minutes. Remove jars and cool.

SWEET TEA—POACHED PEACHES

MAKES ABOUT 5 (1-PT./500-ML) JARS

Pack your peaches in fresh-brewed sweet tea as a tasty alternative to plain water or sugar syrup.

1	lemon*
3½	lb. (1.6 kg) peaches
3½	cups (875 mL) water
4	regular-size tea bags*
1	cup (250 mL) sugar
1	cup (250 mL) honey
3	Tbsp. (45 mL) lemon juice

★

Simple Switch

You can use all honey, if preferred, and add your favorite spices such as vanilla beans or cinnamon. Try a different tea, such as Earl Grey or Jasmine, for a flavor twist.

1. Bring a large pot of water to a boil. Fill a large bowl two-thirds full of ice water. Cut lemon in half, and squeeze juice into ice water. Cut an X in the bottom (opposite stem end) of each peach. Working in batches, place peaches in a wire basket; lower into boiling water and blanch 60 seconds, or just until skins loosen or curl. Place immediately in lemon juice mixture. When cool enough to handle, peel peaches, cut in half, and remove pits. Cut halves in half, if desired; return to lemon juice mixture.

2. Bring 3½ cups (875 mL) water to a boil in a medium saucepan. Remove from heat. Add tea bags; cover and steep 15 minutes. Remove tea bags. Stir in sugar, honey, and 3 Tbsp. (45 mL) lemon juice; bring to a simmer. Keep hot.

3. Pack peach halves or quarters tightly into a hot jar, cavity side down, leaving ½-inch (1-cm) headspace. Ladle hot tea mixture over peaches, leaving ½-inch (1-cm) headspace. Remove air bubbles. Wipe jar rim. Center lid on jar. Apply band, and adjust to fingertip-tight. Place jar in boiling-water canner. Repeat until all jars are filled.

4. Process jars 25 minutes, adjusting for altitude. Turn off heat; remove lid, and let jars stand 5 minutes. Remove jars and cool.

*Ball® Fruit-Fresh® may be substituted for the lemon juice. You can use 2 Tbsp. loose tea placed in a tea ball instead of the tea bags.

BLUEBERRY SYRUP

MAKES ABOUT 4 (¹/₂-PT./250-ML) JARS

Fruit syrups certainly have an esteemed place as a pantry staple, with their fresh fruit tastes, simple preparation, and incredible versatility. They are also an excellent way to use up bumper crops of fruit. Save your leftover blueberry pulp from this recipe to make the delicious Blueberry Butter (page 136).

4¹/₄ lb. (about 2 kg) fresh blueberries

3 cups (750 mL) water, divided

Cheesecloth

3 cups (375 mL) sugar

1¹/₂ Tbsp. (22 mL) bottled lemon juice

1. Wash and drain blueberries. Combine blueberries and 2 cups water in an 8-qt. (8-L) stainless steel or enameled Dutch oven; bring to a boil over medium-high heat, crushing berries with a potato masher. Reduce heat, and simmer 12 minutes, stirring occasionally.

2. Line a fine wire-mesh strainer with 3 layers of dampened cheesecloth. Place strainer over a bowl. Pour blueberry mixture into strainer. (Do not press mixture.) Let stand 30 minutes or until collected juice measures 2¹/₂ cups (625 mL) and mixture no longer drips. Reserve pulp (you should have 5¹/₂ cups/1.3 L) for Blueberry Butter (page 136) or another use.

3. Combine 3 cups sugar and remaining 1 cup water in a large stainless steel saucepan. Bring to a boil, stirring until sugar dissolves. Boil, uncovered, 20 minutes or until mixture registers 220°F (104°C) on a candy thermometer, stirring occasionally. Stir in blueberry juice and lemon juice. Return to a boil; reduce heat, and simmer, uncovered, 5 minutes, stirring once. Remove from heat. Skim off and discard any foam.

4. Ladle syrup into a hot jar, leaving ¹/₄-inch (.5-cm) headspace. Remove air bubbles. Wipe jar rim. Center lid on jar. Apply band, and adjust to fingertip-tight. Place jar in boiling-water canner. Repeat until all jars are filled.

5. Process jars 10 minutes, adjusting for altitude. Turn off heat; remove lid, and let jars stand 5 minutes. Remove jars and cool.

RASPBERRY SYRUP

MAKES ABOUT 4 (1-PT./500-ML) JARS

Feeling adventurous? Try adding a splash of syrup to your morning cup of coffee. The raspberry pairs perfectly with rich coffee notes.

3 lb. (1.5 kg) raspberries

2 cups (500 mL) water

Cheesecloth

2¾ cups (675 mL) sugar

½ cup (125 mL) light corn syrup

2 Tbsp. (30 mL) bottled lemon juice

———— ★ ————

Perfect Pairing
Mix with club soda for a refreshing drink.

1. Place raspberries and water in a 6-qt. (6-L) stainless steel or enameled Dutch oven. Bring to a simmer over medium-low heat. Cook, uncovered, 20 minutes, stirring occasionally. (Do not boil.)

2. Remove from heat. Line a wire-mesh strainer with 2 layers of dampened cheesecloth or a jelly bag. Place over a bowl. Pour berry mixture into strainer, and let drain 2 hours or as needed to extract 4½ cups (1.13 L) juice. (Do not press or squeeze mixture.) Discard solids. Rinse Dutch oven.

3. Combine raspberry juice, sugar, and next 2 ingredients in Dutch oven, stirring until sugar dissolves. Bring mixture to a full rolling boil over medium-high heat; boil 1 minute.

4. Ladle hot syrup into a hot jar, leaving ½-inch (1-cm) headspace. Remove air bubbles. Wipe jar rim. Center lid on jar. Apply band, and adjust to fingertip-tight. Place jar in boiling-water canner. Repeat until all jars are filled.

5. Process jars 10 minutes, adjusting for altitude. Turn off heat; remove lid, and let jars stand 5 minutes. Remove jars and cool.

STRAWBERRY SYRUP

MAKES ABOUT 5 (1-PT./500-ML) JARS

Recipe testers agreed, this makes an awesome margarita; see below!

3½ lb. (1.7 kg) strawberries

3 cups (750 mL) water

1 (3-inch/7.5-cm) cinnamon stick

Cheesecloth

6 cups (1.5 L) sugar

¾ cup (175 mL) light corn syrup

⅓ cup (75 mL) bottled lemon juice

1. Place first 3 ingredients in a 6-qt. (6-L) stainless steel or enameled Dutch oven. Bring to a simmer over medium-low heat. Cook, uncovered, 20 minutes, stirring occasionally. (Do not boil.)

2. Remove from heat. Line a wire-mesh strainer with 2 layers of dampened cheesecloth or a jelly bag. Place over a bowl. Pour berry mixture into strainer, and let drain 2 hours or as needed to extract 6 cups (1.5 mL) juice. (Do not press or squeeze mixture.) Discard solids. Rinse Dutch oven.

3. Combine strawberry juice, sugar, and next 2 ingredients in Dutch oven, stirring until sugar dissolves. Bring mixture to a full rolling boil over medium-high heat; boil 1 minute.

4. Ladle hot syrup into a hot jar, leaving ¼-inch (.5-cm) headspace. Remove air bubbles. Wipe jar rim. Center lid on jar. Apply band, and adjust to fingertip-tight. Place jar in boiling-water canner. Repeat until all jars are filled.

5. Process jars 10 minutes, adjusting for altitude. Turn off heat; remove lid, and let jars stand 5 minutes. Remove jars and cool.

STRAWBERRY MARGARITAS »

MAKES 2 SERVINGS

Kosher salt

¼ cup (60 mL) tequila

¼ cup (60 mL) Strawberry Syrup

2 Tbsp. (30 mL) fresh lime juice

6 to 8 ice cubes

Garnishes: fresh strawberries, lime slices or wedges

1. Rim 2 chilled margarita glasses, or rocks glasses, with salt.

2. Combine tequila and next 3 ingredients in a cocktail shaker. Cover with lid, and shake vigorously 1 minute or until shaker is frosted. Pour evenly into prepared glasses.

FROZEN STRAWBERRY MARGARITAS: Rim 2 chilled margarita glasses with salt. Process tequila, next 3 ingredients, and 7 to 8 fresh strawberries, hulled and frozen, in a blender until smooth. Pour evenly into prepared glasses.

STRAWBERRY COCKTAIL: Omit salt. Combine tequila and next 3 ingredients in a cocktail shaker. Cover with lid, and shake vigorously 1 minute or until shaker is frosted. Strain evenly into 2 chilled martini or cocktail glasses.

BLACKBERRY SYRUP

MAKES ABOUT 3 (1-PT./500-ML) JARS

During the peak of summer, try adding a splash of syrup to iced lemonade for a refreshing cooldown.

3 lb. (1.5 kg) blackberries

2 cups (500 mL) water

Cheesecloth

2¾ cups (675 mL) sugar

¼ cup (60 mL) light corn syrup

2 Tbsp. (30 mL) bottled lemon juice

1. Place blackberries and water in a 6-qt. (6-L) stainless steel or enameled Dutch oven. Bring to a simmer over medium-low heat. Cook, uncovered, 20 minutes, stirring occasionally. (Do not boil.)

2. Remove from heat. Line a wire-mesh strainer with 2 layers of dampened cheesecloth or a jelly bag. Place over a bowl. Pour berry mixture into strainer, and let drain 2 hours or as needed to extract 4½ cups (1.13 L) juice. (Do not press or squeeze mixture.) Discard solids. Rinse Dutch oven.

3. Combine blackberry juice, sugar, and next 2 ingredients in Dutch oven, stirring until sugar dissolves. Bring mixture to a full rolling boil over medium-high heat; boil 1 minute.

4. Ladle hot syrup into a hot jar, leaving ½-inch (1-cm) headspace. Remove air bubbles. Wipe jar rim. Center lid on jar. Apply band, and adjust to fingertip-tight. Place jar in boiling-water canner. Repeat until all jars are filled.

5. Process jars 10 minutes, adjusting for altitude. Turn off heat; remove lid, and let jars stand 5 minutes. Remove jars and cool.

« WATERMELON-BLACKBERRY GRANITA

MAKES 6 SERVINGS

Try this as a kid-friendly fruit ice or as an adult libation; just add a splash of vodka or rum, and garnish with melon slices and mint.

8 cups (2 L) seeded watermelon cubes

½ cup (125 mL) Blackberry Syrup

2 Tbsp. (30 mL) fresh lime juice

1. Process watermelon, in batches, in a blender until liquified. Pour into a 13- x 9-inch (3.5-L) baking dish. Stir in syrup and lime juice.

2. Freeze 3 hours or until ice crystals form, stirring every 30 minutes.

3. Place a 2-qt. (2-L) container with a tight-fitting lid in freezer for 10 minutes. Transfer granita to chilled container. Store in freezer. Let stand in refrigerator 15 minutes before serving.

Homemade Pie Filling in 3 Easy Steps

Refer to water bath canning procedures on pages 26-27
and follow recipe guidelines in steps and chart below.

Makes 1 (1-qt./1-L) jar filling for 1 (9-inch/23-cm) pie

STEP 1: See Fruit Pie Fillings chart below. Bring prepared fruit and sugar to a boil in large saucepan; reduce heat, and simmer, uncovered, 5 minutes, stirring often. Remove from heat and stir in flavorings.

STEP 2: Ladle hot fruit mixture into a hot jar, leaving ½-inch (1-cm) headspace. Remove air bubbles.

STEP 3: Process jars 30 minutes, adjusting for altitude.

TIP: To thicken pie filling out of the pantry, drain ⅓ cup (75 mL) liquid from 1 (1-qt./1-L) jar of Homemade Pie Filling into a medium saucepan. Whisk 3 Tbsp. (45 mL) cornstarch into liquid until smooth. Add remaining contents of jar to cornstarch mixture and stir gently to blend. Bring to a boil over medium-high heat. Reduce heat and simmer for 1 minute. Serve as a warm topping for ice cream or custard. To make a **QUICK-AND-EASY FRUIT PIE,** follow the recipe below.

Fruit Pie Fillings

For each 1-qt./1-L jar

FRUIT	PREPARATION	SUGAR	FLAVORINGS
Apples (2 lb./1 kg)	Peel, core, and slice (about 6 cups/1.5 L).	½ cup (125 mL)	2 Tbsp. (30 mL) lemon juice ½ tsp. (2 mL) ground cinnamon ¼ tsp. (1 mL) ground nutmeg
Blueberries (6 cups/1.5 L)	Wash; remove stems.	¾ cup (175 mL)	½ tsp. (2 mL) lemon zest 2 Tbsp. (30 mL) lemon juice ½ tsp. (2 mL) ground cinnamon
Cherries, Dark, Sweet (6 cups/1.5 L)	Wash; remove stems, and pit.	½ cup (125 mL)	2 Tbsp. (30 mL) lemon juice ½ tsp. (2 mL) ground cinnamon ¼ tsp. (1 ml) almond extract
Cherries, Tart, Red (4 cups/1 L)	Wash; remove stems, and pit.	1¼ cups (300 mL)	¼ tsp. (1 mL) almond extract
Peaches or Nectarines (2 lb./1 kg)	Peel peaches* (leave nectarines unpeeled); halve, remove pits, and slice (about 6 cups/1.5 L).	½ cup (125 mL)	2 Tbsp. (30 mL) lemon juice ½ tsp. (2 mL) ground cinnamon

*See Canning Guidelines for Fruit chart, pages 113-114.

QUICK-AND-EASY FRUIT PIE: Preheat oven to 450°F (230°C). Prepare Flaky Piecrust (page 315) and fit rolled out piecrust into a 9-inch (23-cm) pie plate. Drain ⅓ cup (75 mL) liquid from 1 (1-qt./1-L) jar of Homemade Pie Filling into a medium bowl. Whisk 3 Tbsp. (45 mL) cornstarch and ⅛ tsp. (.2 mL) salt into liquid in bowl until smooth. Add remaining contents of jar to cornstarch mixture, stirring gently to blend. Pour into prepared piecrust. Top with remaining piecrust; fold edges under and crimp. Cut slits in top for steam to escape. Bake at 450°F (230°C) for 15 minutes; reduce heat to 350°F (180°C); bake 25 to 30 minutes or until crust is golden and filling is bubbly.

PEAR-AND-SOUR CHERRY PIE FILLING

MAKES ABOUT 3 (1-QT./1-L) JARS

Sweet pears balance tart cherries for a lovely all-season pie filling.

---

3 cups (750 mL) sugar

2 tsp. (10 mL) ground cinnamon

3¾ lb. (1.75 kg) ripe Bosc pears, peeled, cored, and sliced

2½ lb. (1.25 kg) fresh tart red cherries, pitted

3 Tbsp. (45 mL) bottled lemon juice

1. Whisk together sugar and cinnamon in a 6-qt. (6-L) stainless steel or enameled Dutch oven until blended. Add pear slices and cherries, and sprinkle with lemon juice. Bring to a simmer over medium heat, stirring gently; cover and cook 10 minutes or until fruit releases its juices, stirring occasionally.

2. Ladle hot fruit mixture into a hot jar, leaving 1-inch (2.5-cm) headspace. Remove air bubbles. Wipe jar rim. Center lid on jar. Apply band, and adjust to fingertip-tight. Place jar in boiling-water canner. Repeat until all jars are filled.

3. Process jars 30 minutes, adjusting for altitude. Turn off heat; remove lid, and let jars stand 5 minutes. Remove jars and cool.

PEAR-AND-SOUR CHERRY PIE: Preheat oven to 400°F (200°C). Prepare Flaky Piecrust (page 315) and fit rolled out piecrust into a 9-inch (23-cm) pie plate. Drain ⅓ cup syrup from 1 jar of pie filling into a medium bowl. Whisk in 2 Tbsp. (30 mL) cornstarch until smooth. Add remaining pie filling, gently stirring to blend into cornstarch mixture. Pour into pie shell in a 9-inch (23-cm) pie plate set on a baking sheet. Bake at 400°F (200°C) for 30 minutes. Reduce oven temperature to 350°F (190°C); bake 25 more minutes or until golden brown.

APPLE-PEAR-CRANBERRY PIE FILLING

MAKES ABOUT 3 (1-QT./1-L) JARS

Make pie filling a snap! This trifruit filling is great for crisps and turnovers too.

---

4 cups (1 L) water

¾ cup (175 mL) bottled lemon juice, divided

5 cups (1.25 L) thinly sliced peeled apples (2 lb./1 kg apples)

5 cups (1.25 L) thinly sliced peeled pears (2¼ lb./1 kg pears)

2 cups (500 mL) cranberries, fresh or frozen, thawed

2½ cups (625 mL) sugar

1 tsp. (5 mL) ground cinnamon

⅛ tsp. (.5 mL) ground nutmeg

1. Combine water and ¼ cup (60 mL) lemon juice in a large bowl. Submerge apple and pear slices in lemon water; drain.

2. Combine fruit slices, cranberries, next 3 ingredients, and remaining ½ cup (125 mL) lemon juice in a 6-qt. (6-L) stainless steel or enameled Dutch oven. Bring to a simmer over medium heat; cover and cook 10 minutes or until fruit releases its juices, stirring occasionally.

3. Ladle hot fruit mixture into a hot jar, leaving ½-inch (1-cm) headspace. Remove air bubbles. Wipe jar rim. Center lid on jar. Apply band, and adjust to fingertip-tight. Place jar in boiling-water canner. Repeat until all jars are filled.

4. Process jars 30 minutes, adjusting for altitude. Turn off heat; remove lid, and let jars stand 5 minutes. Remove jars and cool.

APPLE-PEAR-CRANBERRY PIE: Preheat oven to 400°F (200°C). Prepare Flaky Piecrust (page 315) and fit rolled out piecrust into a 9-inch (23-cm) pie plate. Drain ⅓ cup syrup from 1 jar of pie filling into a medium bowl. Whisk in 2 Tbsp. (30 mL) cornstarch until smooth. Add remaining pie filling, gently stirring to blend into cornstarch mixture. Pour into an unbaked pie shell in a 9-inch (23-cm) pie plate set on a baking sheet. Bake at 400°F (200°C) for 30 minutes. Reduce oven temperature to 350°F (190°C); bake 25 more minutes or until golden brown.

Fruit Butter in 5 Easy Steps

Refer to water bath canning procedures on pages 26-27
and follow recipe guidelines in steps and chart below.

Makes 6 (½-pt./250-mL) or 3 (1-pt./500-mL) jars

STEP 1: Prepare desired fruit as described in the Fruit Preparation for Fruit Butter chart below.

STEP 2: Choose 1 liquid, 1 sweetener, and 1 spice (or a combination, as desired) from the Liquids, Sweeteners, and Spices for Fruit Butter chart below.

STEP 3: Combine prepared fruit and ¼ cup (60 mL) bottled lemon juice in a Dutch oven. Bring to a boil; reduce heat, cover, and simmer until very soft. Puree mixture. Return to Dutch oven; stir in desired liquid, sweetener, and spice. Bring to a boil; reduce heat and simmer, uncovered, until mixture holds its shape in a spoon, stirring often.

STEP 4: Ladle hot fruit mixture into a hot jar, leaving ¼-inch (.5-cm) headspace for ½-pt. (250-mL) jars, or ½-inch (1-cm) headspace for 1-pt. (500-mL) jars. Remove air bubbles.

STEP 5: Process jars 10 minutes, adjusting for altitude.

Fruit Preparation for Fruit Butter

FRUIT	PREPARATION
Apples	12 to 16 medium (4 lb./2 kg): Wash, peel, core, and chop.
Apricots	35 medium (4½ lb./2 kg): Wash, pit, and chop.
Nectarines	18 medium (6 lb./3 kg): Wash, halve, pit, and chop.
Peaches	18 to 24 medium (6 lb./3 kg): Wash and peel. Halve, pit, and chop.
Pears	18 to 24 medium (6 lb./3 kg): Wash, peel, core, and chop.
Plums	55 to 60 medium (6 lb./3 kg): Wash, halve, pit, and chop.

Liquids, Sweeteners, and Spices for Fruit Butter

¾ cup (75 mL)	1 to 2 cups (250 to 500 mL)*	To taste
Apple cider Apple juice Cranberry juice Orange juice Pineapple juice Water	Agave nectar Brown sugar Granulated sugar Honey Maple syrup	Balsamic vinegar Citrus zest Dry sherry Ground allspice Ground cinnamon Ground ginger Liqueur Star anise Vanilla extract Wine

*Start with 1 cup (250 mL) sweetener. If desired, gradually add more to taste up to 2 cups (500 mL).

SLOW-COOKER METHOD: Combine desired prepared fruit and lemon juice in an electric slow cooker. Cover and cook on HIGH setting 1 hour or until fruit is very soft. Puree; stir in desired liquid, sweetener, and spices, and return to slow cooker. Partially cover and cook on HIGH setting until mixture is thick and holds its shape in a spoon (about 6 to 10 hours), stirring occasionally. If desired, cook, partially covered, on LOW setting 8 hours or overnight. Fill jars and process according to steps 4 and 5 above.

PEAR–STAR ANISE BUTTER

MAKES ABOUT 4 (½-PT./250-ML) JARS

Star anise adds a unique burst of flavor to pears cooked down into this scrumptious butter. Wonderful as a glaze for a roast, stirred into hot cereal on a winter day, or use as a delicious spread on sandwiches.

- 3½ lb. (1.6 kg) firm, ripe d'Anjou pears, peeled, cored, and coarsely chopped (6½ cups/1.6 L)
- 2 Tbsp. (30 mL) orange zest
- ½ cup (125 mL) fresh orange juice
- ⅓ cup (75 mL) water
- 1½ Tbsp. (22 mL) lemon zest
- 3 Tbsp. (45 mL) fresh lemon juice
- 2 cups (500 mL) sugar
- ¾ tsp. (3 mL) freshly grated nutmeg
- 4 star anise

★

Tricks of the Trade

The peels of green pears can make a butter have a grainy texture, so be sure not to skip the peeling!

1. Bring first 6 ingredients to a boil in a large stainless steel or enameled saucepan. Reduce heat, and simmer, uncovered, 20 to 25 minutes or until pears are soft, stirring occasionally. Remove from heat and let cool slightly (about 5 minutes).

2. Place pear mixture in a food processor; pulse 12 times or until coarsely pureed.

3. Bring pear puree, sugar, and nutmeg to a boil in same pan, stirring until sugar dissolves. Reduce heat; simmer, uncovered, 20 minutes or until mixture is thickened and holds its shape on a spoon.

4. Place 1 star anise into a hot jar. Spoon hot mixture into jar, leaving ¼-inch (.5-cm) headspace. Remove air bubbles. Wipe rim. Center lid on jar. Apply band and adjust to fingertip-tight. Repeat until all jars are filled.

5. Process jars 10 minutes, adjusting for altitude. Turn off heat; remove lid, and let jars stand 5 minutes. Remove jars and cool.

BLUEBERRY BUTTER

MAKES ABOUT 6 (1/2-PT./250-ML) JARS

Two appealing recipes with one batch of blueberries! First make our Blueberry Syrup (page 122), then use the pulp to make this smooth fruity butter.

5½ cups (1.4 L) blueberry pulp reserved from Blueberry Syrup (page 122)

3 cups (750 mL) sugar

1 Tbsp. (15 mL) lemon zest

1½ Tbsp. (22 mL) fresh lemon juice

¼ tsp. (1 mL) ground nutmeg

1. Process blueberry pulp in a food processor 1 minute or until very smooth. Combine pureed pulp, sugar, and remaining ingredients in a 6-qt. (6-L) stainless steel or enameled Dutch oven. Bring to a boil over medium heat, stirring often. Reduce heat, and simmer, stirring constantly, 1 hour or until mixture thickens and holds its shape on a spoon.

2. Ladle hot blueberry butter into a hot jar, leaving ¼-inch (.5-cm) headspace. Remove air bubbles. Wipe jar rim. Center lid on jar. Apply band, and adjust to fingertip-tight. Place jar in boiling-water canner. Repeat until all jars are filled.

3. Process jars 10 minutes, adjusting for altitude. Turn off heat; remove lid, and let jars stand 5 minutes. Remove jars and cool.

APPLE-PLUM BUTTER

MAKES ABOUT 8 (¹/₂-PT./250-ML) JARS

Lightly spiced apples and plums combine to make this inspiring seasonal fruit butter.

- 2 lb. (1 kg) unpeeled apples, cored and cut into thick slices
- 2 lb. (1 kg) plums, quartered and pitted
- 1 cup (250 mL) apple juice
- 6 cups (1.5 L) sugar
- ¼ tsp. (1 mL) ground cinnamon

★

Peak of Freshness

Use a mix of heirloom apples, such as Cortland, Gala, Jonagold, or Jonathan. Leaving the skins on helps the butter retain beautiful color.

1. Bring first 3 ingredients to a boil in a 4-qt. (4-L) stainless steel or enameled Dutch oven over medium heat; reduce heat, cover, and simmer 18 to 20 minutes or until apple slices disintegrate, stirring occasionally.

2. Press apple mixture through a food mill, in batches, until pureed to measure 8 cups (2 L). Pour each batch of puree into a bowl.

3. Pour puree into Dutch oven; add sugar and cinnamon, stirring until sugar dissolves. Cook over low heat 1 hour to 1 hour and 15 minutes or until mixture is thick and holds its shape in a spoon, stirring often. Remove from heat. Skim foam, if necessary.

4. Ladle hot butter into a hot jar, leaving ¼-inch (.5-cm) headspace. Remove air bubbles. Wipe jar rim. Center lid on jar. Apply band, and adjust to fingertip-tight. Place jar in boiling-water canner. Repeat until all jars are filled.

5. Process jars 10 minutes, adjusting for altitude. Turn off heat; remove lid, and let jars stand 5 minutes. Remove jars and cool.

APPLESAUCE

MAKES ABOUT 4 (1-PT./500-ML) JARS

A quintessential recipe for every home canner, this recipe is rewarding and easily adapted to personal tastes with added spices or sugar.

---

6 lb. (3 kg) apples, peeled, cored, and quartered

²/₃ cup (150 mL) sugar

½ cup (125 mL) water

½ cup (125 mL) bottled lemon juice

★

Tricks of the Trade

If a smooth sauce is desired, cool apple mixture slightly, and process in batches in a food processor. Return applesauce to Dutch oven, and bring to a boil, stirring often, before filling jars.

1. Combine all ingredients in a 6-qt. (6-L) stainless steel or enameled Dutch oven. Cook over medium-low heat 25 minutes or until apple is very tender, stirring occasionally.

2. Mash apple mixture with a potato masher to desired consistency.

3. Ladle hot applesauce into a hot jar, leaving ½-inch (1-cm) headspace. Remove air bubbles. Wipe jar rim. Center lid on jar. Apply band, and adjust to fingertip-tight. Place jar in boiling-water canner. Repeat until all jars are filled.

4. Process jars 20 minutes, adjusting for altitude. Turn off heat; remove lid, and let jars stand 5 minutes. Remove jars and cool.

APPLESAUCE STREUSEL CAKE

MAKES 16 SERVINGS

A delectable moist streusel-topped cake that uses your homemade applesauce, lightly spiced and perfect for afternoon tea. For a decadent treat, spread Caramel Sauce (page 318) on each slice.

STREUSEL TOPPING

- ⅔ cup (150 mL) firmly packed light brown sugar
- ½ cup (125 mL) all-purpose flour
- 1 tsp. (5 mL) ground cinnamon
- ¼ cup (60 mL) cold unsalted butter

CAKE

- ½ cup (125 mL) unsalted butter, softened
- 1½ cups (375 mL) firmly packed light brown sugar
- 2 large eggs
- 2½ cups (625 mL) all-purpose flour
- 1 tsp. (5 mL) baking soda
- 2 tsp. (10 mL) ground cinnamon
- ¼ tsp. (1 mL) salt
- ¼ tsp. (1 mL) ground cloves
- ⅛ tsp. (.5 mL) ground nutmeg
- 2 cups (500 mL) Applesauce (page 139)
- ½ cup (125 mL) raisins or cranberries
- ½ cup (125 mL) chopped walnuts (optional)

1. Preheat oven to 325°F (160°C). Prepare Streusel: Stir together brown sugar, flour, and cinnamon in a medium bowl until blended; cut in butter with a pastry blender until crumbly. Set aside.

2. Prepare Cake: Beat butter at medium speed with an electric mixer until creamy; gradually add brown sugar, beating well. Add eggs, beating just until blended.

3. Combine flour and next 5 ingredients; add to butter mixture alternately with Applesauce, beginning and ending with flour mixture. Beat at low speed just until blended after each addition, stopping to scrape bowl as needed. (Batter will be very thick.) Fold in raisins and walnuts, if desired.

4. Spoon batter into a greased 9- x 5-inch (23- x 13-cm) loaf pan. Sprinkle Streusel Topping evenly over batter.

5. Bake at 325°F (160°C) for 1 hour and 15 minutes or until a wooden pick inserted in center comes out clean. Cool completely in pan on a wire rack (about 1 hour).

HABANERO-CARROT BUTTER

MAKES ABOUT 5 (½-PT./250-ML) JARS

Fresh carrots are transformed in this surprisingly delicious spicy, savory butter.

---

2 lb. (1 kg) carrots, peeled and sliced

1 cup (250 mL) water

1 cup (250 mL) white wine vinegar (5% acidity)

¾ cup (175 mL) finely chopped onion

½ cup (125 mL) fresh lime juice (about 3 limes)

1 tsp. (5 mL) salt

4 garlic cloves, chopped

3 habanero peppers, seeded and chopped

⅓ cup (75 mL) chopped fresh cilantro

1. Bring all ingredients, except cilantro, to a boil in a 4-qt. (4-L) stainless steel or enameled Dutch oven; reduce heat, cover and simmer 30 minutes or until carrot is very soft. Remove from heat, and cool slightly (about 5 minutes).

2. Process carrot mixture and cilantro in a blender or food processor in batches until smooth, stopping to scrape down sides as needed.

3. Return carrot mixture to Dutch oven. Bring to a boil; reduce heat, and simmer, uncovered, 10 to 15 minutes or until mixture thickens and holds its shape on a spoon.

4. Fill a hot jar with hot carrot mixture, leaving ¼-inch (.5-cm) headspace. Remove air bubbles. Wipe jar rim. Center lid on jar. Apply band, and adjust to fingertip-tight. Repeat until all jars are filled.

5. Process jars 10 minutes, adjusting for altitude. Turn off heat; remove lid, and let jars stand 5 minutes. Remove jars and cool.

SPICY SHRIMP TACOS

MAKES 4 SERVINGS

A chunky mango guacamole spiced with our Habanero-Carrot Butter is served with shrimp and a spicy vegetable sauté in this outstanding take on tacos.

- 1 ripe avocado, diced
- 1 medium mango, finely diced
- ¼ cup (60 mL) minced red onion
- ¼ cup (60 mL) chopped fresh cilantro, divided
- ¼ cup (60 mL) lime juice (about 3 large limes), divided
- 10 Tbsp. Habanero-Carrot Butter (page 142), divided
- 1½ tsp. (7 mL) salt, divided
- 1 tsp. (5 mL) ground black pepper, divided
- 1 red or yellow bell pepper, sliced
- 1 large zucchini, sliced
- 2 garlic cloves, minced
- 2 Tbsp. (30 mL) olive oil
- 1 lb. medium-size raw shrimp, peeled and deveined
- 8 (6-inch/15-cm) corn or flour tortillas, warmed

Crumbled queso fresco or feta cheese

Lime wedges

1. Combine first 3 ingredients in a medium bowl. Stir in 2 Tbsp. (30 mL) each cilantro, lime juice, and Habanero-Carrot Butter. Stir in ½ tsp. (2 mL) salt and ¼ tsp. (1 mL) pepper.

2. Sauté bell pepper, zucchini, and garlic in hot olive oil in a large skillet over medium-high heat until crisp-tender.

3. Sprinkle shrimp with remaining 1 tsp. (5 mL) salt and remaining ¾ tsp. (3 mL) pepper. Add to vegetable mixture; cook, stirring often, 4 to 5 minutes or until shrimp turn pink. Remove from heat and stir in remaining ½ cup (125 mL) Habanero-Carrot Butter, remaining 2 Tbsp. (60 mL) cilantro, and remaining 2 Tbsp. (60 mL) lime juice.

4. Divide shrimp mixture among tortillas. Top with mango mixture, and sprinkle with cheese. Serve with lime wedges.

PEACH-GINGER BUTTER

MAKES ABOUT 6 (½-PT./250-ML) JARS

Nothing quite beats a fresh in-season peach, except maybe a whole bushel of them to use in preserves. Luscious peach butter with a zing of ginger creates a decidedly satisfying flavor.

- 10 cups (2.4 mL) coarsely chopped fresh peaches (about 12 medium)
- ½ cup (125 mL) water
- ½ cup (125 mL) finely chopped crystallized ginger
- 2 tsp. (10 mL) lemon zest
- 2 Tbsp. (30 mL) fresh lemon juice
- 3 cups (750 mL) sugar

★

Perfect Pairing

Try this butter mixed with mustard as a glaze for grilled or roasted meats or on sliced baguette with Balsamic-Onion Jam (page 59) and herbed goat cheese.

1. Combine first 5 ingredients in a 6-qt. (6-L) stainless steel or enameled Dutch oven. Bring to a boil over medium-high heat, stirring often. Reduce heat, and simmer, uncovered, 15 minutes or until peaches are tender, stirring occasionally. Remove from heat, and let cool slightly.

2. Pulse peach mixture, in batches, in a food processor until almost smooth. Pour each batch into a large bowl.

3. Return peach puree to Dutch oven; stir in sugar. Bring to a boil over medium heat, stirring until sugar dissolves. Cook, stirring constantly, 25 to 30 minutes or until mixture thickens and holds its shape on a spoon.

4. Ladle hot peach mixture into a hot jar, leaving ¼-inch (.5-cm) headspace. Remove air bubbles. Wipe jar rim. Center lid on jar. Apply band, and adjust to fingertip-tight. Place jar in boiling-water canner. Repeat until all jars are filled.

5. Process jars 10 minutes, adjusting for altitude. Turn off heat; remove lid, and let jars stand 5 minutes. Remove jars and cool.

PEAR-MAPLE-BOURBON BUTTER

MAKES ABOUT 6 (¹/₂-PT./250-ML) JARS

Pears are a warming reminder of fall, leaves turning joyful colors, cozy mornings with oatmeal and hot tea, pies baking in the oven. Pear butter is all that on a spoon. Eat this on toast, with your oatmeal, or generously spread on pork roast.

- ¹/₂ cup (125 mL) maple syrup
- ¹/₂ cup (125 mL) bourbon
- 4 lb. (2 kg) pears, peeled, cored, and coarsely chopped

★

Tricks of the Trade

Fruit butters can be used in baking to cut the fat quantity. Try replacing half the butter or fat called for with a flavorful fruit butter in your favorite cake or muffin recipe.

1. Bring all ingredients to a boil in a 6-qt. (6-L) stainless steel or enameled Dutch oven; reduce heat, and simmer, uncovered, 35 minutes or until pear is very soft, stirring often to prevent scorching. Remove from heat; cool slightly.

2. Process pear mixture, in batches, in a food processor until pureed, pouring each batch of puree into a bowl. Return mixture to Dutch oven. Bring to a boil; reduce heat, and simmer, uncovered, until puree thickens, darkens in color, and holds its shape on a spoon, stirring occasionally. (Stir more often as puree thickens.)

3. Ladle hot pear butter into a hot jar, leaving ¹/₄-inch (.5-cm) headspace. Remove air bubbles. Wipe jar rim. Center lid on jar. Apply band, and adjust to fingertip-tight. Place jar in boiling-water canner. Repeat until all jars are filled.

4. Process jars 10 minutes, adjusting for altitude. Turn off heat; remove lid, and let jars stand 5 minutes. Remove jars and cool.

HOT PEACH-LIME CHUTNEY

MAKES ABOUT 4 (1/2-PT./250-ML) JARS

Loaded with lime juice and ripe peaches, this chutney has a nice balance of tart and sweet with a hit of heat.

12 peaches (3 lb./1.5 kg), peeled, pitted, and cut into 1/2-inch (1-cm) cubes

3 cups (750 mL) sugar

1 3/4 cups (425 mL) white vinegar (5% acidity)

1/4 cup (60 mL) fresh lime juice (about 3 large limes)

1 cup (250 mL) 1/2-inch (1-cm) diced onion

2 Tbsp. (30 mL) (1/2-inch/ 1-cm x 1/8-inch/3-mm) lime peel strips

1 tsp. (5 mL) salt

1 tsp. (5 mL) dried crushed red pepper

1. Bring all ingredients to a boil in a 4-qt. (4-L) stainless steel or enameled Dutch oven. Reduce heat, and simmer, uncovered, 1 hour or until thick, stirring occasionally.

2. Ladle hot chutney into a hot jar, leaving 1/2-inch (1-cm) headspace. Remove air bubbles. Wipe jar rim. Center lid on jar. Apply band, and adjust to fingertip-tight. Place jar in boiling-water canner. Repeat until all jars are filled.

3. Process jars 10 minutes, adjusting for altitude. Turn off heat; remove lid, and let jars stand 5 minutes. Remove jars and cool.

★

Tricks of the Trade

A citrus zester will make quick work of zesting rinds. Line up the slivers and proceed according to the recipe.

FIG-AND-LEMON CHUTNEY

MAKES ABOUT 4 (1-PT./500-ML) JARS

This recipe makes use of wonderful Meyer lemons. With their sweet-tart flavor and thin skins, they meld perfectly with figs.

- 8 Meyer lemons
- 1 Tbsp. (15 mL) salt
- ½ cup (125 mL) apple cider vinegar
- ¼ cup (60 mL) bottled lemon juice
- 2 lb. (1 kg) fresh green figs
- 1½ cups (375 mL) firmly packed light brown sugar
- 1 Tbsp. (15 mL) grated fresh ginger
- 1 tsp. (5 mL) ground cardamom
- 1 tsp. (5 mL) ground coriander
- ½ tsp. (2 mL) dried crushed red pepper
- 3 large shallots, diced
- 2 garlic cloves, chopped
- 1 cup (250 mL) diced dried Calimyrna figs

--- ★ ---

Tricks of the Trade
If using regular lemons instead of Meyer lemons, sprinkle with the salt and let stand 1 hour.

1. Quarter lemons lengthwise; remove seeds, and cut crosswise into ⅛-inch (3-mm)-thick slices to measure 2 cups (500 mL). Place lemon slices in a 6-qt. (6-L) stainless steel or enameled Dutch oven. Sprinkle lemon slices with salt; let stand 30 minutes.

2. Add vinegar and lemon juice; cook, uncovered, over medium heat 10 minutes or until lemon rind is soft.

3. Add green figs and next 7 ingredients. Cook, uncovered, over medium heat 30 minutes or until mixture thickens, stirring often.

4. Add dried figs; reduce heat to low, and simmer, uncovered, 10 minutes or until dried figs are soft and chutney holds its shape on a spoon.

5. Ladle hot chutney into a hot jar, leaving ½-inch (1-cm) headspace. Remove air bubbles. Wipe jar rim. Center lid on jar. Apply band, and adjust to fingertip-tight. Place jar in boiling-water canner. Repeat until all jars are filled.

6. Process jars 15 minutes, adjusting for altitude. Turn off heat; remove lid, and let jars stand 5 minutes. Remove jars and cool.

THAI GREEN TOMATO CHUTNEY

MAKES ABOUT 5 (1-PT./500-ML) JARS

This end-of-summer chutney combines late-season green tomatoes with sweet ripe plums and has all the tangy, spicy notes of Thai cuisine. Serve with grilled eggplant, cherry peppers, and cilantro.

2 lb. (1 kg) red plums, pitted and coarsely chopped

1½ lb. (750 g) green tomatoes, cored and coarsely chopped

1⅓ cups (325 mL) diced onion (1 large onion)

¾ cup (175 mL) firmly packed light brown sugar

½ cup (125 mL) rice vinegar

¼ cup (60 mL) fresh lemon juice (about 2 large)

2 garlic cloves, minced

2 Thai chile peppers, minced*

1 tsp. (5 mL) salt

¼ cup (60 mL) chopped fresh cilantro

1. Bring first 7 ingredients to a boil in a 6-qt. (6-L) stainless steel or enameled Dutch oven; reduce heat, and simmer, uncovered, 20 minutes or until fruit begins to soften. Add chile peppers and salt; simmer, stirring constantly, 25 minutes or until very thick. Stir in cilantro. Remove from heat.

2. Ladle hot chutney into a hot jar, leaving ½-inch (.5-cm) headspace. Remove air bubbles. Wipe jar rim. Center lid on jar. Apply band, and adjust to fingertip-tight. Place jar in boiling-water canner. Repeat until all jars are filled.

3. Process jars 15 minutes, adjusting for altitude. Turn off heat; remove lid, and let jars stand 5 minutes. Remove jars and cool.

* ½ to 1 tsp. (2 to 5 mL) ground red pepper may be substituted.

★

Simple Switch

Other varieties of plums, such as Italian prune plums, pluots, and green damson plums work nicely in this recipe too.

GREEN APPLE–SHALLOT CHUTNEY

MAKES ABOUT 6 (1/2-PT./250-ML) JARS

A tart and chewy treat thanks to green apples and dried apricots seasoned with ginger, cinnamon, and pickling spices.

- **6** Granny Smith apples (about 3½ lb./1.6 kg), peeled, cored, and halved
- **1½** cups (375 mL) apple cider vinegar
- **1** cup (250 mL) sugar
- **½** cup (125 mL) firmly packed light brown sugar
- **2** tsp. (10 mL) mustard seeds
- **2** tsp. (10 mL) dried crushed red pepper
- **1** tsp. (5 mL) grated fresh ginger
- **¼** tsp. (1 mL) ground cinnamon
- **¼** tsp. (1 mL) ground black pepper
- **1** tsp. (5 mL) butter or olive oil
- **2** cups (500 mL) thinly sliced shallots
- **¼** cup (60 mL) water
- **1** cup (250 mL) chopped dried apricots

1. Cut each apple half vertically into 6 slices. Cut slices crosswise into ½-inch (1-cm) pieces. Place apple, vinegar, and next 7 ingredients in a 6-qt. (6-L) stainless steel or enameled Dutch oven. Cook, stirring often, over medium-low heat 30 minutes or until apple is tender.

2. Meanwhile, melt butter in a large skillet over medium-high heat. Add shallots and water; cook, stirring often, 15 to 20 minutes or until shallots are caramel colored.

3. Add shallots and apricots to apple mixture. Cook, stirring often, 15 to 20 minutes or until thickened.

4. Ladle hot apple mixture into a hot jar, leaving ½-inch (1-cm) headspace. Remove air bubbles. Wipe jar rim. Center lid on jar. Apply band, and adjust to fingertip-tight. Place jar in boiling-water canner. Repeat until all jars are filled.

5. Process jars 15 minutes, adjusting for altitude. Turn off heat; remove lid, and let jars stand 5 minutes. Remove jars and cool.

CURRIED GRILLED PORK TENDERLOIN

MAKES 6 SERVINGS

Tangy chutney is a perfect topping for marinated and grilled pork tenderloin. Serve this with buttered basmati rice and salad for a simple dinner.

½ cup (125 mL) chopped onion

2 Tbsp. (30 mL) lime juice (1 large lime)

2 Tbsp. (30 mL) olive oil

1 tsp. (5 mL) curry powder

1 tsp. (5 mL) minced fresh garlic

½ tsp. (2 mL) salt

½ tsp. (2 mL) dried thyme

½ tsp. (2 mL) dried oregano

½ tsp. (2 mL) freshly ground black pepper

2 (1¼-lb./625 g) pork tenderloins

Green Apple–Shallot Chutney (page 150)

1. Process first 9 ingredients in a blender until smooth. Pour mixture into large shallow dish or large zip-top plastic freezer bag; add pork, turning to coat. Cover or seal, and chill at least 4 hours.

2. Preheat grill to medium-high (350° to 400°F/180° to 200°C) heat. Remove pork from marinade, discarding marinade. Grill pork, covered with grill lid, 15 to 20 minutes or until a meat thermometer inserted in thickest portion registers 155°F (68°C), turning every 5 minutes. Let stand 10 to 12 minutes or until thermometer registers 160°F (70°C).

3. Cut pork into slices and serve with Green Apple–Shallot Chutney.

TAMARIND CHUTNEY

MAKES ABOUT 4 (1-PT./500-ML) JARS

This authentic South Asian condiment is a perfect balance of sweet and sour. It's a great counterpoint to potatoes and grilled meats.

- 3/4 lb. (350 g) whole tamarinds
- 2 cups (500 mL) water
- 1 Tbsp. (15 mL) cumin seeds
- 1 1/2 cups (375 mL) firmly packed light brown sugar
- 1 Tbsp. (15 mL) salt
- 1 1/2 tsp. (7 mL) dried crushed red pepper
- 1/2 tsp. (2 mL) ground ginger
- 1/2 tsp. (2 mL) Himalayan black salt (kala namak) or sea salt

★

Tricks of the Trade

Himalayan black salt, also known as *kala namak,* is a pungent, sulfur-rich rock salt used in South Asian cooking. It can be found in Asian grocery stores.

1. Crack open tamarind bark; remove pods, discarding bark and, if possible, any seeds and strings. Break pods into pieces; place in a small 3-qt. (3-L) stainless steel or enameled saucepan. Add water, and bring to a boil; cover, reduce heat, and simmer 15 minutes. Remove from heat. Let stand 20 minutes or until cool enough to handle.

2. While tamarind cools, heat cumin seeds in a small skillet over medium-low heat, stirring constantly, until lightly toasted and fragrant. Transfer seeds to a medium saucepan. Set aside.

3. Remove pulp from pieces of pod, discarding seeds and strings. Place pulp in a wire-mesh strainer set over a medium bowl. Press pulp through strainer with the back of a wooden spoon to measure 2 cups (500 mL). Discard any solids.

4. Add pulp, brown sugar, and next 4 ingredients to cumin seeds. Bring to a boil, stirring constantly over high heat; reduce heat, and simmer until sugar dissolves, stirring often.

5. Ladle hot chutney into a hot jar, leaving 1/2-inch (1-cm) headspace. Remove air bubbles. Wipe jar rim. Center lid on jar. Apply band, and adjust to fingertip-tight. Place jar in boiling-water canner. Repeat until all jars are filled.

6. Process jars 10 minutes, adjusting for altitude. Turn off heat; remove lid, and let jars stand 5 minutes. Remove jars and cool.

Tamarind Chutney (at left)

Mint-Cilantro
Chutney (page 329)

Green Apple-
Shallot Chutney
(page 150)

MANGO CHUTNEY

MAKES ABOUT 4 (1-PT./500-ML) JARS

Toasting the spices until aromatic adds intense flavor to this sublime traditional Indian chutney.

- 1 tsp. (5 mL) mustard seeds
- 1 tsp. (5 mL) fennel seeds
- 1 tsp. (5 mL) cumin seeds
- ½ tsp. (2 mL) fenugreek seeds
- 6 cups (1.5 L) finely diced mango (4 to 5 large mangoes)
- 6 Tbsp. (90 mL) granulated sugar
- ¼ cup (60 mL) fresh lime juice (about 3 large limes)
- 2 tsp. (10 mL) salt
- 2 tsp. (10 mL) garam masala
- 2 tsp. (10 mL) grated fresh ginger
- ¼ tsp. (.5 mL) ground red pepper

1. Heat mustard seeds in a 4-qt. (4-L) stainless steel or enameled Dutch oven over medium-high heat, stirring often, until they begin to pop.

2. Add fennel seeds and next 2 ingredients; heat, stirring constantly, until fragrant. Stir in mango and next 6 ingredients. Bring to a simmer; cook, stirring constantly, 15 minutes or until thick.

3. Ladle hot chutney into a hot jar, leaving ½-inch (.5-cm) headspace. Remove air bubbles. Wipe jar rim. Center lid on jar. Apply band, and adjust to fingertip-tight. Place jar in boiling-water canner. Repeat until all jars are filled.

4. Process jars 10 minutes, adjusting for altitude. Turn off heat; remove lid, and let jars stand 5 minutes. Remove jars and cool.

★

Perfect Pairing

This classic chutney is superb with curried chicken or vegetable dishes or simply spooned onto basmati rice.

CUCUMBER-AND-CHARRED RED ONION RELISH

MAKES ABOUT 5 (1-PT./500-ML) JARS

This chunky relish gets its smoky flavor from red onions broiled to a desirable char, while cucumbers bathed in a pickle brine offer a cool, crunchy contrast. Serve the relish in traditional style with hot dogs or offer it alongside fried chicken with corn on the cob.

3 lb. (1.5 kg) red onions (about 4 large), cut into ¼-inch (.5-cm)-thick slices

Vegetable cooking spray

1½ cups (375 mL) white vinegar (5% acidity)

1 cup (250 mL) fresh lime juice (about 10 limes)

1 cup (250 mL) sugar

1 Tbsp. (15 mL) mustard seeds

¼ cup (60 mL) kosher salt

2 tsp. (10 mL) coriander seeds

2 tsp. (10 mL) dried crushed red pepper

1 tsp. (5 mL) ground turmeric

1 tsp. (5 mL) smoked paprika

2 lb. (1 kg) pickling cucumbers, cut into ⅛- to ¼-inch (3-mm to .5-cm) cubes (about 6 cups/1.5 L)

1. Preheat broiler with oven rack 6 inches from heat. Arrange onion slices in a single layer on a large baking sheet coated with cooking spray. Broil 5 minutes on each side or until onion begins to char. Place pan on a wire rack until onion is cool enough to handle; chop onion into ¼-inch (.5-cm) pieces.

2. Combine vinegar and next 8 ingredients in a 6-qt. (6-L) stainless steel or enameled Dutch oven. Bring to a boil, stirring until sugar dissolves. Add cucumber and onion; return to a boil. Cook, uncovered, 10 minutes, stirring occasionally.

3. Using a slotted spoon, fill a hot jar with hot vegetables, leaving ½-inch (1-cm) headspace. Ladle hot pickling liquid over vegetables, leaving ½-inch (1-cm) headspace. Remove air bubbles. Wipe jar rim. Center lid on jar. Apply band, and adjust to fingertip-tight. Place jar in boiling-water canner. Repeat until all jars are filled.

4. Process jars 15 minutes, adjusting for altitude. Turn off heat; remove lid, and let jars stand 5 minutes. Remove jars and cool.

CHOWCHOW

MAKES ABOUT 12 (1-PT./500-ML) OR 6 (1-QT./1-L) JARS

This piquant condiment has roots in Southern states.

1½ lb. (750 g) pickling cucumbers

2 lb. (1 kg) Vidalia, or other sweet onions, finely chopped

1½ lb. (750 g) green tomatoes, cored and finely chopped

1 small head cabbage (about 2½ lb./1.25 kg), cut into 1-inch (2.5-cm) dice

¾ cup (175 mL) Ball® Salt for Pickling and Preserving

2 qt. (2 L) water

4 tsp. (60 mL) kosher salt, divided

½ lb. green beans, cut into 1-inch (2.5-cm) pieces

1 small head cauliflower (about 1½ lb./750 g), broken into florets

2 qt. (2 L) apple cider vinegar (5% acidity)

½ cup (125 mL) prepared horseradish

2 Tbsp. (30 mL) mustard seeds

½ tsp. (2 mL) celery seeds

4 garlic cloves, minced

3 medium-size green bell peppers, finely chopped

2 medium-size red bell peppers, finely chopped

3 jalapeño peppers, seeded and finely chopped

2 cups (500 mL) firmly packed light brown sugar

½ cup (125 mL) Dijon mustard

1 Tbsp. (15 mL) ground turmeric

1 tsp. (5 mL) curry powder

1. Quarter cucumbers lengthwise; cut crosswise into ¼-inch (.5-cm) slices. Layer cucumber slices, onions, tomatoes, and cabbage in a 1-gal. (4-L) food-grade plastic container with a tight-fitting lid.

2. Dissolve pickling salt in 2 qt. (2-L) water. Pour salt water over vegetables in container, adding up to 2 cups (500 mL) additional water, if necessary, to cover vegetables; secure lid on container. Chill overnight. Drain; rinse 2 or 3 times under cold running water. Drain and place in a large bowl.

3. Bring a 6-qt. (6-L) pot of water and 1 Tbsp. (15 mL) kosher salt to a boil. Fill a large bowl with ice water. Blanch green beans in boiling salted water for 2 minutes; transfer beans to ice water with a slotted spoon. Drain and add to cabbage mixture. Repeat procedure with cauliflower.

4. Bring vinegar to a boil in a large stainless steel or enameled stock pot. Add horseradish and next 3 ingredients; reduce heat, and simmer 3 minutes. Add bell peppers and jalapeño peppers. Return to a boil; add brown sugar, next 3 ingredients, and remaining 1 tsp. (15 mL) kosher salt. Return to a boil; carefully add drained vegetables. Bring to a boil, stirring often. Reduce heat, and simmer, uncovered, 10 minutes or until vegetables are thoroughly heated.

5. Ladle hot chowchow into a hot jar, leaving ½-inch (1-cm) headspace. Remove air bubbles. Wipe jar rim. Center lid on jar. Apply band, and adjust to fingertip-tight. Place jar in boiling-water canner. Repeat until all jars are filled.

6. Process 1-pt. (500-L) jars 25 minutes or 1-qt. (1-L) jars 30 minutes, adjusting for altitude. Turn off heat; remove lid, and let jars stand 5 minutes. Remove jars and cool.

EASTERN SHORE CORN RELISH

MAKES ABOUT 5 (1-PT./500-ML) JARS

Plump ripe corn, peppers, and cucumbers combine with Old Bay seasoning to give this relish its "Eastern" twist.

- 4 cups (1 L) fresh corn kernels (about 6 ears)
- 2 cups (500 mL) diced green bell pepper
- 2 cups (500 mL) diced sweet onion
- 2 cups (500 mL) apple cider vinegar (5% acidity)
- 1 cup (250 mL) diced unpeeled cucumber
- 1 cup (250 mL) sugar
- 2 Tbsp. (30 mL) Old Bay seasoning
- 1 Tbsp. (15 mL) kosher salt
- 3 cups (750 mL) diced seeded peeled tomatoes

★

Perfect Pairing
From crab cakes to lobster rolls, this relish adds a Maryland flavor twist to your favorite seafood dishes.

1. Bring all ingredients, except tomatoes, to a boil in a 6-qt. (6-L) stainless steel or enameled Dutch oven, stirring often. Reduce heat, and simmer 10 minutes, stirring often.

2. Stir in tomatoes; cook 10 minutes. Remove from heat.

3. Ladle hot relish into a hot jar, leaving ½-inch (1-cm) headspace. Remove air bubbles. Wipe jar rim. Center lid on jar. Apply band, and adjust to fingertip-tight. Place jar in boiling-water canner. Repeat until all jars are filled.

4. Process jars 15 minutes, adjusting for altitude. Turn off heat; remove lid, and let jars stand 5 minutes. Remove jars and cool.

CRAB CAKES

MAKES 8 SERVINGS

Fresh lump crabmeat defines these fantastic crab cakes, served with Eastern Shore Corn Relish (page 158), and are sure to transport you to the mid-Atlantic coast.

- 3 Tbsp. (45 mL) olive oil, divided
- ½ cup (125 mL) finely chopped red bell pepper
- ⅓ cup (75 mL) finely chopped sweet onion
- ¼ cup (60 mL) finely chopped celery
- ½ tsp. (2 mL) Old Bay seasoning
- 1 lb. (450 g) fresh lump crabmeat, drained
- ½ cup (125 mL) mayonnaise
- 1½ tsp. (7 mL) chopped fresh cilantro
- 1 tsp. (5 mL) salt
- ½ tsp. (2 mL) freshly ground black pepper
- 2 cups (500 mL) fresh white breadcrumbs, divided

Eastern Shore Corn Relish (page 158)

Lemon wedges

1. Heat 2 tsp. (10 mL) olive oil in a medium skillet over medium-low heat. Add bell pepper and next 2 ingredients. Cook 8 minutes or until very tender, but not brown, stirring occasionally. Stir in Old Bay seasoning. Remove from heat and cool completely.

2. Meanwhile, pick crabmeat, removing any bits of shell.

3. Combine vegetable mixture, mayonnaise, and next 3 ingredients in a large bowl. Gently fold in crabmeat and ½ cup (125 mL) breadcrumbs. With moist hands, shape mixture into 8 (½-inch/1-cm) cakes. Place remaining 1½ cups (375 mL) breadcrumbs in a shallow dish. Dredge cakes in breadcrumbs, pressing lightly to adhere; place on a baking sheet. Cover and chill 30 minutes or until firm.

4. Heat half of remaining oil in a large skillet over medium-high heat. Add 4 crab cakes, and cook 2 to 3 minutes on each side or until golden. Drain on paper towels. Repeat procedure with remaining oil and remaining 4 crab cakes. Serve with Eastern Shore Corn Relish and lemon wedges.

SUMMER BOUNTY ZUCCHINI RELISH

MAKES ABOUT 4 (¹/₂-PT./125-ML) JARS

This delightful relish, loaded with zucchini, peppers, and traditional pickling spices, can easily be doubled if you're overrun with summer squash.

- 3 cups (750 mL) grated zucchini (about 4 small)
- 1¹/₂ cups (375 mL) (¹/₄-inch/.5-cm) diced red, orange, and yellow bell peppers (about 8 oz./250 g)
- ¹/₂ cup (125 mL) grated onion
- 2 Tbsp. (30 mL) Ball® Salt for Pickling & Preserving
- 1¹/₂ cups (375 mL) sugar
- 1 cup (250 mL) white vinegar (5% acidity)
- 2 tsp. (10 mL) celery seeds
- 1 tsp. (5 mL) mustard seeds

Ball® Pickle Crisp (optional)

★

Perfect Pairing
This is delicious served on top of fried fish and black-eyed peas.

1. Combine first 3 ingredients in a large glass or stainless steel bowl. Sprinkle with salt; cover with cold water. Let stand for 2 hours. Drain. Rinse; drain, pressing slightly to remove excess water.

2. Bring sugar and next 3 ingredients in a 4-qt. (4-L) stainless steel or enameled Dutch oven to a boil. Add drained vegetables, and return to a boil. Reduce heat, and simmer, uncovered, 10 minutes.

3. Ladle hot relish into a hot jar, leaving ¹/₂-inch (1-cm) headspace. Remove air bubbles. Wipe jar rim. Top mixture with ¹/₁₆ tsp. (.25 mL) Pickle Crisp, if desired. Center lid on jar. Apply band, and adjust to fingertip-tight. Place jar in boiling-water canner. Repeat until all jars are filled.

4. Process jars 10 minutes, adjusting for altitude. Turn off heat; remove lid, and let jars stand 5 minutes. Remove jars and cool.

BEET RELISH WITH HORSERADISH

MAKES ABOUT 4 (1-PT./500-ML) JARS

Give those beets an extra scrubbing because they hold onto dirt more than other vegetables.

- 3 lb. (1.4 kg) 3-inch (7.5 cm)-diameter beets
- 2½ cups (625 mL) apple cider vinegar (5% acidity)
- 2 cups (500 mL) finely diced onion (1 large)
- 1¼ cups (300 mL) sugar
- ⅔ cup (150 mL) prepared horseradish
- 2 tsp. (10 mL) Ball® Salt for Pickling & Preserving
- 1½ tsp. (7 mL) freshly ground black pepper
- ½ to 1 tsp. (2 to 5 mL) ground red pepper

★

Perfect Pairing
The saltiness of grilled sausages serves as a nice counterpoint to this slightly sweet and savory relish.

1. Trim beets, leaving 1 inch (2.5 cm) of stem, and scrub. Bring beets to a boil in water to cover in a large saucepan; reduce heat, and simmer 25 to 30 minutes or until tender. Drain, rinse, and cool slightly. Trim off roots and stems; peel beets. Finely dice beets to measure 8 cups.

2. Combine beets, vinegar, and remaining 6 ingredients in a 4-qt. (4-L) stainless steel or enameled Dutch oven. Bring to a boil, stirring often. Reduce heat, and simmer 12 minutes, stirring occasionally.

3. Ladle hot beet mixture into a hot jar, leaving ½-inch (1-cm) headspace. Remove air bubbles. Wipe jar rim. Center lid on jar. Apply band, and adjust to fingertip-tight. Place jar in boiling-water canner. Repeat until all jars are filled.

4. Process jars 15 minutes, adjusting for altitude. Turn off heat; remove lid, and let jars stand 5 minutes. Remove jars and cool.

Salsa in 3 Easy Steps

Refer to water bath canning procedures on pages 26-27
and follow recipe guidelines in steps and chart below.

Makes about 6 (½-pt./250-mL) jars

STEP 1: Combine ingredients for desired salsa (see chart below) and bring to a boil in large stainless steel or enameled saucepan. Reduce heat and simmer 5 minutes.

STEP 2: Ladle hot salsa into a hot jar, leaving ½-inch (1-cm) headspace. Remove air bubbles.

STEP 3: Process jars 15 minutes, adjusting for altitude.

SALSA RECIPES	INGREDIENTS	SEASONINGS	ACID
Corn and Cherry Tomato	1¾ lb. (.75 kg) cherry tomatoes, quartered 1 cup (250 mL) fresh corn kernels (about 2 large ears) ½ cup (125 mL) red onion, finely chopped 1 to 2 jalapeño peppers, seeded and minced	3 Tbsp. (45 mL) chopped fresh cilantro 1 tsp. (5 mL) salt	¼ cup (60 mL) fresh lime juice (about 3 limes)
Green Tomato Salsa Verde	2 lb. (1 kg) green tomatoes, finely chopped 1 cup (250 mL) finely chopped red onion 1 to 2 jalapeño or serrano peppers, seeded and finely chopped	½ cup (125 mL) chopped fresh cilantro 1 tsp. (5 mL) salt 2 garlic cloves, minced	⅓ cup (75 mL) fresh lime juice (about 4 limes)
Habanero-Tomatillo	2½ lb. (1.25 kg) tomatillos, husks removed, roasted*, and chopped 4 habanero peppers, seeded and minced 1 red onion, quartered, roasted*, peeled, and chopped	3 Tbsp. (45 mL) chopped fresh cilantro 1 tsp. (5 mL) salt	¼ cup (60 mL) fresh lime juice (about 3 limes)
Mango-Chipotle	3 mangoes, peeled and cut into ½-inch (1-cm) chunks 1 red bell pepper, diced 1 small white onion, finely chopped	3 Tbsp. (45 mL) chopped fresh cilantro 1 tsp. (5 mL) salt 2 canned chipotle peppers in adobo sauce, chopped	½ cup (125 mL) fresh lime juice (about 6 limes)
Tomato-Jalapeño	2 lb. (1 kg) plum tomatoes, chopped 1 medium onion, finely chopped 2 jalapeño peppers, seeded and minced	¼ cup (60 mL) finely chopped fresh cilantro 1 tsp. (5 mL) salt ½ tsp. (2 mL) black pepper 2 garlic cloves, minced	½ cup (125 mL) fresh lime juice (about 6 limes)

*To roast tomatillos and onion: Preheat oven to 425°F (220°C). Arrange tomatillos, stem side down, and onion quarters, skin side down, on a large rimmed baking sheet. Bake at 425°F (220°C) for 20 minutes or until tomatillos and onion are beginning to char and soften.

CARAMELIZED PINEAPPLE-HABANERO SALSA

MAKES ABOUT 4 (1-PT./500-ML) JARS

Caramelizing pineapple plays up its golden sweet flavor in this simple, spicy salsa.

2 (2-lb./1-kg) ripe pineapples, peeled, quartered lengthwise, and cored

Vegetable cooking spray

6 Tbsp. (90 mL) sugar, divided

2 cups (500 mL) chopped red onion

½ cup (125 mL) fresh lime juice

1 habanero pepper, seeded and minced

½ cup (125 mL) chopped fresh cilantro

1½ tsp. (7 mL) salt

───── ★ ─────

Tricks of the Trade
Be sure to wear gloves when seeding the peppers, and do not touch your face or eyes to avoid burning.

1. Preheat oven to 400°F/200°C. Cut each pineapple quarter crosswise into 1-inch slices. Place slices in a single layer on 2 baking sheets coated with cooking spray. Sprinkle evenly with ¼ cup (60 mL) sugar.

2. Bake at 400°F/200°C for 15 minutes. Turn slices over, and bake 10 to 15 more minutes or until beginning to caramelize. Remove from oven; cool.

3. Coarsely chop pineapple slices to measure 6½ cups (1.6 L). Combine pineapple, onion, and next 2 ingredients in a large stainless steel or enameled saucepan. Bring to a boil over medium heat. Cook 5 minutes, stirring occasionally. Stir in cilantro, salt, and remaining 2 Tbsp. (30 mL) sugar.

4. Transfer half of pineapple mixture to a food processor; process until chopped. (Do not puree.) Return chopped mixture to coarsely chopped pineapple mixture remaining in pan. Cook over medium heat 5 minutes or until thoroughly heated, stirring occasionally.

5. Ladle hot salsa into a hot jar, leaving ½-inch (1-cm) headspace. Remove air bubbles. Wipe jar rim. Center lid on jar. Apply band, and adjust to fingertip-tight. Place jar in boiling-water canner. Repeat until all jars are filled.

6. Process jars 15 minutes, adjusting for altitude. Turn off heat; remove lid, and let jars stand 5 minutes. Remove jars and cool.

SALSA ROJA

MAKES ABOUT 3 (½-PT./250-ML) JARS

Ancho chiles give this salsa its deep hue and deep rich and slightly smoky flavor.

1¼ lb. (625 g) plum tomatoes, cored

1 small onion, quartered

6 garlic cloves, peeled

6 ancho chiles

2 cups (500 mL) boiling water

¼ cup (60 mL) fresh lime juice (about 3 large)

Salt

Black pepper

—————— ★ ——————

Tricks of the Trade

Toasting dried chile peppers before using brings out the natural sugars and makes the flavor much deeper.

1. Preheat oven to 425°F (220°C). Place tomatoes and onion quarters, skin side down, on a large rimmed baking sheet. Wrap garlic in a small piece of aluminum foil. Place foil pouch on 1 corner of baking sheet.

2. Bake at 425°F (220°C) for 20 minutes or until tomatoes and onion are beginning to char and soften. Transfer baking sheet to a wire rack to cool.

3. While vegetables are baking, toast ancho chiles on a very hot griddle, or in a skillet, 8 or 9 seconds on each side or just until beginning to puff and blister. (Do not allow to burn or they will become bitter.) When chiles are cool enough to handle, remove stems and seeds; tear into large pieces and place in a medium bowl. Cover with boiling water. Let stand 15 minutes or until softened. Drain, reserving soaking liquid.

4. When roasted vegetables are cool enough to handle, remove peels, and place in a food processor. Add lime juice and ancho chiles; process until pureed, adding some of reserved soaking liquid, if necessary, to desired consistency. Adjust seasoning with salt and pepper.

5. Transfer salsa to a large stainless steel or enameled saucepan. Bring to a boil. Remove from heat.

6. Ladle hot salsa into a hot jar, leaving ½-inch (1-cm) headspace. Remove air bubbles. Wipe jar rim. Center lid on jar. Apply band, and adjust to fingertip-tight. Place jar in boiling-water canner. Repeat until all jars are filled.

7. Process jars 25 minutes, adjusting for altitude. Turn off heat; remove lid, and let jars stand 5 minutes. Remove jars and cool.

ROASTED SALSA VERDE

MAKES ABOUT 3 (1-PT./500-ML) JARS

This traditional salsa is equally delicious served with tortilla chips or as a base for enchiladas.

- 4 lb. (2 kg) tomatillos, husks removed
- 2 medium-size white onions, each cut into 8 wedges
- 2 jalapeño or serrano peppers
- 6 garlic cloves, peeled
- ½ cup (125 mL) lime juice (about 6 limes)
- ¼ cup (60 mL) coarsely chopped fresh cilantro leaves
- 2 tsp. (10 mL) salt
- 1 tsp. (5 mL) black pepper

1. Preheat oven to 425°F (220°C). Arrange tomatillos, stem side down, on a large rimmed baking sheet lined with aluminum foil. Place onions, jalapeño peppers, and garlic on prepared baking sheet. Bake at 425°F (220°C) for 15 minutes or until garlic is softened. Remove garlic from baking sheet. Bake onion mixture 15 more minutes or until onion is tender and tomatillos and peppers are slightly charred. Remove from oven and cool slightly. When peppers are cool enough to handle, remove stems and seeds.

2. Process roasted vegetables and garlic, in batches, in a food processor until smooth. Transfer to a 4-qt. (4-L) stainless steel or enameled saucepan. Stir in lime juice and remaining ingredients. Bring to a simmer. Remove from heat.

3. Ladle hot salsa into a hot jar, leaving ½-inch (1-cm) headspace. Remove air bubbles. Wipe jar rim. Center lid on jar. Apply band, and adjust to fingertip-tight. Place jar in boiling-water canner. Repeat until all jars are filled.

4. Process jars 20 minutes, adjusting for altitude. Turn off heat; remove lid, and let jars stand 5 minutes. Remove jars and cool.

ENCHILADAS SUIZAS

MAKES 6 SERVINGS

A beloved Mexican dish of soft corn tortillas rolled around chicken and cheese is transformed by bathing and baking it in our Roasted Salsa Verde (page 167) with a touch of cream.

¼ cup (60 mL) canola oil

2 cups (500 mL) Roasted Salsa Verde (page 167), divided

12 (6-inch/15-cm) corn tortillas

4 cups (1 L) shredded cooked chicken

3 cups/750 mL (12 oz./ 350 g) crumbled queso fresco or shredded Monterey Jack cheese, divided

Vegetable cooking spray

½ cup (125 mL) heavy cream

½ cup (125 mL) thinly sliced red onion, rinsed

½ cup (125 mL) thinly sliced radishes

3 Tbsp. (45 mL) chopped fresh cilantro

1. Preheat oven to 350°F (180°C). Heat oil in an 8-inch (20-cm) skillet over medium-low heat. Heat 1 cup (250 mL) Roasted Salsa Verde in a medium skillet over medium-low heat until thoroughly heated.

2. Fry tortillas, 1 at a time, in hot oil 15 seconds on each side to soften; drain on paper towels. Dip fried tortillas, 1 at a time, in salsa, allowing excess to drip back into skillet. Place tortillas, 1 at a time, on a plate, and spoon ¼ cup (125 mL) chicken and 1 Tbsp. (15 mL) cheese down center of each. Roll up and place seam side down in a 13- x 9-inch (3.5-L) baking dish coated with cooking spray.

3. Bring remaining 1 cup (250 mL) salsa to a simmer in a small stainless steel or enameled saucepan. (Do not boil.) Stir in cream.

4. Pour salsa and cream mixture over enchiladas, and sprinkle with remaining 2¼ cups (550 mL) cheese.

5. Bake, uncovered, at 350°F (180°C) for 15 to 20 minutes or until sauce is bubbly and edges are lightly browned.

6. Sprinkle with onion, radishes, and cilantro. Serve immediately.

SMOKY SOUR CHERRY–TEQUILA SALSA

The tart flavor of sour cherries is fantastic in savory condiments like this chipotle-and-tequila-spiked salsa.

- 2 cups (500 mL) diced onion
- ½ cup (125 mL) firmly packed brown sugar
- ¼ cup (60 mL) fresh lime juice
- 1 garlic clove, minced
- 4 lb. (2 kg) fresh tart cherries, pitted and chopped (about 13 cups/3.25 L)
- ½ cup (125 mL) chopped fresh cilantro
- 2 canned chipotle peppers in adobo sauce, minced
- 1 small red serrano pepper, seeded and minced
- ¼ cup (60 mL) tequila
- 1½ tsp. (7 mL) salt
- ½ tsp. (2 mL) ground black pepper

★

Perfect Pairing
Serve with grilled halibut and roasted haricots verts.

1. Combine first 4 ingredients in a large stainless steel or enameled Dutch oven. Cook, stirring often, over medium heat 5 minutes. Add cherries and next 3 ingredients; cook 5 minutes, stirring often. Stir in tequila, salt, and pepper. Bring to a boil. Remove from heat.

2. Ladle hot salsa into a hot jar, leaving ½-inch (1-cm) headspace. Remove air bubbles. Wipe jar rim. Center lid on jar. Apply band, and adjust to fingertip-tight. Place jar in boiling-water canner. Repeat until all jars are filled.

3. Process jars 15 minutes, adjusting for altitude. Turn off heat; remove lid, and let jars stand 5 minutes. Remove jars and cool.

CHIPOTLE TOMATILLO SALSA

MAKES ABOUT 4 (½-PT./250-ML) JARS

Charred tomatillos and chipotles in adobo make a truly special tart and smoky pairing for this salsa.

- 2 lb. (1 kg) fresh tomatillos, husks removed
- 1 small onion, unpeeled and quartered
- 4 garlic cloves, peeled
- ¼ cup (60 mL) fresh lime juice (about 3 large limes)
- ½ tsp. (2 mL) salt
- 3 to 4 canned chipotle peppers in adobo sauce

★

Peak of Freshness

Tomatillos, also called husk tomatoes, are a Mexican fruit related to tomatoes. They have a papery shell that comes off easily when they are ripe. Look for either green or purple husks as they taste the same.

1. Preheat oven to 425°F (220°C). Arrange tomatillos, stem side down, and onion quarters, skin side down, on a large rimmed baking sheet. Wrap garlic cloves in a small piece of aluminum foil. Place foil pouch on 1 corner of baking sheet.

2. Bake at 425°F (220°C) for 20 minutes or until tomatillos and onion are beginning to char and soften. Transfer baking sheet to a wire rack to cool. When vegetables are cool enough to handle, remove peels, and place in a food processor. Add lime juice and remaining ingredients; process until pureed.

3. Transfer mixture to a large stainless steel or enameled saucepan. Bring to a boil. Remove from heat.

4. Ladle hot salsa into a hot jar, leaving ½-inch (1-cm) headspace. Remove air bubbles. Wipe jar rim. Center lid on jar. Apply band, and adjust to fingertip-tight. Place jar in boiling-water canner. Repeat until all jars are filled.

5. Process jars 25 minutes, adjusting for altitude. Turn off heat; remove lid, and let jars stand 5 minutes. Remove jars and cool.

FIERY PEACH SALSA

MAKES ABOUT 7 (½-PT./250-ML) JARS

A habanero pepper makes this salsa extra spicy. It's delicious as a garnish on grilled salmon and adds just the right amount of sweet heat to pork or seafood tacos.

- 6 cups (1.5 L) peeled, diced, hard under-ripe peaches
- 1 cup (250 mL) sugar
- 1 cup (250 mL) chopped red bell pepper
- 1 cup (250 mL) apple cider vinegar (5% acidity)
- ½ cup (125 mL) chopped red onion
- ½ cup (125 mL) water
- ¼ cup (60 mL) lime juice (about 3 limes)
- ¼ tsp. (1 mL) salt
- 2 jalapeño peppers, seeded and finely chopped
- 2 garlic cloves, minced
- 1 habanero pepper, seeded and minced
- ¼ cup (60 mL) chopped fresh cilantro

1. Combine all ingredients, except cilantro, in a 6-qt. (6-L) stainless steel or enameled Dutch oven. Bring to a boil over high heat, stirring until sugar dissolves. Reduce heat, and simmer, uncovered, 5 minutes. Remove from heat; stir in cilantro.

2. Ladle hot mixture into a hot jar, leaving ½-inch (1-cm) headspace. Remove air bubbles. Wipe jar rim. Center lid on jar. Apply band, and adjust to fingertip-tight. Place jar in boiling-water canner. Repeat until all jars are filled.

3. Process jars 10 minutes, adjusting for altitude. Turn off heat; remove lid, and let jars stand 5 minutes. Remove jars and cool.

★

Peak of Freshness

During tomato season, puree some salsa with tomatoes into a fresh gazpacho for a quick, spicy cold soup. Thin with chicken broth, if desired.

ROASTED TOMATO GUAJILLO SALSA

MAKES ABOUT 4 (1/2-PT./250-ML) JARS

Guajillo chiles are a medium heat Mexican chile with a smoky sweet flavor, making this an addictive salsa when paired with roasted tomatoes, garlic, and onions.

---

2 lb. (1 kg) plum tomatoes, cored

1 medium onion, quartered

4 garlic cloves, peeled

12 large guajillo chile peppers

2 cups (500 mL) boiling water

2 Tbsp. (30 mL) malt vinegar (5% acidity), or apple cider vinegar (5% acidity)

1/2 tsp. (2 mL) ground cumin

1/4 tsp. (1 mL) dried oregano

★

Tricks of the Trade
Look for Mexican oregano in specialty shops or buy it online. It has a bolder flavor than Mediterranean oregano. Dried Ancho chiles may be substituted if guajillo are hard to find.

1. Preheat oven to 425°F (220°C). Place tomatoes and onion quarters, skin side down, on a large rimmed baking sheet. Wrap garlic in a small piece of aluminum foil. Place foil pouch on 1 corner of baking sheet.

2. Bake at 425°F (220°C) for 20 minutes or until tomatoes and onion are beginning to char and soften. Transfer baking sheet to a wire rack to cool.

3. While vegetables are baking, rinse any dirt from guajillo chiles, and pat dry with a paper towel. Toast peppers on a very hot griddle, or in a skillet, 8 to 10 seconds on each side or just until beginning to puff and blister. (Do not allow peppers to burn or they will become bitter.) When cool enough to handle, remove stems and seeds from chiles; tear into large pieces and place in a medium bowl. Cover with boiling water. Let stand 15 minutes or until softened. Drain, reserving soaking liquid.

4. When roasted vegetables are cool enough to handle, remove skins and place in a food processor. Add vinegar, next 2 ingredients, and chiles; process until pureed, adding some of reserved soaking liquid, if necessary, to desired consistency.

5. Transfer salsa to a large stainless steel or enameled saucepan. Bring to a boil. Remove from heat.

6. Ladle hot salsa into a hot jar, leaving 1/2-inch (1-cm) headspace. Remove air bubbles. Wipe jar rim. Center lid on jar. Apply band, and adjust to fingertip-tight. Place jar in boiling-water canner. Repeat until all jars are filled.

7. Process jars 30 minutes, adjusting for altitude. Turn off heat; remove lid, and let jars stand 5 minutes. Remove jars and cool.

SUMMER CORN AND PEACH SALSA

MAKES ABOUT 6 (¹/₂-PT./250-ML) JARS

Chipotle peppers, malt vinegar, and a splash of maple syrup round out the smoky flavor in this sweet peach and corn salsa.

- ¼ cup (60 mL) malt vinegar (5% acidity)
- ¼ cup (60 mL) lime juice (about 4 limes)
- 3 Tbsp. (45 mL) chopped canned chipotle pepper in adobo sauce (optional)
- 2 Tbsp. (30 mL) maple syrup
- 2 tsp. (10 mL) salt
- 1 tsp. (5 mL) chopped fresh thyme
- 1½ lb. (750 g) peaches, peeled, pitted, and finely chopped (3½ cups/875 mL) (see page 114)
- 3⅓ cups (825 mL) fresh or frozen corn kernels
- 2 garlic cloves, minced
- 1 cup (250 mL) finely chopped red bell pepper

★

Simple Switch
Substitute nectarines for the peaches for an equally delicious summer salsa.

1. Combine all ingredients in a 6-qt. (6-L) stainless steel or enameled Dutch oven. Bring to a boil over high heat. Reduce heat to medium-low, and cook, stirring often, 5 minutes or until thoroughly heated.

2. Ladle hot salsa into a hot jar, leaving ½-inch (1-cm) headspace. Remove air bubbles. Wipe jar rim. Center lid on jar. Apply band, and adjust to fingertip-tight. Place jar in boiling-water canner. Repeat until all jars are filled.

3. Process jars 15 minutes, adjusting for altitude. Turn off heat; remove lid, and let jars stand 5 minutes. Remove jars and cool.

SALSA RANCHERA

MAKES ABOUT 4 (1-PT./500-ML) JARS

- 3 lb. (1.5 kg) plum tomatoes, cored
- ¾ lb. (350 g) jalapeño peppers
- 4 garlic cloves
- 1 medium-size white onion, cut into ½-inch (1-cm)-thick slices
- 2 tsp. (10 mL) salt
- ½ cup (125 mL) chopped fresh cilantro
- ⅓ cup (75 mL) fresh lime juice (about 4 limes)

1. Preheat oven to 425°F (220°C). Arrange first 4 ingredients on a large rimmed baking sheet lined with aluminum foil. Bake at 425°F (220°C) for 20 minutes. Remove garlic from baking sheet. Bake 20 more minutes or until vegetables are very soft and beginning to char.

2. Transfer jalapeño peppers to a bowl; cover bowl with plastic wrap. Let stand 15 minutes.

3. Meanwhile, remove skins from tomatoes, and coarsely chop. Coarsely chop onion. Place tomato, onion, and salt in a medium stainless steel or enameled saucepan.

4. Peel peppers; remove and discard seeds, if desired. Finely chop peppers; add to tomato mixture. Bring to a boil, stirring often. Reduce heat, and simmer 2 minutes. Stir in cilantro and lime juice.

5. Ladle hot salsa into a hot jar, leaving ½-inch (1-cm) headspace. Remove air bubbles. Wipe jar rim. Center lid on jar. Apply band, and adjust to fingertip-tight. Place jar in boiling-water canner. Repeat until all jars are filled.

6. Process jars 20 minutes, adjusting for altitude. Turn off heat; remove lid, and let jars stand 5 minutes. Remove jars and cool.

HUEVOS RANCHEROS

MAKES 4 SERVINGS

- 4 (6-inch/15-cm) corn tortillas
- 3 Tbsp. (45 mL) olive oil, divided
- 8 large eggs
- 1 cup (250 mL) refried beans, warmed
- 1 cup (250 mL) Salsa Ranchera, warmed

Toppings: grated Cotija cheese, avocado slices, fresh cilantro leaves

1. Cook tortillas in 2 batches in 1 Tbsp. (15 mL) hot olive oil in a large nonstick skillet 2 minutes on each side or just until crisp, adding more oil if necessary. Drain on paper towels.

2. Heat remaining 1 Tbsp. (15 mL) oil in skillet until hot. Break 4 eggs into hot oil. Season with salt and black pepper to taste; cook 2 minutes on each side or to desired degree of doneness. Repeat procedure with remaining 1 Tbsp. oil, remaining 4 eggs, and salt and pepper.

3. Spread ¼ cup (60 mL) refried beans on each tortilla. Top each with 2 eggs and ¼ cup (60 mL) salsa. Serve immediately with desired toppings.

MANGO-HABANERO WING AND DIPPING SAUCE

MAKES ABOUT 5 (½-PT./250-ML) JARS

If you like a tongue-tingling sauce for chicken wings, then try this. The searing heat of habanero peppers is tempered ever so slightly by the addition of mango and honey.

1 cup (250-mL) white vinegar (5% acidity)

¼ cup (60 mL) hot sauce

2 Tbsp. (30 mL) sugar

2 Tbsp. (30 mL) honey

5 habanero peppers, halved and seeded

4 garlic cloves, crushed

4 cups (1 L) chopped peeled fresh or frozen mango, thawed

1. Process first 6 ingredients in a blender or processor until peppers are minced. Gradually add mango, processing until smooth.

2. Pour mango mixture into a 4-qt. (4-L) stainless steel or enameled saucepan. Bring to a boil; reduce heat, and simmer, uncovered, 10 minutes or until slightly thickened.

3. Ladle hot mango sauce into a hot jar, leaving ¼-inch (.5-cm) headspace. Remove air bubbles. Wipe jar rim. Center lid on jar. Apply band, and adjust to fingertip-tight. Place jar in boiling-water canner. Repeat until all jars are filled.

4. Process jars 10 minutes, adjusting for altitude. Turn off heat; remove lid, and let jars stand 5 minutes. Remove jars and cool.

MANGO HABANERO CHICKEN WINGS: Preheat oven to 425°F (220°C). Arrange wings on baking pan sprayed with non-stick cooking spray and bake 50 minutes or until wings are thoroughly cooked and crispy, turning once during baking. Toss with desired amount of Mango-Habanero Wing and Dipping Sauce (the more sauce, the hotter the wings!) and serve.

PAW PAW'S BYWATER BBQ SAUCE

MAKES ABOUT 6 (1-PT./500-ML) JARS

Take your BBQ to New Orleans! This spectacular sauce has all that mouthwatering Deep South spice with hints of sweet and a hot, spicy kick. Stock up, you'll want BBQ every day.

- 2½ cups (625 mL) firmly packed light brown sugar
- 3 Tbsp. (45 mL) kosher salt
- 3 Tbsp. (45 mL) garlic powder
- 3 Tbsp. (45 mL) onion powder
- 3 Tbsp. (45 mL) dry mustard
- 1 Tbsp. (15 mL) black pepper
- 2 tsp. (10 mL) paprika
- 2 tsp. (10 mL) ground red pepper
- ½ tsp. (2 mL) chili powder
- 8 cups (2 L) ketchup
- 2 cups (500 mL) water
- 1¼ cups (300 mL) apple cider vinegar (5% acidity)
- ¾ cup (175 mL) apple cider
- ⅓ cup (75 mL) honey
- ¼ cup (60 mL) Creole mustard or Dijon mustard
- 2½ Tbsp. (38 mL) Worcestershire Sauce (page 257)
- 2 Tbsp. (30 mL) bottled lemon juice
- 1 Tbsp. (15 mL) Fiery Fermented Hot Sauce (page 264)

1. Stir together first 9 ingredients in a 6-qt. (6-L) stainless steel or enameled Dutch oven. Add ketchup and remaining ingredients, stirring until blended.

2. Bring to a boil; reduce heat to medium, and simmer, uncovered, 20 minutes or until sauce is slightly thickened, stirring often.

3. Ladle hot sauce into a hot jar, leaving ½-inch (1-cm) headspace. Remove air bubbles. Wipe jar rim. Center lid on jar. Apply band, and adjust to fingertip-tight. Place jar in boiling-water canner. Repeat until all jars are filled.

4. Process jars 15 minutes, adjusting for altitude. Turn off heat; remove lid, and let jars stand 5 minutes. Remove jars and cool.

ROASTED EGGPLANT AND PEPPER PUTTANESCA SAUCE

MAKES ABOUT 6 (1-PT./500-ML) JARS

This sauce is super quick to make, and the roasted eggplant and peppers give it a velvety texture.

6 lb. (3 kg) plum tomatoes

Vegetable cooking spray

2 lb. (1 kg) eggplant, cut into 1-inch (2.5-cm) cubes

3 large onions, unpeeled and quartered

3 red bell peppers, halved and seeded

2 cups (500 mL) dry red wine

½ cup (125 mL) balsamic vinegar

1½ cups (375 mL) chopped pitted kalamata olives

1 Tbsp. (15 mL) anchovy paste or chopped anchovies (optional)

2 tsp. (10 mL) salt

2 tsp. (2 mL) dried oregano

1 tsp. (5 mL) ground black pepper

6 garlic cloves, minced

1 (3.5-oz./105-mL) jar capers, drained

1. Preheat oven to 400°F (200°C). Core tomatoes and cut in half lengthwise. Arrange tomato halves on 2 large rimmed baking sheets lined with aluminum foil. Bake at 400°F (200°C) for 45 minutes or until softened and beginning to char. Remove from oven. Let cool in pan on a wire rack. When tomatoes are cool enough to handle, peel and coarsely chop. Place tomatoes and accumulated juice in a 6-qt. (6-L) stainless steel or enameled Dutch oven.

2. Replace foil on baking sheets; coat foil with cooking spray. Arrange eggplant on 1 baking sheet; onion and bell pepper halves on another. Bake at 400°F (200°C) for 30 minutes or until edges of eggplant are golden brown and onion and bell pepper are crisp-tender.

3. Add eggplant to tomatoes. Remove peel and coarsely chop onion and bell pepper; add to tomato mixture. Stir in wine and remaining ingredients. Bring to a boil; reduce heat, and simmer, uncovered, 15 minutes.

4. Ladle hot sauce into a hot jar, leaving ½-inch (1-cm) headspace. Remove air bubbles. Wipe jar rim. Center lid on jar. Apply band, and adjust to fingertip-tight. Place jar in boiling-water canner. Repeat until all jars are filled.

5. Process jars 45 minutes, adjusting for altitude. Turn off heat; remove lid, and let jars stand 5 minutes. Remove jars and cool.

ASIAN POMEGRANATE BBQ AND STIR-FRY SAUCE

MAKES ABOUT 4 (½-PT./250-ML) JARS

Pomegranate molasses, commonly found in Middle Eastern stores, adds tartness to Asian spices and soy sauce, creating a flavorful and adaptable sauce.

3	cups (750 mL) chicken stock
1½	cups (375 mL) ketchup
½	cup (125 mL) firmly packed light brown sugar
½	cup (125 mL) soy sauce
½	cup (125 mL) pomegranate molasses
1	Tbsp. (15 mL) Worcestershire Sauce (page 257)
2	tsp. (10 mL) coarsely chopped fresh ginger
2	garlic cloves, sliced
2	small serrano chiles
1	(3-inch/7.5-cm) cinnamon stick
½	star anise
½	cup (125 mL) granulated sugar

1. Combine first 11 ingredients in a large stainless steel or enameled saucepan. Bring to a boil over medium heat; reduce heat, and simmer, uncovered, 20 minutes.

2. Pour mixture through a wire-mesh strainer into a bowl; discard solids. Return sauce to pan.

3. Stir in sugar, and bring to a boil, whisking constantly until sugar dissolves. Remove from heat.

4. Ladle hot sauce into a hot jar, leaving ¼-inch (.5-cm) headspace. Remove air bubbles. Wipe jar rim. Center lid on jar. Apply band, and adjust to fingertip-tight. Place jar in boiling-water canner. Repeat until all jars are filled.

5. Process jars 10 minutes, adjusting for altitude. Turn off heat; remove lid, and let jars stand 5 minutes. Remove jars and cool.

BEEF-AND-VEGETABLE STIR-FRY WITH SOBA NOODLES

MAKES 4 SERVINGS

The addition of fresh garlic, ginger, sesame oil, and soy sauce to our Asian Pomegranate BBQ and Stir-Fry Sauce (page 182) gives this vegetable and beef stir-fry ramped-up Asian flavor.

1 (8-oz./250-g) package soba noodles

1 cup (250 mL) fresh snow peas

⅓ cup (75 mL) Asian Pomegranate BBQ and Stir-Fry Sauce (page 182)

3 Tbsp. (45 mL) lite soy sauce

1 Tbsp. (15 mL) rice vinegar

2 tsp. (10 mL) dark sesame oil

1 lb. (450 g) boneless sirloin steak 1 inch (2.5 cm) thick, cut into thin strips*

½ tsp. (2 mL) salt

¼ tsp. (1 mL) freshly ground black pepper

3 Tbsp. (45 mL) peanut oil, divided

2 cups (500 mL) broccoli florets

2 cups (500 mL) sliced carrot

1 cup (250 mL) sliced fresh mushrooms

½ cup (125 mL) vertically sliced red onion

1 Tbsp. (15 mL) minced fresh garlic

1 Tbsp. (15 mL) minced fresh ginger

½ cup (125 mL) sliced green onions

1. Prepare soba noodles according to package directions. Drain and rinse with cold water. Drain noodles, and leave in colander.

2. Trim ends and remove strings from snow peas; discard ends and strings. Combine stir-fry sauce and next 3 ingredients in a small bowl.

3. Sprinkle beef with salt and pepper. Stir-fry beef in 1 Tbsp. (15 mL) hot peanut oil in a large skillet or wok over medium-high heat 2 to 3 minutes or until lightly browned. Transfer to a bowl.

4. Add remaining 2 Tbsp. (30 mL) peanut oil to skillet; stir-fry broccoli and carrot 2 minutes. Add snow peas, mushrooms, and onion; stir-fry 3 to 4 minutes or until vegetables are crisp-tender. Add garlic and ginger; stir-fry 30 seconds.

5. Return beef and any accumulated juices to skillet. Add sauce mixture, stirring to coat beef and vegetables.

6. Rinse noodles with warm water; drain and gently stir into vegetable mixture. Sprinkle with green onions, and serve immediately.

*1 lb. (450 g) skinned and boned chicken breasts; boneless center-cut pork chops 1 inch (2.5 cm) thick, cut into thin strips; or peeled and deveined shrimp may be substituted.

CHERRY-BOURBON BBQ SAUCE

MAKES ABOUT 3 (½-PT./250-ML) JARS

Dried tart cherries and bourbon create the "wow" factor in this barbecue sauce that's full of smoky, spicy goodness.

1 cup (250 mL) dried tart cherries

⅓ cup (75 mL) bourbon

1 cup (250 mL) finely chopped onion

1 Tbsp. (15 mL) olive oil

1 tsp. (5 mL) smoked paprika

1 garlic clove, minced

½ cup (125 mL) apple cider vinegar (5% acidity)

½ cup (125 mL) firmly packed dark brown sugar

1½ cups (625 mL) tomato sauce

1 Tbsp. (15 mL) dry mustard

1 Tbsp. (15 mL) Worcestershire Sauce (page 257)

1 tsp. (5 mL) salt

¼ tsp. (1 mL) freshly ground black pepper

1 tsp. (5 mL) prepared horseradish (optional)

1. Combine cherries and bourbon in a microwave-safe bowl. Cover and microwave at HIGH 30 seconds. Set aside.

2. Sauté onion in hot olive oil in a medium stainless steel or enameled saucepan over medium-high heat 5 to 7 minutes or until onion is tender. Add paprika and garlic; cook, stirring constantly, 1 minute. Stir in vinegar and brown sugar; cook 2 to 3 minutes or until syrupy.

3. Stir in tomato sauce, next 4 ingredients, and, if desired, horseradish. Bring to a simmer; cover and cook 20 minutes, stirring occasionally. Add reserved cherry mixture; simmer, uncovered, 5 minutes, stirring often. Remove from heat; cool slightly.

4. Process sauce in a blender until smooth. Return to saucepan; bring to a boil.

5. Ladle hot sauce into a hot jar, leaving ¼-inch (.5-cm) headspace. Remove air bubbles. Wipe jar rim. Center lid on jar. Apply band, and adjust to fingertip-tight. Place jar in boiling-water canner. Repeat until all jars are filled.

6. Process jars 15 minutes, adjusting for altitude. Turn off heat; remove lid, and let jars stand 5 minutes. Remove jars and cool.

★

Perfect Pairing
Use this barbecue sauce when you want something a little more refined.

SPICY ASIAN PLUM SAUCE

MAKES ABOUT 4 (1-PT./500-ML) JARS

Made with slightly sweetened plums that are spiced with warm notes of cinnamon and cloves and heated with chile peppers, this sauce is redolent of Asian cuisine and much better than store-bought.

- 4 lb. (2 kg) black or red plums, pitted and coarsely chopped
- 1½ cups (375 mL) firmly packed light brown sugar
- ½ cup (125 mL) rice vinegar or apple cider vinegar (5% acidity)
- ¼ cup (60 mL) lite soy sauce
- 1 tsp. (5 mL) grated fresh ginger
- 1 medium onion, chopped
- 3 garlic cloves, minced
- 1 tsp. (5 mL) salt
- 1 tsp. (5 mL) dried crushed red pepper, or more to taste
- ½ tsp. (2 mL) fennel seeds
- ½ tsp. (2 mL) freshly ground Szechuan peppercorns or black peppercorns
- ½ tsp. (2 mL) ground cinnamon
- ½ tsp. (2 mL) ground ginger
- ½ tsp. (2 mL) ground red pepper
- ⅛ tsp. ground cloves (.5 mL)
- 2 star anise

1. Bring first 7 ingredients to a boil in a 4-qt. (4-L) stainless steel or enameled Dutch oven over medium heat; reduce heat, and simmer, stirring often, 20 minutes or until plums and onion are very soft.

2. Stir in salt and remaining ingredients. Simmer, uncovered, 20 minutes or until plums disintegrate and mixture thickens. Remove and discard star anise.

3. Process plum mixture, in batches, in a food processor. Pour each batch of puree into a bowl. Pour puree into Dutch oven. Bring to a simmer over medium heat. Remove from heat.

4. Ladle hot sauce into a hot jar, leaving ¼-inch (.5-cm) headspace. Remove air bubbles. Wipe jar rim. Center lid on jar. Apply band, and adjust to fingertip-tight. Place jar in boiling-water canner. Repeat until all jars are filled.

5. Process jars 10 minutes, adjusting for altitude. Turn off heat; remove lid, and let jars stand 5 minutes. Remove jars and cool.

CACCIATORE SIMMER SAUCE

MAKES ABOUT 4 (1-PT./500-L) JARS

Cacciatore sauce has never been easier than with this rich, enticing homemade sauce seasoned with capers and wine. A pantry staple you'll want to make again and again.

12	lb. (6 kg) tomatoes
1½	cups (375 mL) diced onion (about 2 medium)
1	red bell pepper, diced
1	cup (250 mL) diced baby portobello mushrooms
½	cup (125 mL) dry red or dry white wine
2	tsp. (10 mL) salt
1	tsp. (5 mL) dried thyme
1	tsp. (5 mL) dried oregano
½	tsp. (2 mL) freshly ground black pepper
½	tsp. (2 mL) dried crushed red pepper (optional)
3	garlic cloves, minced
1	bay leaf
1	tsp. (5 mL) Ball® Citric Acid*

★

Tricks of the Trade
Roasting tomatoes brings out their natural sweetness and heightens their flavor; a good way to start all sauce bases.

1. Preheat oven to 375°F (190°C). Wash tomatoes; pat dry with paper towels. Cut tomatoes in halves or quarters to make uniform-sized pieces. Arrange pieces in a single layer on large baking sheets. Bake at 375°F (190°C) for 45 minutes or until very soft and beginning to brown. Cool.

2. Place onion, red bell pepper, and mushrooms in a single layer on a large baking sheet. Bake at 375°F (190°C) for 20 minutes or just until beginning to brown. Transfer onion mixture to a 6-qt. (6-L) stainless steel or enameled Dutch oven.

3. Remove skins and seeds from tomatoes by pressing through a food mill into Dutch oven. Discard skins and seeds.

4. Stir in wine and next 7 ingredients. Bring to a boil; reduce heat, and simmer, uncovered, 20 minutes. Stir in citric acid. Remove and discard bay leaf.

5. Ladle hot sauce into a hot jar, leaving ½-inch (1-cm) headspace. Remove air bubbles. Wipe jar rim. Center lid on jar. Apply band, and adjust to fingertip-tight. Place jar in boiling-water canner. Repeat until all jars are filled.

6. Process jars 40 minutes, adjusting for altitude. Turn off heat; remove lid, and let jars stand 5 minutes. Remove jars and cool.

*¼ cup bottled lemon juice may be substituted for the citric acid.

CHICKEN CACCIATORE: Heat oil in a large skillet and brown 1 lb. sliced chicken breasts or thighs. Stir in 1 jar of Cacciatore Simmer Sauce, cover, and simmer until chicken is thoroughly cooked, about 10 minutes. Serve over hot cooked pasta or rice.

SAUCY SLOPPY JOE STARTER

MAKES ABOUT 4 (1-PT./500-ML)

Have plenty of napkins on hand! This rich sauce is kid-friendly, but we bet the adults will go for seconds too.

Vegetable cooking spray

- 3 cups (750 mL) finely chopped green bell pepper (about 2 large)
- 3 cups (750 mL) finely chopped red bell pepper (about 2 large)
- 2 cups (500 mL) diced onion (about 2 large)
- 4 tsp. (20 mL) salt
- 2 tsp. (10 mL) ground black pepper
- ½ cup (125 mL) Roasted Tomato Paste (page 206)*
- 4 cups (1 L) Tomato Sauce (page 200)*
- ½ cup (125 mL) apple cider vinegar (5% acidity)
- ½ cup (125 mL) Dijon mustard
- ¼ cup (60 mL) firmly packed brown sugar

1. Preheat oven to 375°F (190°C). Line a large rimmed baking sheet with aluminum foil; coat foil with cooking spray. Spread green bell pepper and next 2 ingredients on prepared pan. Stir in salt and pepper. Bake at 375°F (190°C) for 20 minutes or until vegetables are very tender and beginning to brown, stirring occasionally.

2. Transfer onion mixture to a large skillet. Stir in tomato paste; cook, uncovered, stirring often, 5 minutes until mixture begins to thicken. Stir in Tomato Sauce and remaining ingredients. Bring to a boil; reduce heat, and simmer, uncovered, stirring often, 5 minutes or until sauce is slightly thickened.

3. Ladle hot sauce into a hot jar, leaving ½-inch (1-cm) headspace. Remove air bubbles. Wipe jar rim. Center lid on jar. Apply band, and adjust to fingertip-tight. Place jar in boiling-water canner. Repeat until all jars are filled.

4. Process jars 20 minutes, adjusting for altitude. Turn off heat; remove lid, and let jars stand 5 minutes. Remove jars and cool.

*1 (6-oz./170-g) can tomato paste and 4 (8-oz./227-g) cans tomato sauce, respectively, may be substituted.

SOUTHEAST ASIAN SWEET-AND-SOUR SAUCE

MAKES ABOUT 6 (½-PT./500-ML) JARS

This apricot-based sauce gets its Asian accent from ginger and lemongrass and its kick from sambal oelek, a chile paste. Try it as a dipping sauce for pot stickers or chicken wings, or as a stir-fry sauce or barbecue sauce.

- 1 cup (250 mL) water
- 3 Tbsp. (45 mL) minced fresh ginger
- 2 Tbsp. (30 mL) minced lemongrass
- 2 Tbsp. (30 mL) minced garlic
- 2½ lb. (1.25 kg) apricots (about 20 apricots), pitted and chopped
- 2½ cups (625 mL) sugar
- 1 cup (250 mL) finely chopped red bell pepper (about 1 medium)
- ¼ cup (60 mL) fresh lime juice (about 4 limes)
- ¼ cup (60 mL) sambal oelek (ground fresh chile paste)
- 3 Tbsp. (45 mL) fish sauce

★

Perfect Pairing

Terrific as a dipping sauce, but also try mixing a tablespoonful with ½ cup mayonnaise and serve alongside sweet potato fries, or spread on grilled chicken.

1. Place first 5 ingredients in a 4-qt. (4-L) stainless steel or enameled saucepan; bring to a boil. Reduce heat to medium; cover and simmer 15 minutes or until apricots are very tender, stirring occasionally. Remove from heat; cool slightly.

2. Process apricot mixture, in batches, in a blender until smooth. Pour each batch into a bowl. Return apricot mixture to saucepan. Stir in sugar and remaining ingredients. Bring to a boil over medium heat, stirring until sugar dissolves; reduce heat and simmer, uncovered, 5 minutes.

3. Ladle hot apricot mixture into a hot jar, leaving ½-inch (1-cm) headspace. Remove air bubbles. Wipe jar rim. Center lid on jar. Apply band, and adjust to fingertip-tight. Place jar in boiling-water canner. Repeat until all jars are filled.

4. Process jars 10 minutes, adjusting for altitude. Turn off heat; remove lid, and let jars stand 5 minutes. Remove jars and cool.

DIJON MUSTARD

MAKES ABOUT 6 (4-OZ./125-ML) JARS

2 cups (500 mL) chopped onion

2 cups (500 mL) Pinot Grigio or other dry white wine

1 cup (250 mL) white wine vinegar (5% acidity)

1 tsp. (5 mL) salt

6 garlic cloves, coarsely chopped

4 black peppercorns

1 rosemary sprig

1 cup (250 mL) yellow mustard seeds

$1/3$ cup (75 mL) dry mustard

$2^2/3$ cups (650 mL) water

1. Combine first 7 ingredients in a large stainless steel or enameled saucepan. Bring to a boil over high heat; reduce heat, and simmer, uncovered, 15 to 20 minutes or until onion is very soft, stirring occasionally. Remove pan from heat; pour onion mixture through a wire-mesh strainer into a glass or stainless steel bowl. Discard solids.

2. Stir mustard seeds and dry mustard into wine mixture. Cover and let stand at room temperature at least 24 hours, but no longer than 48 hours.

3. Process mustard mixture in a blender or food processor, adding water until consistency of cooked oatmeal.

4. Transfer mustard to a small saucepan. Bring to a boil, stirring often; reduce heat, and simmer, uncovered 5 minutes.

5. Ladle hot mustard into a hot jar, leaving $1/4$-inch (.5-cm) headspace. Remove air bubbles. Wipe jar rim. Center lid on jar. Apply band, and adjust to fingertip-tight. Place jar in boiling-water canner. Repeat until all jars are filled.

6. Process jars 10 minutes, adjusting for altitude. Turn off heat; remove lid, and let jars stand 5 minutes. Remove jars and cool.

DIJON-GLAZED HAM

MAKES ABOUT 25 SERVINGS

1 (10-lb./5-kg) fully cooked, bone-in ham

$3/4$ cup (175 mL) Rhubarb Jelly (page 86)

$1/2$ cup (125 mL) Dijon mustard

$1/8$ tsp. (.5 mL) ground cloves

1. Preheat oven to 325°F (160°C). Remove skin from ham, and trim fat to $1/4$-inch (.5-cm) thickness. Place a rack in a roasting pan. Pour water to a depth of $1/2$ inch (1 cm) into roasting pan. Place ham on rack; cover loosely with aluminum foil.

2. Bake at 325°F (160°C) on lower oven rack 2 hours or until a meat thermometer registers 140°F (60°C), basting with pan juices every 30 minutes. Remove ham from oven.

3. Increase oven temperature to 425°F (220°C). Place jelly, mustard, and cloves in a small saucepan; cook over medium heat, whisking until jelly melts. Baste ham with pan juices. Brush half of jelly mixture over surface of ham. Bake at 425°F (220°C) for 10 minutes. Baste ham with pan juices, and brush with remaining half of jelly mixture. Bake 10 more minutes. Remove from oven and let stand 15 minutes before serving.

CRANBERRY MOSTARDA

MAKES ABOUT 4 (½-PT./250 ML) JARS

A Northern Italian condiment often made of dried fruit in a mustard syrup, today's mostardas are being reinvented to use fresh ingredients, spices, and herbs.

- ¾ cup (175 mL) red wine
- 2 Tbsp. (30 mL) yellow mustard seeds
- 2 Tbsp. (30 mL) brown mustard seeds
- 2 (12-oz./350-g) packages fresh or frozen cranberries
- 1 cup (250 mL) sugar
- ¼ cup (60 mL) red wine vinegar (5% acidity)
- 2 tsp. (10 mL) salt
- ½ medium-size red onion, diced (6 oz./180 g)
- 2 Tbsp. (30 mL) Dijon mustard
- ½ tsp. (2 mL) freshly ground black pepper

1. Bring first 3 ingredients to a simmer in a small stainless steel or enameled saucepan over medium-high heat. Remove from heat and let stand 10 minutes or until seeds are slightly softened.

2. Bring cranberries and next 4 ingredients to a boil in a large stainless steel saucepan. Cook 10 minutes or until most of cranberry skins begin to split and mixture begins to thicken.

3. Stir in mustard seed mixture, Dijon mustard, and pepper. Reduce heat to medium-low, and simmer 15 minutes or until mixture begins to thicken.

4. Ladle hot mixture into a hot jar, leaving ¼-inch (.5-cm) headspace. Remove air bubbles. Wipe jar rim. Center lid on jar. Apply band, and adjust to fingertip-tight. Repeat until all jars are filled.

5. Process jars 15 minutes, adjusting for altitude. Turn off heat; remove lid, and let jars stand 5 minutes. Remove jars and cool.

★

Simple Switch

Impress your guests by serving this mostarda with roasted pork loin or your next Thanksgiving turkey.

PEACH-ALE MUSTARD

MAKES ABOUT 4 (¹/₂-PT./250-ML) JARS

2¹/₂ lb. (1.25 kg) peaches (about 10 peaches), halved and pitted

²/₃ cup (150 mL) white balsamic vinegar (6% acidity)

¹/₂ cup (125 mL) maple syrup

¹/₂ cup (125 mL) dry mustard

2 Tbsp. (30 mL) brown mustard seeds

1 tsp. (5 mL) salt

1 (12-oz./355-g) bottle ale

1. Preheat oven to 425°F (220°C). Arrange peach halves, cut sides up, on a large rimmed baking sheet lined with aluminum foil. Bake at 425°F (220°C) for 30 minutes or until peaches are very soft and lightly browned. Remove pan from oven, and place on a wire rack. When peaches are cool enough to handle, peel and chop.

2. Combine vinegar and next 5 ingredients in a 6-qt. (6-L) stainless steel or enameled Dutch oven. Bring to a boil, stirring constantly; reduce heat, and simmer, uncovered, 10 minutes, stirring often. Remove from heat; cool completely (about 1 hour). Transfer peach mixture to a large bowl. Cover and chill overnight.

3. Process peach mixture in a food processor until pureed. Pour puree into a large stainless steel or enameled saucepan. Bring to a boil, stirring often.

4. Ladle hot mustard into a hot jar, leaving ¹/₄-inch (.5-cm) headspace. Remove air bubbles. Wipe jar rim. Center lid on jar. Apply band, and adjust to fingertip-tight. Place jar in boiling-water canner. Repeat until all jars are filled.

5. Process jars 10 minutes, adjusting for altitude. Turn off heat; remove lid, and let jars stand 5 minutes. Remove jars and cool.

CURED SALMON CROSTINI

MAKES 12 APPETIZER SERVINGS

12 (¹/₄-inch/6-mm) diagonally cut French bread baguette slices

3 Tbsp. (45 mL) olive oil

Salt and black pepper to taste

12 thin slices (about ¹/₄ lb./125 g) Cold-Cured Salmon (page 359)

¹/₄ cup (60 mL) Peach-Ale Mustard

¹/₄ cup (60 mL) paper-thin onion slices

1. Preheat oven to 350°F (180°C). Arrange baguette slices on a large baking sheet. Brush with olive oil and sprinkle with salt and pepper. Bake at 350°F (180°C) for 10 minutes or until crisp and golden. Remove from oven; cool.

2. Top crostini evenly with salmon slices, mustard, and onion. Serve immediately.

NOTHING SAYS SUMMER LIKE GARDEN-FRESH TOMATOES.

The bright, showy colors promise juicy, fresh eating in salads and sandwiches, and the tantalizing flavors are equally enticing in cozy winter meals of pasta, chili, and stews. Though tomatoes are a fruit, they are just on the cusp of proper pH levels so they need a little extra attention to ensure that they are perfectly safe for water bath canning. This is especially true for some of the sweet heirloom varieties. For this reason, we've added a touch of Ball® Citric Acid or bottled lemon juice to each recipe to ensure a safe and successful preserving experience every time.

Canned Tomatoes in 4 Easy Steps

Refer to water bath canning procedures on pages 26-27
and follow recipe guidelines in steps and chart below.

Makes 2 (1-pt./500-mL) jars or 1 (1-qt./1-L) jar*

STEP 1: Wash 8 to 10 tomatoes (2½ to 3½ lb./ 1.25 to 1.5 kg). Cut a small "X" in the blossom end of each tomato with a paring knife. Dip in boiling water 30 to 60 seconds; immediately plunge into cold water. Core and peel. Halve, quarter, or leave whole, as desired.

STEP 2: Choose 1 packing method according to the Packing Methods for Canned Tomatoes chart below.

STEP 3: Before adding tomatoes to 1-pt. (500-mL) jars, working with one hot jar at a time, add ¼ tsp. (1 mL) Ball® Citric Acid or 1 Tbsp. (15 mL) bottled lemon juice and ¼ tsp. (1 mL) salt (optional). Add tomatoes. Remove air bubbles.

STEP 4: Process jars for time indicated in chart below, adjusting for altitude. Turn off heat; remove lid, and let jars stand 5 minutes. Remove jars and cool.

*If making 1-qt. (1-L) jars, add ½ tsp. (2 mL) Ball® Citric Acid or 2 Tbsp. (30 mL) bottled lemon juice and 1 tsp. (5 mL) salt (optional) to each hot jar. Add tomatoes. Remove air bubbles. Proceed with Step 4.

Packing Methods for Canned Tomatoes

PACKED IN OWN JUICE	PACKED IN WATER (RAW PACK)	PACKED IN WATER (HOT PACK)
Pack raw peeled tomatoes into hot jars, 1 at a time, pressing gently on tomatoes until the natural juice fills spaces between tomatoes, leaving ½-inch (1-cm) headspace. Process 1-pt. (500-mL) or 1-qt. (1-L) jars 1 hour and 25 minutes.	Bring 2 cups (500 mL) water to a boil; reduce heat, and keep hot. Pack raw peeled tomatoes into hot jars, 1 at a time, leaving ½-inch (1-cm) headspace. Ladle hot water over tomatoes, leaving ½-inch (1-cm) headspace. Process 1-pt. (500-mL) jars 40 minutes, or 1-qt. (1-L) jars 45 minutes.	Bring tomatoes and just enough water to cover to a boil in a large stainless steel or enameled Dutch oven; reduce heat, and simmer 5 minutes. Pack hot tomatoes into hot jars, 1 at a time, with a slotted spoon, leaving ½-inch (1-cm) headspace. Ladle hot cooking liquid over tomatoes, leaving ½-inch (1-cm) headspace. Process 1-pt. (500-mL) jars 40 minutes, or 1-qt. (1-L) jars 45 minutes.

TOMATO SAUCE

MAKES ABOUT 6 (1-PT./500-ML) OR 3 (1-QT./1-L) JARS

This basic tomato sauce lets the natural sweetness of summer shine through all year long. Use it unseasoned as a base for your recipes or simmer in one of the Seasoning Blends (page 201) to add global flair to your meals.

15 lb. (6.8 kg) ripe plum tomatoes, cored and quartered

Choice of Seasoning Blend for Canned Tomatoes (page 199) or Tomato Juice (page 202) (optional)

1½ tsp. Ball® Citric Acid or ⅓ cup (75 mL) bottled lemon juice

1 Tbsp. (15 mL) salt (optional)

★

Perfect Pairing

This sauce is meant for all recipes that call for a simple tomato sauce as an ingredient.

1. Bring tomatoes to a boil in a large stainless steel or enameled stockpot; reduce heat, and simmer, uncovered, 15 minutes, stirring occasionally. Press tomato mixture, in batches, through a food mill, into a large bowl; discard skins and seeds. Return each batch of tomato puree to stockpot. Add Seasoning Blend, if desired. Bring to a boil; reduce heat, and simmer 45 minutes or until reduced by half. Stir in citric acid, and, if desired, salt.

2. Ladle hot tomato sauce into a hot jar, leaving ½-inch (1-cm) headspace. Remove air bubbles. Wipe jar rim. Center lid on jar. Apply band, and adjust to fingertip-tight. Place jar in boiling-water canner. Repeat until all jars are filled.

3. Process 1-pt. (500-mL) jars 35 minutes and 1-qt. (1-L) jars 40 minutes, adjusting for altitude. Turn off heat; remove lid, and let jars stand 5 minutes. Remove jars and cool.

SEASONING BLENDS

Longing for Italian? Or maybe Mexican? With a sprinkle, you can customize our Tomato Sauce (page 200) to satisfy your cravings. Stir in one of these spice blends after tomatoes have been pureed. These blends will season three quarts of sauce or three quarts of canned whole, crushed, or diced tomatoes. If seasoning tomatoes, divide seasoning evenly between six pints or three quarts.

ITALIAN SEASONING BLEND

MAKES ABOUT 6 TBSP. (90 ML)

- 2 Tbsp. (30 mL) dried oregano
- 2 Tbsp. (30 mL) dried basil
- 1 Tbsp. (15 mL) garlic powder
- 2 tsp. (10 mL) dried thyme
- 2 tsp. (10 mL) dried crushed red pepper (optional)

1. Combine all ingredients in a small bowl.

SMOKY MEXICAN SEASONING BLEND

MAKES ⅓ CUP (75 ML)

- 2 tsp. (10 mL) cumin seeds
- 2 tsp. (10 mL) coriander seeds
- 4 tsp. (20 mL) chili powder
- 4 tsp. (20 mL) ground chipotle chile powder
- 2 tsp. (10 mL) dried oregano
- 2 tsp. (10 mL) garlic powder

1. Heat cumin seeds and coriander seeds in a small nonstick skillet over medium-low heat, 5 minutes, stirring often, until toasted and fragrant.

2. Remove skillet from heat; cool seeds slightly. Process seeds in a spice grinder, blender, or with a mortar and pestle until finely ground. Place in a bowl; stir in chili powder and remaining ingredients.

CURRY SEASONING BLEND

MAKES ABOUT 6 TBSP. (90 ML)

- 1 Tbsp. (15 mL) cumin seeds
- 1 Tbsp. (15 mL) coriander seeds
- 2 tsp. (10 mL) black mustard seeds
- 2 tsp. (10 mL) black peppercorns
- 1 tsp. (5 mL) fennel seeds
- 1 tsp. (5 mL) fenugreek seeds
- 1 tsp. (5 mL) ground cardamom
- 2 tsp. (10 mL) turmeric powder
- 2 tsp. (10 mL) ground red pepper
- ½ tsp. (2 mL) ground cinnamon
- 6 fresh curry leaves (optional)

1. Heat first 6 ingredients in a small nonstick skillet over medium-low heat, 5 minutes, stirring often, until toasted and fragrant. Cool slightly. Remove skillet from heat; process seed mixture in a spice grinder, blender, or with a mortar and pestle until finely ground. Place ground seeds in a small bowl; stir in cardamom and next 3 ingredients.

2. If desired, add 1 curry leaf for each 1-pt. (500-mL) jar, or 2 leaves for each 1-qt. (1-L) jar of canned tomatoes or tomato sauce.

CREOLE SEASONING BLEND

MAKES ABOUT ½ CUP (125 ML)

- 1 Tbsp. (15 mL) sweet paprika
- 1 Tbsp. (15 mL) hot paprika
- 1 Tbsp. (15 mL) ground red pepper
- 1 Tbsp. (15 mL) dried oregano
- 2 tsp. (10 mL) garlic powder
- 2 tsp. (10 mL) onion powder
- 2 tsp. (10 mL) ground black pepper
- 2 tsp. (10 mL) dried thyme
- 1 tsp. (5 mL) celery seed
- 1 tsp. (5 mL) ground white pepper

1. Combine all ingredients in a small bowl.

TOMATO JUICE

MAKES ABOUT 4 (1-QT./1-L) JARS

When end-of-summer bounty finds you with glorious heaps of tomatoes, turn to this flavorful "new" classic recipe. The addition of one beet adds extra sweetness and superb color.

14 lb. (7 kg) tomatoes,

1 large red beet, peeled and cut into ¼-inch (.5-cm) cubes

1 Tbsp. (15 mL) salt or celery salt

2 tsp. (10 mL) Ball® Citric Acid or ½ cup (125 mL) bottled lemon juice

———— ★ ————

Peak of Freshness
Tomatoes that are very ripe and bursting with juice can be used here.

1. Core tomatoes and cut into quarters. Bring tomatoes, any accumulated juice, and diced beet to a boil in a large stainless steel or enameled stockpot, stirring often; reduce heat, and simmer, uncovered, 15 minutes or until vegetables are very tender, stirring often.

2. Press tomato mixture, in batches, through a food mill, into a large bowl; discard skins and seeds. Return tomato juice to stockpot. Cook over medium heat, stirring often, until a thermometer registers 190°F (88°C); remove from heat. Stir in salt and citric acid or lemon juice.

3. Ladle hot juice into a hot jar, leaving 1-inch (2.5-cm) headspace. Remove air bubbles. Wipe jar rim. Center lid on jar. Apply band, and adjust to fingertip-tight. Place jar in boiling-water canner. Repeat until all jars are filled.

4. Process jars 40 minutes, adjusting for altitude. Turn off heat; remove lid, and let jars stand 5 minutes. Remove jars and cool.

BLOODY MARY MIX

MAKES ABOUT 5 (1-PT./500-ML) JARS

For an eye-opening experience, try this Bloody Mary concoction made with delicate celery hearts and dill pickle juice. Enjoy it as a Virgin Mary or shot with vodka. As a twist, pair it with tequila.

2   qt. (2 L) Tomato Juice (page 202)

½   cup (125 mL) finely minced celery hearts (light green leafy centers)

6   Tbsp. (90 mL) Worcestershire Sauce (page 257)

6   Tbsp. (90 mL) dill pickle juice

¼   cup (60 mL) prepared horseradish

2   Tbsp. (30 mL) hot sauce

2   tsp. (10 mL) salt

2   tsp. (10 mL) garlic powder

1   tsp. (5 mL) black pepper

1   tsp. (5 mL) celery seeds

1   tsp. (5 mL) smoked paprika

1   cup (250 mL) bottled lemon juice

1. Combine all ingredients, except lemon juice, in an 8-qt. (8-L) stainless steel or enameled Dutch oven. Bring to a boil; reduce heat, and simmer 5 minutes. Remove from heat; stir in lemon juice.

2. Ladle hot tomato juice mixture into a hot jar, leaving ½-inch (1-cm) headspace. Remove air bubbles. Wipe jar rim. Center lid on jar. Apply band, and adjust to fingertip-tight. Place jar in boiling-water canner. Repeat until all jars are filled.

3. Process jars 35 minutes, adjusting for altitude. Turn off heat; remove lid, and let jars stand 5 minutes. Remove jars and cool.

OVEN-ROASTED MARINARA

MAKES ABOUT 8 (1-PT./500-ML) OR 4 (1-QT./1-L) JARS

Roasting tomatoes and onions intensifies the flavor, drawing out the inherent sweetness of both. This is a versatile base sauce that can be used on its own or as the starting point for other sauce variations.

20 lb. (9 kg) plum tomatoes

1½ cups (375 mL) chopped onion (about 2 medium)

Vegetable cooking spray

1 cup (250 mL) dry red, or white, wine

1 Tbsp. (15 mL) salt

1 Tbsp. (15 mL) dried oregano

2 tsp. (10 mL) black pepper

6 garlic cloves, minced

2 bay leaves

2 tsp. (10 mL) Ball® Citric Acid or ½ cup (125 mL) bottled lemon juice

---
★

Peak of Freshness

Use a mix of heirloom tomatoes with different textures and colors. Look for a balance of juicy and meaty ones at your local farmers' market.

1. Preheat oven to 375°F (190°C). Cut tomatoes into halves or quarters, as necessary, to create uniform size. Arrange tomatoes in a single layer on large rimmed baking sheets. Bake, in batches, at 375°F (190°C) for 45 minutes or until tomatoes are very soft and beginning to brown. Cool.

2. Spread onion on a separate large baking sheet coated with cooking spray. Bake at 375°F (190°C) for 20 minutes or until onions are golden brown, stirring occasionally.

3. Press tomatoes, in batches, through a food mill into a large bowl; discard skins and seeds. Place tomato puree and caramelized onion in a large stainless steel or enameled stock pot. Stir in wine and next 5 ingredients. Bring to a boil; reduce heat, and simmer, uncovered, 15 to 20 minutes or until reduced to desired texture. Remove and discard bay leaves. Stir in citric acid or lemon juice.

4. Ladle hot marinara sauce into a hot jar, leaving ½-inch (1-cm) headspace. Remove air bubbles. Wipe jar rim. Center lid on jar. Apply band, and adjust to fingertip-tight. Place jar in boiling-water canner. Repeat until all jars are filled.

5. Process jars 40 minutes, adjusting for altitude. Turn off heat; remove lid, and let jars stand 5 minutes. Remove jars and cool.

MEATBALLS IN MARINARA SAUCE

MAKES 8 SERVINGS

Italian meatballs simmered in hearty homemade marinara sauce are sure to make this recipe a Sunday supper classic.

- ½ cup (125 mL) soft, fresh breadcrumbs
- ¼ cup (60 mL) milk
- 1½ lb. (700 g) lean ground beef
- 1½ lb. (700 g) ground pork
- ⅓ cup (75 mL) grated Parmesan cheese
- 2 Tbsp. (30 mL) chopped fresh parsley
- 1 tsp. (5 mL) dried Italian seasoning
- 2 tsp. (10 mL) salt
- 1 tsp. (5 mL) freshly ground black pepper
- 2 large eggs, beaten
- ¼ cup (60 mL) olive oil
- 2 (1-qt./1-L) jars Oven-Roasted Marinara (page 204)

Hot cooked pasta

1. Combine breadcrumbs and milk in a large bowl; let stand until milk is absorbed. Add beef and next 7 ingredients, mixing with hands just until combined. Shape mixture by ¼ (60-mL) cupfuls into 24 balls, and place on a rimmed baking sheet. Cover with plastic wrap and chill for at least 1 hour but no longer than 4 hours. Reshape meatballs, if necessary.

2. Cook meatballs, in batches, in hot olive oil in a large skillet over medium-high heat. Drain on paper towels. Wipe skillet with paper towels; return to heat. Add Oven-Roasted Marinara and meatballs to skillet. Bring to a boil; reduce heat, partially cover, and simmer 35 to 40 minutes or until meatballs are done, stirring occasionally. Serve over hot cooked pasta.

ROASTED TOMATO PASTE

MAKES ABOUT 4 (4-OZ./125-ML) JARS

Plum tomatoes have more flesh, fewer seeds, and give off less water than heirloom tomatoes, making them perfect for paste, but a combination of plum tomatoes and heirloom tomatoes may be substituted. Omit citric acid if freezing tomato paste.

12 lb. (6 kg) plum tomatoes or other paste tomatoes, stems removed and halved crosswise

1 Tbsp. (15 mL) salt, or more to taste (optional)

1 tsp. (5 mL) Ball® Citric Acid or ¼ cup (60 mL) bottled lemon juice

1. Preheat oven to 350°F (180°C). Gently squeeze seeds from tomato halves. Cut halves in half vertically. Place tomato quarters in single layers on large rimmed baking sheets. Sprinkle evenly with 1 Tbsp. (15 mL) salt, if desired.

2. Bake at 350°F (180°C) for 1½ hours. (Begin checking every 20 minutes after the first 40 minutes to prevent burning.) Remove from oven; cool slightly.

3. Process tomato, in batches, in a food processor until smooth. Pour into a large bowl; stir in citric acid or lemon juice. Adjust salt to taste, if using. Return puree to baking sheets. Bake at 350°F (180°C) until tomato mixture is deep red in color and very thick, stirring every 20 to 30 minutes. (This may take from 2½ to 3½ hours, depending upon type of tomatoes used.)

4. Spoon hot tomato paste into a hot jar, leaving ¼-inch (.5-cm) headspace. Remove air bubbles. Wipe jar rim. Center lid on jar. Apply band, and adjust to fingertip-tight. Place jar in boiling-water canner. Repeat until all jars are filled.

5. Process jars 40 minutes, adjusting for altitude. Turn off heat; remove lid, and let jars stand 5 minutes. Remove jars and cool.

TO FREEZE: Spoon hot tomato paste into jars, leaving ½-inch (1-cm) headspace. Center lid on jars. Apply bands, and adjust loosely. Once paste is frozen, adjust bands to fingertip-tight. Store in freezer six months.

VODKA SAUCE BASE

MAKES ABOUT 4 (1-PT./500-ML) OR 2 (1-QT./1-L) JARS

This quick, small-batch sauce gets its classic flavor from simmering the onions in vodka, which brings out their natural sweetness. The sauce is finished right before canning by simmering whole sprigs of fresh basil, infusing even more flavor into the tomato sauce.

1½ cups (375 mL) finely chopped onion (about 1 large)

1 cup (250 mL) vodka

½ cup (125 mL) water

2 tsp. (10 mL) salt

1 tsp. (5 mL) black pepper

5 garlic cloves, minced

6 lb. (3 kg) plum tomatoes, cored and coarsely chopped

2 large basil sprigs

1 tsp. (5 mL) Ball® Citric Acid or ¼ cup (60 mL) bottled lemon juice

1. Bring first 6 ingredients to a boil in an 8-qt. (8-L) stainless steel or enameled Dutch oven; reduce heat, and simmer, uncovered, 10 minutes.

2. Stir in tomatoes and any accumulated juice. Return to a boil; reduce heat and simmer, uncovered, until onion and tomatoes are very soft. Press tomato mixture, in batches, through a food mill into a large bowl; discard skins and seeds.

3. Return tomato mixture to Dutch oven; add basil. Cook, stirring constantly, over medium-high heat 45 minutes or until reduced by half. Remove basil; stir in citric acid or lemon juice.

4. Ladle hot sauce base into a hot jar, leaving ½-inch (1-cm) headspace. Remove air bubbles. Wipe jar rim. Center lid on jar. Apply band, and adjust to fingertip-tight. Place jar in boiling-water canner. Repeat until all jars are filled.

5. Process jars 40 minutes, adjusting for altitude. Turn off heat; remove lid, and let jars stand 5 minutes. Remove jars and cool.

VODKA SAUCE: Heat Vodka Sauce Base in a saucepan over medium heat until thoroughly heated. Stir in 2 Tbsp. (30 ml) heavy cream for a 1-pt. (500-mL) jar or ¼ cup (60 mL) heavy cream for a 1-qt. (1-L) jar and desired amount of chopped fresh basil. Serve immediately over pasta or grilled meat. Sprinkle with shaved Parmesan cheese.

MEXICAN TOMATO SAUCE

MAKES ABOUT 4 (1-PT./500-ML) JARS

Go south-of-the-border with this simple and tasty sauce. Amp up the heat by adding one or two chipotle peppers in adobo sauce before pureeing the tomato sauce.

- 2 cups (500 mL) chopped white onion (about 2 large)
- 1 cup (250 mL) chicken stock
- 1/3 cup (75 mL) lime juice (about 4 limes)
- 2 tsp. (10 mL) salt
- 4 1/3 lb. (2 kg) plum tomatoes, coarsely chopped
- 6 garlic cloves, chopped
- 1/4 cup (60 mL) chopped fresh cilantro

———— ★ ————

Perfect Pairing

This is a great starter sauce for tacos, fajitas, enchiladas, or any of your favorite Mexican recipes. Simply simmer sauce to heat, and reduce to desired thickness before using.

1. Combine all ingredients, except cilantro, in a 6-qt. (6-L) stainless steel or enameled Dutch oven. Cover and cook over medium-low heat 45 minutes or until onion is very tender, stirring occasionally. Remove from heat; cool slightly.

2. Process tomato mixture in a blender or food processor, in batches, until very smooth. Pour through a wire-mesh strainer into a bowl, pressing with the back of a spoon to remove small bits of tomato peel and seeds. Discard seeds and peel.

3. Pour tomato puree into a large skillet. Bring to a boil; reduce heat, and simmer, uncovered, until thickened to desired consistency. Stir in cilantro.

4. Ladle hot tomato sauce into a hot jar, leaving 1/2-inch (1-cm) headspace. Remove air bubbles. Wipe jar rim. Center lid on jar. Apply band, and adjust to fingertip-tight. Place jar in boiling-water canner. Repeat until all jars are filled.

5. Process jars 40 minutes, adjusting for altitude. Turn off heat; remove lid, and let jars stand 5 minutes. Remove jars and cool.

PICKLING MAY BE CONSIDERED A RETRO CRAFT, BUT ITS POPULARITY TODAY IS VERY MUCH ON-TREND.

Thanks to our ancestors who discovered they could preserve food for long winters by submerging it beneath a high-acid, often salty brine, we can build on old techniques with new concepts tested to achieve the perfect balance of vinegar and salt that creates safe pH levels without overwhelming the true flavors of the vegetables and fruits. In this section, you'll find delicious recipes for old favorites along with fresh takes on spicy pickled okra, curried cauliflower, eggplant with artichoke, and other options influenced by traditional heritage and updated for today's tastes. These beauties will deserve a display shelf all their own.

DILL PICKLE SPEARS

MAKES ABOUT 6 (1-PT./500-ML) WIDE MOUTH JARS

A traditional pickle loaded with dill flavor, this is a great recipe to start with if you're new to cucumber pickles. A pinch of Ball® Pickle Crisp added to each jar will ensure extra crunch.

- 4 lb. (2 kg) (3- to 5-inch/7.5- to 12.5-cm) pickling cucumbers
- 1 gal. (4 L) water
- 10 Tbsp. (150 mL) Ball® Salt for Pickling & Preserving, divided
- 1 qt. (1 L) water
- 3 cups (750 mL) white vinegar (5% acidity)
- 2 Tbsp. (30 mL) sugar
- 1 Tbsp. (15 mL) pickling spice
- 12 dill sprigs
- 2 Tbsp. (30 mL) mustard seeds

Ball® Pickle Crisp (optional)

★

Tricks of the Trade

Pickling cucumbers are small, crisp, unwaxed, and needn't be peeled. Wide mouth jars aren't essential for pickles, but they do make for easier packing.

---

1. Wash cucumbers, and trim any that are longer than 5 inches (12.5 cm) so that they'll fit comfortably in the jar. Cut each cucumber lengthwise into quarters. Place spears in a large, clean container (such as a 12- to 18-qt. [12- to 18-L] food-safe plastic pail or basin). Combine 1 gal. (4 L) water and 6 Tbsp. (90 mL) salt in a large pitcher, stirring until salt dissolves. Pour over cucumbers; cover and let stand at room temperature 24 hours. Drain.

2. Combine 1 qt. (1 L) water, next 3 ingredients, and remaining ¼ cup (60 mL) salt in a 3-qt. (3-L) stainless steel or enameled saucepan. Bring to a boil.

3. Place 2 dill sprigs and 1 tsp. mustard seeds into a hot jar, and pack tightly with cucumber spears. Ladle hot pickling liquid over spears, leaving ½-inch (1-cm) headspace. Add ⅛ tsp. (.5 mL) Ball® Pickle Crisp to jar, if desired. Remove air bubbles. Wipe rim. Center lid on jar. Apply band, and adjust to fingertip-tight. Repeat until all jars are filled.

4. Process jars 10 minutes, adjusting for altitude. Turn off heat; remove lid, and let jars stand 5 minutes. Remove jars and cool.

PICKLED PEPPERS AND ONIONS

MAKES ABOUT 6 (1-PT./500-ML) JARS

2 cups (500 mL) ¼-inch (.5-cm)-thick vertically sliced red onion

4 cups (1 L) white vinegar (5% acidity)

4 cups (1 L) water

1½ (375 mL) cups sugar

½ cup (125 mL) Ball® Salt for Pickling & Preserving

2 tsp. (10 mL) dried crushed red pepper

2 medium-size red bell peppers, cut into ¼-inch (.5-cm)-thick strips

2 medium yellow bell peppers, cut into ¼-inch (.5-cm)-thick strips

2 large green bell peppers, cut into ¼-inch (.5-cm)-thick strips

Ball® Pickle Crisp (optional)

1. Soak onion slices in ice water to cover 10 minutes. Bring vinegar and next 4 ingredients to a boil in a 2-qt. (2-L) stainless steel or enameled saucepan over medium-high heat, stirring until sugar dissolves.

2. Drain onion slices; pat dry. Toss together onions and bell peppers.

3. Pack vegetables tightly into a hot jar, leaving ½-inch (1-cm) headspace. Add ⅛ tsp. (.5 mL) Ball® Pickle Crisp to jar, if desired. Ladle hot pickling liquid over vegetables, leaving ½-inch (1-cm) headspace. Remove air bubbles. Wipe jar rim. Center lid on jar. Apply band, and adjust to fingertip-tight. Place jar in boiling-water canner. Repeat until all jars are filled.

4. Process jars 10 minutes, adjusting for altitude. Turn off heat; remove lid, and let jars stand 5 minutes. Remove jars and cool.

CUBAN SANDWICHES

MAKES 4 SERVINGS

8 oz. (250 g) roast pork

8 (1-oz./30-g) Swiss cheese

¼ cup (60 mL) mayonnaise

2 Tbsp. (30 mL) yellow mustard

4 (4- to 5-inch/10- to 12.5-cm) kaiser or club rolls, halved lengthwise

1 cup (250 mL) drained Pickled Peppers and Onions

8 oz. (250 g) deli ham slices

1. Cut roast pork and Swiss cheese into thin slices. Stir together mayonnaise and mustard in a small bowl until blended.

2. Spread cut sides of each roll with 1 rounded Tbsp. (about 15 mL) mayonnaise mixture. Place 1 cheese slice on each roll bottom. Top evenly with roast pork, Pickled Peppers and Onions, ham, and remaining cheese slices. Cover with roll tops.

3. Tightly wrap each sandwich in aluminum foil and place in a large skillet. Place a large cast-iron skillet on top of sandwiches. Cook over medium heat 12 to 15 minutes or until toasted and cheese melts, turning every 3 minutes.

PICKLED DILLED BEANS

MAKES ABOUT 6 (1-PT./500-L) WIDE MOUTH JARS

Crushed red pepper gives these beans a kick. A mix of green and yellow beans makes for a pretty jar.

- 3½ lb. (1.6 kg) fresh green or yellow beans (5 to 6 inches long/12.5 to 15 cm long)
- 5 cups (1.25 L) white vinegar (5% acidity)
- 2 cups (500 mL) water
- ⅓ cup (75 mL) Ball® Salt for Pickling & Preserving
- 1½ tsp. (7 mL) dried crushed red pepper
- 12 fresh dill sprigs
- 6 garlic cloves, peeled and crushed

Ball® Pickle Crisp (optional)

★

Tricks of the Trade

Green beans only need their stem ends snapped, the "tail" end is the tender part of the bean. For quick prep, stack the beans with their stem ends lined up; working in batches, use a sharp heavy knife to cut them all off.

1. Wash beans, trim stem ends, and cut into 4-inch (10-cm) lengths. Combine vinegar and next 3 ingredients in a 3-qt. (3-L) stainless steel or enameled saucepan. Bring to a boil.

2. Place 2 dill sprigs and 1 crushed garlic clove into a hot jar. Pack whole beans tightly into jar. Ladle hot pickling liquid over beans, leaving ½-inch (1-cm) headspace. Add ⅛ tsp. (.5 mL) Ball® Pickle Crisp to jar, if desired. Remove air bubbles. Wipe jar rim. Center lid on jar. Apply band, and adjust to fingertip-tight. Place jar in boiling-water canner. Repeat until all jars are filled.

3. Process jars 10 minutes, adjusting for altitude. Turn off heat; remove lid, and let jars stand 5 minutes. Remove jars and cool.

PICKLED ASPARAGUS

MAKES ABOUT 6 (1½-PT./750-ML) JARS

When asparagus is in season, pickling is the best way to extend it throughout the year. Delicate spears enhanced with garlic and dill will remain flavorful and crisp.

- 5 cups (1.24 L) white vinegar (5% acidity)
- 1 qt. (1 L) water
- ⅔ cup (150 mL) sugar
- ½ cup (125 mL) Ball® Salt for Pickling & Preserving
- 4 tsp. (20 mL) dried crushed red pepper
- 2 tsp. (10 mL) pickling spice
- 7 lb. (3.25 kg) fresh asparagus
- 12 dill sprigs
- 6 garlic cloves, crushed

Ball® Pickle Crisp (optional)

★

Peak of Freshness

Asparagus comes in three colors that range in thickness depending on when they are harvested and the age of the plant. Choose very fresh medium-thickness spears and mix the colors up for interest!

---

1. Bring first 6 ingredients to a boil in a 3-qt. (3-L) stainless steel or enameled saucepan over medium-high heat, stirring until sugar and salt dissolve.

2. Rinse asparagus. Cut spears into 5-inch (13-cm) lengths to fit jars, discarding tough ends. Place 2 dill sprigs and 1 garlic clove into a hot jar. Tightly pack asparagus, cut ends down, in jar, leaving ½-inch (1-cm) headspace. Add ⅛ tsp. (.5 mL) Ball® Pickle Crisp to jar, if desired. Ladle hot pickling liquid over asparagus, leaving ½-inch (1-cm) headspace. Remove air bubbles. Wipe jar rim. Center lid on jar. Apply band, and adjust to fingertip-tight. Place jar in boiling-water canner. Repeat until all jars are filled.

3. Process jars 10 minutes, adjusting for altitude. Turn off heat; remove lid, and let jars stand 5 minutes. Remove jars and cool.

PICKLED GOLDEN BEETS

MAKES ABOUT 4 (1-PT./500-ML) WIDE MOUTH JARS

This recipe works with red beets, too, but golden beets are less likely to stain your fingers or your apron.

---

4 lb. (2 kg) (3-inch/7.5-cm-diameter) golden beets

2½ cups (625 mL) white vinegar (5% acidity)

1¼ cups (300 mL) water

1¼ cups (300 mL) sugar

1 tsp. (5 mL) Ball® Salt for Pickling & Preserving

8 whole cloves

1 (3-inch/7.5-cm) cinnamon stick

2 (2- to 2½-inch/5- to 6-cm-diameter) onions, thinly sliced

1. Trim beets, leaving 1 inch (2.5 cm) of stem, and scrub. Bring beets to a boil in water to cover in a large saucepan; reduce heat, and simmer 25 to 30 minutes or until tender. Drain, rinse, and cool slightly. Trim off roots and stems; peel beets. Cut beets in half vertically; cut halves crosswise into ¼-inch (.5-cm)-thick slices to measure 6 cups (1.5 L).

2. Stir together vinegar and next 5 ingredients in a 6-qt. (6-L) stainless steel or enameled Dutch oven. Bring mixture to a boil. Add beets and onion; reduce heat, and simmer 5 minutes. Remove and discard spices.

3. Pack beets and onion into a hot jar with a slotted spoon, leaving ½-inch (1-cm) headspace. Ladle hot pickling liquid over beet mixture, leaving ½-inch (1-cm) headspace. Remove air bubbles. Wipe jar rim. Center lid on jar. Apply band, and adjust to fingertip-tight. Place jar in boiling-water canner. Repeat until all jars are filled.

4. Process jars 30 minutes, adjusting for altitude. Turn off heat; remove lid, and let jars stand 5 minutes. Remove jars and cool.

PICKLED FENNEL WITH ORANGES

MAKES ABOUT 5 (1-PT./500-ML) JARS

Thinly sliced fennel gets star treatment in this pickle seasoned with orange, turmeric, and ginger.

2½ lb. (1.1 kg) fennel bulbs (2 to 3 large)

1 Tbsp. (15 mL) Ball® Salt for Pickling & Preserving

1 (8-oz./250-g) orange, quartered

2 cups (500 mL) apple cider vinegar (5% acidity)

1 cup (250 mL) fresh orange juice (about 4 oranges)

½ cup (125 mL) water

¼ cup (60 mL) sugar or honey

1¼ tsp. (6 mL) cumin seeds

1¼ tsp. (6 mL) ground black pepper

1 (1-inch/2.5-cm) piece peeled fresh ginger, thinly sliced*

1 (1-inch/2.5-cm) piece peeled fresh turmeric, thinly sliced*

───── ★ ─────

Peak of Freshness

Fennel is an herb with a distinct anise flavor whose bulbous stalks are used as a vegetable. Look for fennel that is white and still has stalks of feathery green leaves on it.

1. Rinse fennel thoroughly. Trim and discard root ends of fennel bulbs. Trim stalks from bulbs, and discard. Cut bulbs in half lengthwise; cut halves lengthwise into ¼-inch (.5-cm) slices. Place fennel slices in a large glass bowl. Sprinkle with salt, tossing to coat.

2. Cut orange quarters crosswise into thin slices. Combine vinegar and next 3 ingredients in a medium stainless steel or enameled saucepan. Bring to a boil over medium heat. Reduce heat and simmer while filling jars.

3. Place ¼ tsp. (1 mL) each cumin seeds and pepper, and one-fifth each ginger and turmeric slices in a hot jar. Pack fennel and orange slices tightly in jar, leaving ½-inch (1-cm) headspace. Ladle hot pickling liquid over fennel mixture, leaving ½-inch (1-cm) headspace. Remove air bubbles. Wipe jar rim. Center lid on jar. Apply band, and adjust to fingertip-tight. Place jar in boiling-water canner. Repeat until all jars are filled.

4. Process jars 10 minutes, adjusting for altitude. Turn off heat; remove lid, and let jars stand 5 minutes. Remove jars and cool.

*¼ tsp. (1 mL) ground ginger and ⅛ tsp. (.5 mL) ground turmeric per jar may be substituted.

WATERMELON, CUCUMBER, AND JALAPEÑO PICKLES

MAKES ABOUT 6 (1-PT./500-ML) JARS

A classic watermelon rind pickle taken to new heights with jalapeño slices and cucumbers.

6 Tbsp. (90 mL) Ball®
   Salt for Pickling &
   Preserving, divided

9 cups (2.25 L) water,
   divided

1 (8-lb./4-kg) watermelon

2 lb. (1 kg) medium
   pickling cucumbers,
   such as Kirby

½ lb. (250 g) jalapeño
   peppers

Ice cubes

2 Tbsp. (30 mL) pickling
   spice

Cheesecloth

Kitchen string

4 cups (1 L) sugar

3 cups (750 mL) white
   vinegar (5% acidity)

1½ tsp. (7 mL) mustard
   seeds

18 whole cloves

Ball® Pickle Crisp (optional)

───── ★ ─────

Peak of Freshness
Choose a watermelon
with pickling in mind,
making sure the rind is
firm and bright colored,
free of bruises.

1. Dissolve ¼ cup (60 mL) pickling salt in 1 qt. (1 L) water in a large bowl. Trim green peel and pink flesh from thick watermelon rind. Cut rind into 1-inch (2.5-cm) pieces to measure 8 cups (4 L). Add rind to salt water, adding water, if necessary, to cover rind. Cover with plastic wrap and let stand 6 hours.

2. After 3 hours, dissolve remaining 2 Tbsp. (30 mL) salt in 1 qt. (1 L) water in another large bowl.

3. Scrub cucumbers under cold running water. Cut cucumbers into ¼-inch-thick slices to measure 6 cups (1.5 L). Remove stems from jalapeños; cut into ½-inch (1-cm)-thick slices to measure 2 cups (500 mL). Place cucumber and jalapeño slices in salt water in second bowl. Cover with a thick layer of ice cubes. Cover and let stand 3 hours.

4. Bring a large pot of water to a boil. Drain rind, discarding brine; rinse. Drain. Rinse bowl. Add drained rind to boiling water. Cook 5 to 6 minutes or until crisp-tender. Drain. Rinse with cold water to stop the cooking process. Drain; return rind to rinsed bowl.

5. Drain cucumber mixture, discarding brine and any unmelted ice cubes. Rinse cucumber mixture; drain.

6. Place pickling spice on a 4-inch (10-cm) square of cheesecloth; tie with kitchen string. Bring sugar, vinegar, spice bag, and remaining 1 cup (250 mL) water to a boil in a 6-qt. (6-L) stainless steel or enameled Dutch oven; cover, reduce heat, and simmer 5 minutes. Add rind and cucumber mixture. Bring to a boil; reduce heat, and simmer, uncovered, 10 minutes, stirring occasionally. Remove and discard spice bag.

7. Place ¼ tsp. (1 mL) mustard seeds and 3 whole cloves in a hot jar. Using a slotted spoon, firmly pack rind mixture in jar, leaving ½-inch (1-cm) headspace. Ladle hot pickling liquid over rind mixture, leaving ½-inch (1-cm) headspace. Add ⅛ tsp. (.5 mL) Ball® Pickle Crisp to jar, if desired. Remove air bubbles. Wipe jar rim. Center lid on jar. Apply band, and adjust to fingertip-tight. Place jar in boiling-water canner. Repeat until all jars are filled.

8. Process jars 10 minutes, adjusting for altitude. Turn off heat; remove lid, and let jars stand 5 minutes. Remove jars and cool.

QUICK CONFETTI PICKLES

MAKES ABOUT 3 (1-PT./500-ML) JARS

A beautiful pickle of cucumber, squash, and radishes, glowing with color and a bright lemony taste.

1 English cucumber (about 1½ lb./750 g)

1 medium-size yellow squash (about 7½ oz./ 240 g)

¼ cup (60 mL) Ball® Salt for Pickling & Preserving, divided

2 (7-oz./210-g) pink, purple, or red icicle radishes, or 10 standard-size radishes

1 long, slender carrot (about 2½ oz./75 g), peeled

2 cups (500 mL) water

1 cup (250 mL) apple cider vinegar (5% acidity)

¼ cup (60 mL) sugar

2 Tbsp. (30 mL) lemon juice

1 tsp. (5 mL) dill seeds

6 dill sprigs

Ball® Pickle Crisp (optional)

1. Wash vegetables. Score cucumber and squash lengthwise with a fork, leaving furrows in the peel on all sides. (This makes scalloped edges when vegetables are sliced.) Trim stem and blossom ends of cucumber and squash; cut into ⅛-inch (3-mm) slices. Place in a colander in sink; sprinkle with 2 Tbsp. (30 mL) salt, and toss gently. Let drain 30 minutes.

2. Meanwhile, cut radishes and carrot into ⅛-inch (3-mm)-thick slices; add to drained cucumber and squash, tossing well.

3. Bring water, next 4 ingredients, and remaining 2 Tbsp. (30 mL) salt to a boil in a 1½-qt. (1½-L) stainless steel or enameled saucepan over medium-high heat, stirring until sugar and salt dissolve. Reduce heat to low, and simmer while filling jars.

4. Place 2 dill sprigs in a hot jar. Pack vegetables tightly in jar, leaving ½-inch (1-cm) headspace. Ladle hot pickling liquid over vegetables, leaving ½-inch (1-cm) headspace. Add ⅛ tsp. (.5 mL) Ball® Pickle Crisp to jar, if desired. Remove air bubbles. Wipe jar rim. Center lid on jar. Apply band, and adjust to fingertip-tight. Place jar in boiling-water canner. Repeat until all jars are filled.

5. Process jars 10 minutes, adjusting for altitude. Turn off heat; remove lid, and let jars stand 5 minutes. Remove jars and cool.

★

Simple Switch

You can mix up the assortment and quantity of vegetables, using more carrots, zucchini squash, tiny pickling cucumbers, or hakurei turnips.

PICKLED CHERRIES

MAKES ABOUT 7 (½-PT./250-ML) JARS

Cherries are reconsidered as pickles in this gorgeous dark, sweet, and spicy recipe. Toss these in salads, on cheese plates, and in cocktails.

2½ cups (625 mL) white vinegar (5% acidity)

2 cups (500 mL) sugar

2 Tbsp. (30 mL) Ball® Salt for Pickling & Preserving

1 vanilla bean, split

7 whole cloves

7 star anise

7 (3-inch/7.5-cm) cinnamon sticks

2¾ lb. (1.25 kg) fresh dark, sweet cherries, washed, stemmed, and pitted

---
★

Tricks of the Trade

Use a cherry pitter or a large paper clip to pit cherries while leaving them whole.

---

1. Stir together first 3 ingredients in a medium stainless steel or enameled saucepan. Scrape seeds from vanilla bean; add seeds and bean to vinegar mixture. Bring to a boil, stirring until sugar and salt dissolve.

2. Place 1 clove, 1 star anise, and 1 cinnamon stick into a hot jar. Pack cherries tightly into jar, leaving ½-inch (1-cm) headspace (about 12 cherries). Remove vanilla bean from pan; discard. Ladle hot pickling liquid over cherries, leaving ½-inch (1-cm) headspace. Remove air bubbles. Wipe jar rim. Center lid on jar. Apply band, and adjust to fingertip-tight. Place jar in boiling-water canner. Repeat until all jars are filled.

3. Process jars 10 minutes, adjusting for altitude. Turn off heat; remove lid, and let jars stand 5 minutes. Remove jars and cool.

PICKLED RAINBOW CARROTS WITH CORIANDER

MAKES ABOUT 4 (1-PT./500-ML) WIDE MOUTH JARS

Rainbow carrots are stunning, and these pickles make the most of these heirloom varieties with a coriander and garlic brine.

3½ lb. (1.6 kg) small (3- to 5-inch/7.5- to 12.3-cm) purple, orange, yellow, and white carrots with tops

3½ cups (875 mL) white vinegar (5% acidity)

1 cup (250 mL) water

¼ cup (60 mL) Ball® Salt for Pickling & Preserving

2 tsp. (10 mL) coriander seeds

8 dill sprigs

4 garlic cloves, crushed

★

Simple Switch
For a quick variation increase quantity and use prepackaged baby rainbow carrots.

1. Wash and peel carrots; trim green tops to ¼ inch (.5 cm), and trim any carrots that are longer than 4 inches (10 cm) to fit comfortably within the jars. Cut carrots in half lengthwise.

2. Combine vinegar, water, and salt in a 4-qt. (4-L) stainless steel or enameled saucepan. Bring to a boil over medium heat, stirring until salt dissolves; reduce heat, and simmer until ready to fill jars.

3. Place ½ tsp. (2 mL) coriander seeds, 2 dill sprigs, and 1 garlic clove in a hot jar. Pack jar tightly with carrots. Ladle hot pickling liquid over carrots, leaving ½-inch (1-cm) headspace. Remove air bubbles. Wipe jar rim. Center lid on jar. Apply band, and adjust to fingertip-tight. Repeat until all jars are filled.

4. Process jars 15 minutes, adjusting for altitude. Turn off heat; remove lid, and let jars stand 5 minutes. Remove jars and cool.

BREAD-AND-BUTTER PICKLED ONIONS

MAKES ABOUT 6 (1-PT./500 ML) JARS

This traditional bread-and-butter cucumber pickle has sliced sweet onions and jalapeños added for extra crunch and flavor, making it a superb lunchtime accompaniment.

---

2 lb. (1 kg) sweet onions, halved lengthwise and cut crosswise into ¼-inch (.5-cm)-thick slices

2 lb. pickling cucumbers (such as Kirby), cut into ¼-inch (.5-cm)-thick slices

2 fresh red jalapeño peppers, halved lengthwise, seeded, and thinly sliced crosswise

¼ cup (60 mL) Ball® Salt for Pickling & Preserving

4 garlic cloves, thinly sliced

4 cups (1 L) apple cider vinegar (5% acidity)

3 cups (750 mL) sugar

2 tsp. (10 mL) mustard seeds

1 tsp. (5 mL) ground turmeric

Ball® Pickle Crisp (optional)

1. Toss together first 5 ingredients in a large bowl. Cover and let stand 1 hour. Transfer to a colander; drain 20 minutes. (Do not rinse.)

2. Bring vinegar and next 3 ingredients to a boil in a small stainless steel or enameled saucepan over high heat, stirring constantly, until sugar dissolves. Stir in onion, cucumber, and pickle mixture and return to a boil.

3. Pack hot vegetables into a hot jar, leaving ½-inch (1-cm) headspace. Add ⅛ tsp. (.5 mL) Ball® Pickle Crisp to jar, if desired. Ladle pickling liquid over vegetables, leaving ½-inch (1-cm) headspace. Remove air bubbles. Wipe jar rim. Center lid on jar. Apply band, and adjust to fingertip-tight. Place jar in boiling-water canner. Repeat until all jars are filled.

4. Process jars 10 minutes, adjusting for altitude. Turn off heat; remove lid, and let jars stand 5 minutes. Remove jars and cool.

★

Tricks of the Trade

A mandoline slicer makes excellent and quick work of slicing vegetables. The diagonal-blade style is the safest (the other style is a V blade).

PLOUGHMAN'S PICKLES

MAKES ABOUT 5 (1-PT./500-ML) JARS

The epitome of British pickles, Ploughman's is a spicy, crunchy, tart, and sweet combination of pickles and chutney.

- 3 cups (750 mL) apple cider vinegar (5% acidity)
- 1½ cups (375 mL) sugar
- 1½ cups (375 mL) chopped dried dates
- ¼ cup (60 mL) jarred tamarind paste*
- 1 Tbsp. (15 mL) Ball® Salt for Pickling & Preserving
- 1 Tbsp. (15 mL) grated fresh ginger
- 3 garlic cloves, minced
- 1 Granny Smith apple, peeled and cut into ¼-inch (.5-cm) cubes
- 4 medium carrots
- 1 pickling cucumber (such as Kirby)
- 1 small zucchini
- 1 red onion
- 1 small turnip
- 1½ cups (375 mL) ¼-inch (.5-cm) cauliflower florets

★

Perfect Pairing

The Ploughman is a classic British pub sandwich featuring sharp Cheddar and this vegetable pickle medley. Use these pickles alongside any sandwich or just scoop them up on chips!

1. Combine first 8 ingredients in a 6-qt. (6-L) stainless steel or enameled Dutch oven. Bring to a boil; reduce heat, and simmer, uncovered, 15 minutes or until apples are soft, stirring occasionally.

2. Meanwhile, cut carrots and next 4 ingredients into ¼-inch (.5-cm) cubes.

3. Mash apples and dates with a potato masher. Continue to simmer, stirring constantly, 15 to 20 minutes or until thick. Add cauliflower and diced vegetables. Bring to a simmer; cook, uncovered, 20 minutes or until turnip is fork-tender, stirring often.

4. Ladle hot pickle mixture into a hot jar, leaving ½-inch (1-cm) headspace. Remove air bubbles. Wipe jar rim. Center lid on jar. Apply band, and adjust to fingertip-tight. Place jar in boiling-water canner. Repeat until all jars are filled.

5. Process jars 20 minutes, adjusting for altitude. Turn off heat; remove lid, and let jars stand 5 minutes. Remove jars and cool.

* ½ cup (125 mL) tamarind pulp soaked in ½ cup hot water until softened, then pressed through a sieve, may be substituted.

SQUASH PICKLE MEDLEY

MAKES ABOUT 5 (1-PT./500-ML) JARS

Pickled squash is a favorite where summer squashes take over whole yards. Though it may be a condiment, it's often used as a side dish too.

- 2 lb. (1 kg) small zucchini
- 1 lb. (450 g) small yellow squash
- 1 small onion, halved vertically and cut crosswise into ¼-inch (1-cm) slices (curved strips) (about 5 oz./150 g)
- ⅓ cup (75 mL) Ball® Salt for Pickling & Preserving

Ice cubes

- 2 cups (500 mL) white vinegar (5% acidity)
- 2 cups (500 mL) sugar
- 1 tsp. (5 mL) mustard seeds
- ½ tsp. (2 mL) celery seeds
- ¼ tsp. (1 mL) ground turmeric

★

Simple Switch

Swap in pattypan squash or other varieties of summer squash in this simple, quick recipe.

1. Wash zucchini and yellow squash, and trim stem and blossom ends; cut squash crosswise into ¼-inch (.5-cm) slices. Toss squash and onion with salt in a very large bowl. Cover vegetables with a thick layer of ice cubes. Cover and let stand at room temperature 3 hours.

2. Drain vegetables, but do not rinse, discarding brine and any unmelted ice. Return drained vegetables to bowl. Combine vinegar and next 4 ingredients in a medium stainless steel or enameled saucepan. Bring to a boil over medium-high heat.

3. Tightly pack squash and onion mixture into a hot jar, leaving ½-inch (1-cm) headspace. Cover vegetables with hot pickling liquid, leaving ½-inch (1-cm) headspace. Remove air bubbles. Wipe jar rim. Center lid on jar. Apply band, and adjust to fingertip-tight. Place jar in boiling-water canner. Repeat until all jars are filled.

4. Process jars 20 minutes, adjusting for altitude. Turn off heat; remove lid, and let jars stand 5 minutes. Remove jars and cool.

PICKLED BRUSSELS SPROUTS

MAKES ABOUT 6 (1-PT./500-ML) JARS

These pickled gems make an awesome Bloody Mary garnish or a tangy part of an antipasto platter.

3 lb. (1.5 kg) small Brussels sprouts

5 cups (1.25 L) white vinegar (5% acidity)

2 cups (500 mL) water

1/3 cup (75 mL) Ball® Salt for Pickling & Preserving

24 black peppercorns

12 garlic cloves, smashed

6 dill heads

1 jalapeño pepper, cut into 12 (1/4-inch/.5-cm) slices

1 lemon, cut into 6 (1/4-inch/.5-cm) slices

1. Remove discolored leaves from Brussels sprouts. Cut off stem ends, and cut a shallow X in the bottom of each sprout. Cut large sprouts in half. Cook in boiling water to cover 4 minutes; drain.

2. Combine vinegar, water, and salt in a 3-qt. stainless steel or enameled saucepan. Bring to a boil. Reduce heat to low, and simmer while filling jars.

3. Place 4 peppercorns, 2 garlic cloves, 1 dill head, 2 jalapeño slices, and 1 lemon slice in a hot jar. Pack jar tightly with Brussels sprouts, leaving 1/2-inch (1-cm) headspace. Ladle hot pickling liquid over Brussels sprouts, leaving 1/2-inch (1-cm) headspace. Remove air bubbles. Wipe jar rim. Center lid on jar. Apply band, and adjust to fingertip-tight. Place jar in boiling-water canner. Repeat until all jars are filled.

4. Process jars 10 minutes, adjusting for altitude. Turn off heat; remove lid, and let jars stand 5 minutes. Remove jars and cool.

ASIAN-STYLE CARROT-AND-DAIKON PICKLES

MAKES ABOUT 4 (1-PT./500 ML) JARS

These Vietnamese-style pickles are known as "Do Chun" and can be used as a garnish for many Vietnamese dishes. A classic pairing is in a Bánh Mì sandwich.

1 lb. (450 g) large carrots

¾ lb. (350 g) daikon radishes

2 cups (500 mL) water

2 cups (500 mL) white vinegar (5% acidity)

1 cup (250 mL) sugar

¼ cup (60 mL) Ball® Salt for Pickling & Preserving

8 garlic cloves, crushed

1 (1-inch/2.5-cm) piece fresh ginger, peeled and thinly sliced

¼ cup (60 mL) coriander seeds

4 to 8 small dried red chiles (such as bird's beak peppers or pequin chiles)

Ball® Pickle Crisp (optional)

★

Peak of Freshness
Unlike its other radish cousins, the daikon radish is long and white, resembling a carrot.

---

1. Peel carrots and radishes, and cut into ⅛-inch (3-mm)-thick julienne strips using a mandoline or knife.

2. Bring water and next 5 ingredients to a boil in a 6-qt. (6-L) stainless steel or enameled Dutch oven.

3. Place 1 Tbsp. (15 mL) coriander seeds, 1 to 2 chiles, 2 garlic cloves, and one-fourth of the ginger slices in a hot jar. Pack carrots and radishes tightly in jar, leaving ½-inch (1-cm) headspace.

4. Ladle hot pickling liquid over vegetables, leaving ½-inch (1-cm) headspace. Add ⅛ tsp. (.5 mL) Ball® Pickle Crisp to jar, if desired. Remove air bubbles. Wipe jar rim. Center lid on jar. Apply band, and adjust to fingertip-tight. Place jar in boiling-water canner. Repeat until all jars are filled.

5. Process jars 10 minutes, adjusting for altitude. Turn off heat; remove lid, and let jars stand 5 minutes. Remove jars and cool.

BÁNH MÌ SANDWICHES

MAKES 4 SERVINGS

This take on a Vietnamese favorite, stuffed with roast pork, our Asian-inspired sauces, slivers of jalapeño and pickled daikon with carrots, make this one satisfying sandwich bursting with spicy flavor.

½ cup (125 mL) mayonnaise

1 Tbsp. (15 mL) Asian Pomegranate BBQ and Stir-Fry Sauce (page 182)*

½ tsp. (2 mL) Fiery Fermented Hot Sauce (page 264)*

4 (6-inch/15-cm) pieces French bread baguette, cut in half lengthwise and toasted

2 cups (500 mL) Asian-Style Carrot-and-Daikon Pickles (page 232), drained and chilled

¾ lb. (350 g) roast pork, sliced

12 cilantro sprigs

2 jalapeño peppers, very thinly sliced

Additional Asian Sriracha Sauce (optional)

★

Peak of Freshness

Báhn Mì refers to the type of baguette used in Vietnamese sandwiches, not necessarily the fillings, which can vary from home to home.

1. Stir together first 3 ingredients in a small bowl. Spread mayonnaise mixture evenly on cut side of each baguette half.

2. Divide pickles and pork slices among bottom halves of baguette pieces. Top with cilantro sprigs and jalapeños, and cover with top halves of baguette pieces. Serve with additional Asian Sriracha Sauce, if desired.

*Jarred hoisin sauce and bottled Asian hot chile sauce (such as Sriracha) may be substituted.

HOME-STYLE PICKLED JALAPEÑOS

MAKES ABOUT 6 (1-PT./500 ML) JARS

These long pickled-pepper strips are the perfect fit for tacos, nachos, or any favorite sandwich that needs spicing up.

3½ lb. (1.6 kg) jalapeño peppers, seeded and quartered

1 cup (250 mL) thinly sliced white onion

2 large carrots, thinly sliced

2½ cups (625 mL) white vinegar (5% acidity)

2½ cups (625 mL) water

2 Tbsp. (30 mL) Ball® Salt for Pickling & Preserving

1 Tbsp. (15 mL) sugar

6 garlic cloves, crushed

Ball® Pickle Crisp (optional)

1. Put on gloves, and cut peppers in half lengthwise; remove seeds. Cut halves in half lengthwise to create long strips. Place jalapeño strips in a large bowl. Add onion and carrot; toss well.

2. Combine vinegar and next 3 ingredients in a large stainless steel or enameled saucepan. Bring to a boil.

3. Place 1 crushed garlic clove in a hot jar, and pack jar tightly with vegetable mixture, leaving ½-inch (1-cm) headspace. Add ⅛ tsp. (.5 mL) Ball® Pickle Crisp to jar, if desired. Ladle hot pickling liquid over vegetables, leaving ½-inch (1-cm) headspace. Remove air bubbles. Wipe jar rim. Center lid on jar. Apply band, and adjust to fingertip-tight. Place jar in boiling-water canner. Repeat until all jars are filled.

4. Process jars 10 minutes, adjusting for altitude. Turn off heat; remove lid, and let jars stand 5 minutes. Remove jars and cool.

SPICY PICKLED OKRA WITH CHERRY TOMATOES AND PEARL ONIONS

MAKES ABOUT 6 (1-PT./500-ML) JARS

Pickling okra elevates it to another level of vegetable altogether. Coupled with cayenne peppers and cherry tomatoes, this is pickle perfect.

- 2 lb. (1 kg) (2- to 3-inch/ 5- to 7.5-cm) fresh okra pods
- 1 lb. (450 g) small cherry tomatoes
- 5 cups (1.25 L) white vinegar (5% acidity)
- 1 cup (250 mL) water
- 3 Tbsp. (45 mL) Ball® Salt for Pickling & Preserving
- 1 Tbsp. (15 mL) mustard seeds
- 6 black peppercorns
- 6 medium garlic cloves, crushed
- 6 whole dried cayenne peppers
- ³/₄ lb. (350 g) pearl onions, peeled

★

Perfect Pairing
A Bloody Mary will be completely transformed with these pickles as garnish.

---

1. Wash okra and tomatoes; drain. Trim stems from okra even with tops of caps, leaving caps intact.

2. Bring vinegar, water, and salt to a boil in a 2-qt. (2-L) stainless steel or enameled saucepan; reduce heat, and simmer, uncovered, 5 minutes. Keep hot.

3. Working quickly, place ½ tsp. (2 mL) mustard seeds, 1 peppercorn, 1 garlic clove, and 1 dried cayenne pepper in a hot jar. Top with one-sixth of pearl onions. Tightly pack one-sixth of okra pods, tips down, in jar. Top with one-sixth of tomatoes, leaving ½-inch (1-cm) headspace.

4. Ladle hot pickling liquid over vegetables, leaving ½-inch (1-cm) headspace. Remove air bubbles. Wipe jar rim. Center lid on jar. Apply band, and adjust to fingertip-tight. Place jar in boiling-water canner. Repeat until all jars are filled.

5. Process jars 15 minutes, adjusting for altitude. Turn off heat; remove lid, and let jars stand 5 minutes. Remove jars and cool.

GREEN TOMATO–HOT PEPPER PICKLES

MAKES ABOUT 8 (1-PT./500-ML) JARS

A bounteous early fall garden or farmers' market haul means multiple options for preserving. This spicy pickle makes excellent use of green tomatoes and a profusion of hot peppers.

- 2½ **lb. (1.1 kg) green tomatoes (about 7 medium), cored and cut into eighths**
- 1 **lb. (450 g) yellow, green, and orange hot banana peppers (Hungarian wax), cut into ½-inch (1-cm) rings**
- 1 **lb. (450 g) Anaheim peppers, cut into ½-inch (1-cm) rings**
- 1 **cup (250 mL) sliced onion (about 1 small)**
- 4 **tsp. (20 mL) Ball® Salt for Pickling & Preserving, divided**
- 3 **cups (750 mL) white vinegar (5% acidity)**
- 2 **cups (500 mL) water**
- ½ **cup (125 mL) sugar**
- 4 **tsp. (20 mL) pickling spice**
- 4 **tsp. (20 mL) mustard seeds**
- 8 **small garlic cloves, crushed**

★

Peak of Freshness

Green tomatoes may be used during all phases of ripening. If it's late fall and your plants are done, the very green ones will remain firm once pickled and will have a tart finish.

1. Toss together first 4 ingredients and 1 Tbsp. (15 mL) salt in a very large bowl. Let stand 20 minutes. Drain.

2. Bring vinegar, next 2 ingredients, and remaining 1 tsp. (5 mL) salt to a boil in a 12-qt. (12-L) stainless steel or enameled Dutch oven, stirring until sugar dissolves.

3. Place ½ tsp. (2 mL) pickling spice, ½ tsp. (2 mL) mustard seeds, and 1 garlic clove in a hot jar. Using a slotted spoon, transfer vegetables to hot jar, packing tightly and leaving ½-inch (1-cm) headspace. Ladle hot pickling liquid over vegetables, leaving ½-inch (1-cm) headspace. Remove air bubbles. Wipe jar rim. Center lid on jar. Apply band, and adjust to fingertip-tight. Place jar in boiling-water canner. Repeat until all jars are filled.

4. Process jars 10 minutes, adjusting for altitude. Turn off heat; remove lid, and let jars stand 5 minutes. Remove jars and cool.

PICKLED JICAMA WITH GRAPEFRUIT

MAKES ABOUT 4 (1-PT./500-ML) JARS

Jicama is a little known tuber from Mexico that is finally getting the spotlight it deserves. Juicy and crunchy with a sweet finish, try it here in this twist on a classic south-of-the-border fruit combination.

- 2 (³/₄-lb./350-g) pink grapefruit, divided
- 1½ cups (375 mL) apple cider vinegar (5% acidity)
- ½ cup (125 mL) white vinegar (5% acidity)
- ½ cup (125 mL) sugar
- ¼ cup (60 mL) honey
- 2 Tbsp. (30 mL) Ball® Salt for Pickling & Preserving
- 2 (1¼-lb./1.1-kg) jicamas, peeled and halved
- 1 large shallot (about 3 oz./90 g), cut into thin slices and separated into rings
- 2 star anise, cut in half
- 1 tsp. (5 mL) coriander seeds
- 1 tsp. (5 mL) dried crushed red pepper
- 1 tsp. (5 mL) dried oregano
- 1 tsp. (5 mL) ground black pepper

1. Squeeze juice from 1 grapefruit, adding water, if necessary, to measure 1 cup (250 mL). Combine grapefruit juice, apple cider vinegar, and next 4 ingredients in a large stainless steel or enameled saucepan. Bring to a boil. Reduce heat; keep hot.

2. Cut jicama halves into ½-inch (1-cm) square sticks, the length of each jicama. Using a sharp, thin-bladed knife, cut a ¼-inch (.5-cm) slice from each end of remaining grapefruit. Place flat-end down on a cutting board, and remove and discard rind and peel (bitter white pith) in strips, cutting from top to bottom, and following the curvature of the fruit. Holding peeled fruit in the palm of your hand and working over a bowl to collect juices, slice between membranes, and gently remove whole segments. Discard membranes and seeds.

3. Place one-fourth of shallot rings, 1 star anise half, and ¼ tsp. (1 mL) each coriander seeds and remaining spices into a hot jar. Using a slotted spoon, add one-fourth of grapefruit sections to jar. Add one-fourth of jicama sticks, leaving ½-inch (1-cm) headspace.

4. Ladle hot brine over grapefruit mixture, leaving ½-inch (1-cm) headspace. Remove air bubbles. Wipe jar rim. Center lid on jar. Apply band, and adjust to fingertip-tight. Place jar in boiling-water canner. Repeat until all jars are filled.

5. Process jars 10 minutes, adjusting for altitude. Turn off heat; remove lid, and let jars stand 5 minutes. Remove jars and cool.

★

Tricks of the Trade

Jicama's tough papery peel needs to be cut off with a knife. Start with the top and bottom, then cut down the sides. Jicama flesh will not discolor; wrap leftovers tightly and store in the refrigerator.

MISO PICKLED VEGETABLES

MAKES ABOUT 4 (1-PT./500-ML) JARS

Miso is a savory fermented soybean paste predominantly used in Korean and Japanese cuisines. It adds a richness and an unusual twist to these inspired pickles.

- 2 cups (500 mL) water
- 1½ cups (375 mL) rice vinegar (5% acidity)
- 1 cup (250 mL) apple cider vinegar (5% acidity)
- ½ cup (125 mL) sugar
- ⅓ cup (75 mL) white miso
- 2 Tbsp. (30 mL) Ball® Salt for Pickling & Preserving
- 2 Tbsp. (30 mL) black peppercorns
- 2 Tbsp. (30 mL) mustard seeds
- 2 garlic cloves, minced
- 4 small bay leaves
- 8 to 10 cups (2 to 2.3 L) assorted vegetables (such as small cauliflower florets, thinly sliced red onion, quartered small fresh button mushrooms, ¼-inch [.5-cm]-thick pickling cucumber slices, 1-inch [2.5-cm] eggplant cubes, sliced radishes, sliced okra, or slender green beans, and early spring asparagus, cut into 1-inch [2.5-cm] pieces)

1. Bring first 6 ingredients to a boil in a large stainless steel or enameled saucepan over medium heat.

2. Place 1½ tsp. (7 mL) peppercorns, 1½ tsp. (7 mL) mustard seeds, ½ tsp. (2 mL) garlic, and 1 bay leaf in a hot jar.

3. Tightly pack desired combination of vegetables in jar, leaving ½-inch (1-cm) headspace. Ladle hot pickling liquid over vegetables, leaving ½-inch (1-cm) headspace. Remove air bubbles. Wipe jar rim. Center lid on jar. Apply band, and adjust to fingertip-tight. Place jar in boiling-water canner. Repeat until all jars are filled.

4. Process jars 15 minutes, adjusting for altitude. Turn off heat; remove lid, and let jars stand 5 minutes. Remove jars and cool.

LEMONY EGGPLANT-ARTICHOKE CAPONATA

MAKES ABOUT 8 (1-PT./500-ML) JARS

The combination of roasted eggplant, artichoke hearts, and tangy salted lemon makes this caponata pickle quite addicting and, unlike traditional caponata, perfectly safe for preserving.

2 (1¾-lb./800-g) eggplants

Vegetable cooking spray

2 (5-oz./150-g) lemons

4 tsp. (20 mL) Ball® Salt for Pickling & Preserving, divided

1 cup (250 mL) bottled lemon juice

2 Tbsp. (30 mL) sugar

1 Tbsp. (15 mL) mustard seeds

1 Tbsp. (15 mL) dried crushed red pepper

1 tsp. (5 mL) garlic powder

1½ lb. (750 kg) frozen artichoke hearts, thawed and drained

2 large shallots, cut into thin vertical slices

2½ cups (625 mL) water

1 cup (250 mL) white vinegar (5% acidity)

★

Peak of Freshness

Make this when eggplants are at their peak in August and September; try using different varieties. Fresh or frozen nonmarinated artichoke hearts can be used for this recipe.

1. Preheat oven to 425°F (220°C). Remove stems from eggplants; cut lengthwise into quarters. Place, skin side down, on a large baking sheet. Coat with cooking spray.

2. Cut lemons lengthwise into quarters. Place lemon quarters, rind side down, on baking sheet. Sprinkle eggplant and lemon with 1 tsp. (5 mL) salt.

3. Bake at 425°F (220°C) until eggplant is fork-tender, but keeps its shape. (This will take from 20 to 30 minutes, depending upon the thickness of the eggplant.) Remove from oven, and let stand until cool enough to handle.

4. Cut eggplant into 1-inch (2.5-cm) pieces, and place in a 6-qt. (6-L) stainless steel or enameled Dutch oven. Seed lemon quarters over a bowl to catch juice; discard seeds. Cut lemons crosswise into very thin slices. Add lemon slices and accumulated juice to eggplant. Add bottled lemon juice, next 6 ingredients, and remaining 1 Tbsp. (15 mL) salt. Bring to a simmer over medium heat. Cook 15 to 20 minutes or until lemon rinds are soft.

5. Add water and vinegar. Bring to a boil. Remove from heat.

6. Ladle hot mixture into a hot jar, leaving ½-inch (1-cm) headspace. Remove air bubbles. Wipe jar rim. Center lid on jar. Apply band, and adjust to fingertip-tight. Place jar in boiling-water canner. Repeat until all jars are filled.

7. Process jars 20 minutes, adjusting for altitude. Turn off heat; remove lid, and let jars stand 5 minutes. Remove jars and cool.

FRUIT SHRUB

MAKES ABOUT 1 (1-PT./5-ML) JAR

A shrub is a fruit syrup mixed with vinegar. Historically, shrubs were made as a way to preserve fruit to drink, mixed with soda or flat water. Today, with the addition of different vinegars, sugars, spices, and herbs, shrubs have become a way to preserve and enhance fruit's flavor. Use the shrub traditionally with soda water over ice or mix creatively into cocktails. Each sip will be reminiscent of an era when ingenuity surpassed the simple desire to preserve a summer's bounty.

- 1 cup (250 mL) crushed fruit (such as strawberries, peaches, apricots, Concord grapes, plums, berries, or cherries)
- 1 cup (250 mL) sugar
- 1 (1-qt./500-mL) canning jar
- 1 cup (250 mL) vinegar (such as unfiltered apple cider, balsamic, sherry, or red wine vinegar)

——————— ★ ———————

Perfect Pairing
Get creative with your shrub. Try adding an herb such as lemon verbena or basil to the strawberries or peaches.

1. Combine crushed fruit and sugar in a 1-qt. (1-L) canning jar. Cover and shake to combine. Chill 1 to 3 days or until sugar dissolves and fruit releases its juice.

2. After 1 to 3 days, pour fruit mixture through a wire-mesh strainer into a 2-cup (500-mL) glass measuring cup, pressing with the back of a spoon to release as much juice as possible (about ¾ cup/175 mL); discard solids. Stir in vinegar. Transfer mixture to a 1-pt. (500-mL) jar. Cover with lid and chill 2 weeks before serving.

Refrigerator Pickles in 4 Easy Steps

These globally inspired refrigerator pickles are the ultimate in immediate satisfaction. Because they're refrigerated and not preserved for the pantry, you can get a little creative with fresh vegetables and seasonings.*

Makes about 1 qt. (1 L) or 2 pt. (500 mL) jars

STEP 1: Choose a recipe from the chart below.

STEP 2: Wash and trim 2 lb. (1 kg) desired vegetable or combination of vegetables from the chart below; leave whole (depending on size), halve, quarter, slice, or chop.

STEP 3: Prepare Master Brine by bringing 2 cups (500 mL) vinegar, 1 cup (250 mL) water, 2 Tbsp. (30 mL) sugar, 1 Tbsp. (15 mL) Ball® Salt for Pickling & Preserving, and seasonings from chart below to a boil in a small stainless steel or enameled saucepan; reduce heat, and simmer 3 minutes, stirring to dissolve sugar and salt.

STEP 4: Tightly pack vegetables into 1 hot (1-qt./1-L) or 2 hot (1-pt./500-mL) jars. Pour hot Master Brine over vegetables to cover. Cover jar with lid; let stand 1 hour or until cooled to room temperature. Store in refrigerator at least 1 month for best flavor or up to 3 months. (The longer pickles stand in refrigerator, the more flavorful they will become.)

PICKLE RECIPES	CHOOSE ANY COMBINATION	SEASONINGS	VINEGAR (5% ACIDITY)
Spicy Dill	Asparagus, Bell peppers, Cherry or Grape tomatoes, Green beans, Carrots, Cauliflower, Pickling cucumbers, Green tomatoes, Onions	2 tsp. (10 mL) pickling spice 4 dill sprigs 2 garlic cloves, crushed 1 jalapeño pepper, minced	White vinegar
Mediterranean	Asparagus, Button mushrooms, Green beans, Cauliflower, Eggplant, Onions, Radishes, Bell peppers, Chile peppers, Cherry or Grape tomatoes, Zucchini	2 Tbsp. (30 mL) minced fresh oregano or basil 2 tsp. (10 mL) citrus zest ¼ tsp. (1 mL) dried crushed red pepper 4 garlic cloves, crushed 2 small bay leaves	White wine, red wine, or balsamic vinegar, or a combination
Mexican	Bell peppers, Carrots, Chile peppers, Green beans, Onions, Pickling cucumbers, Radishes, Zucchini	½ cup (120 mL) fresh lime juice ¼ cup (60 mL) chopped fresh cilantro 4 garlic cloves, crushed 2 canned chipotle peppers in adobo sauce, minced	White or apple cider vinegar
Szechuan	Asparagus Cabbage Green Beans Cauliflower Pickling cucumbers Radishes Daikon radishes	2 Tbsp. (30 mL) chopped fresh ginger 1 tsp. (5 mL) Chinese five spice ¼ tsp. (1 mL) dried crushed red pepper 2 garlic cloves, crushed 2 green onions, sliced	White or rice wine vinegar

*Create your own globally inspired refrigerator pickles. Just customize your pickles and the Master Brine recipe with guidance from the recipe chart above. Because these are refrigerator pickles, you can feel safe to experiment by adjusting or varying ingredients as desired.

LIME-PICKLED RADISHES

MAKES ABOUT 1 (1-QT./1-L) JAR

Choose from a traditional pickle brine or give your radishes a new flair with this lime-based brine. It's a perfect topping to any kind of taco.

- ½ cup (125 mL) fresh lime juice (about 6 limes)
- ¼ cup (60 mL) water
- 2 Tbsp. (30 mL) sugar
- 1 tsp. (5 mL) salt
- 1 tsp. (5 mL) coriander seeds
- 1 bunch radishes (about ½ lb./250 g), leaves and roots trimmed and cut into ⅛-inch (3-mm) slices
- ¼ cup (60 mL) thin vertical red onion slices
- 1 Tbsp. (15 mL) chopped fresh cilantro

1. Bring first 5 ingredients to a boil in a small stainless steel or enameled saucepan.

2. Pack radish slices, onion, and cilantro into a hot jar.

3. Pour hot pickling liquid over radish mixture. Center lid on jar. Apply band, and adjust to fingertip-tight. Let cool completely on a wire rack (about 2 hours). Chill for at least 6 hours before serving. Store pickles in refrigerator up to 3 months.

PICKLED GINGER

MAKES ABOUT 4 (4-OZ./125-ML) JARS

If you eat up all the pickled ginger on a sushi plate, this recipe is for you! Keep a jar of this versatile pickle handy in your refrigerator.

- ½ lb. (250 g) fresh ginger
- 1 cup (250 mL) rice vinegar (5% acidity)*
- 6 Tbsp. (90 mL) sugar
- 2 tsp. (10 mL) Ball® Salt for Pickling & Preserving

★

Tricks of the Trade
Using a mandoline is an easy way to slice the ginger very thin.

1. Peel ginger, and cut into paper-thin slices.

2. Bring vinegar, sugar, and salt to a boil in a medium stainless steel or enameled saucepan.

3. Firmly pack ginger slices in hot jars, leaving ½-inch (1-cm) headspace. Ladle hot pickling liquid into jars to cover ginger, leaving ½-inch (1-cm) headspace. Remove air bubbles. Wipe jar rim. Center lid on jar. Apply band, and adjust to fingertip-tight. Cool completely. Chill overnight. Store in refrigerator up to 3 months. (Pickled Ginger will develop a rosy hue during storage.)

*Apple cider vinegar (5% acidity) may be substituted.

SWEET PICKLED RADISH

MAKES ABOUT 1 (1-PT./500 ML) JAR

*Fresh ruby red radishes, with their certain crunch and sharp flavor, make for delicious
and easy refrigerator quick pickles.*

- 1 bunch radishes (about ½ lb./250 g), stem and root ends removed and cut into ⅛-inch (3-mm) slices
- ½ cup (125 mL) white or apple cider vinegar (5% acidity)
- ½ cup (125 mL) sugar
- ¼ cup (60 mL) water
- 1 tsp. (5 mL) Ball® Salt for Pickling & Preserving
- 1 tsp. (5 mL) mustard seeds
- ½ tsp. (2 mL) ground black pepper
- 1 bay leaf
- ½ tsp. (2 mL) dried crushed red pepper (optional)

★

Perfect Pairing
Try this crunchy and tangy radish as an accompaniment with cherry tomatoes and pea shoots.

1. Place radishes in a hot 1-pt. jar. Bring vinegar, next 6 ingredients, and, if desired, crushed red pepper to a boil in a small saucepan.

2. Ladle hot pickling liquid over radishes. Wipe jar rim. Center lid on jar. Apply band, and adjust to fingertip-tight. Let cool on a wire rack (about 1 hour). Chill 6 hours before serving. Store in refrigerator up to 3 months.

Chapter 2

FERMENTING

Fermenting fruits, vegetables, and herbs captures the summer garden's bounty for yearlong enjoyment. With this age-old technique, farm-fresh cabbages become homemade sauerkraut and kimchi; crunchy cucumbers transform into tangy cool-weather treats that impart just-picked goodness with every bite. Salt or brines are used to bring out the natural goodness of vegetables and fruits, and, whether you choose to mix in aromatic spices and seasonings or simply preserve your produce au naturel, you'll find that fermented foods take on deliciously distinctive, crave-worthy flavors—the miracle of salt and probiotic action at work. When beginning the fermenting process, ensure that your container is protected from environmental contaminants with a covering that allows airflow and that your fermenting food is submerged beneath a brine at all times. By following the simple steps in our tried-and-true recipes, you'll be assured of safe, successful, healthy, and positively delicious results.

STEP-BY-STEP FERMENTING

Getting started: Read through recipe before beginning. Visually examine jars for defects and wash in warm soapy water, rinse well and set aside. Wipe down prep area and your fermenting storage place thoroughly to reduce possible contaminants (dust, molds, pet dander). Measure out salt and other spices into small bowls. Remove bruised or tattered parts of vegetables, then rinse under cold running water.

YOU WILL NEED:

- Tested fermented recipe such as Sauerkraut and Kimchi

- Large bowl

- Large spoon

- 2 (1 qt./1 L) glass jars with lids and 2 (4-oz./125-mL) glass jars with lids

STEP 1: Reserve 2 to 4 whole cabbage leaves. Quarter, core, and thinly slice the remaining cabbage.

STEP 2: Place cabbage in a large bowl, sprinkle with Ball® Salt for Pickling & Preserving, and crush the salt into the cabbage, squeezing gently to help the cabbage release water.

STEP 3: Once all the salt has been rubbed in, cover the bowl and set it aside for at least an hour to allow the cabbage to sweat and begin to release liquid.

STEP 4: Squeeze the cabbage to release more liquid. Do not discard the liquid.

STEP 5: Pack the cabbage into your jars with clean hands, firmly pressing down to help the cabbage release more liquid.

STEP 6: Place 1 or 2 of the reserved whole cabbage leaves on top of the shredded cabbage, pushing down and tucking the leaf in. Don't worry if brine doesn't cover the cabbage just yet.

STEP 7: Weigh the cabbage down. A smaller (4-oz.) Ball jar, filled with brine, that fits into the mouth of your fermenting jar may be used as a weight.

STEP 8: After 24 hours check the brine level. It should be higher, covering the cabbage and even billowing out the edges of the jar. If after 36 hours the cabbage does not have enough brine, then you may need to make a small amount to add to the kraut *(see recipe below for additional brine). Cabbage should remain 1 inch below the brine for proper and safe fermentation.

STEP 9: After 1 week, scoop any development of Kahm yeast (see Fermentation, pages 20-21) and wipe around the rim and inside of the jar with a clean damp paper towel. Return to fermenting.

STEP 10: Check your sauerkraut every few days after 1 week for taste, some people like it less fermented and some more. Sauerkraut can safely ferment at cool room temperature for up to 6 weeks. Place a plastic lid on the jar once kraut is to your liking, and store in the refrigerator.

*TO MAKE ADDITIONAL BRINE AS NEEDED, dissolve 2 tsp. (10 mL) Ball® Salt for Pickling & Preserving in 2 cups (500 mL) water. Refrigerate until needed.

SAUERKRAUT

MAKES ABOUT 2 (1-QT./1-L) JARS

Sharp, juicy, and salty describe homemade sauerkraut to a tee.

- 2 tsp. (10 mL), plus 1½ Tbsp. (22 mL) Ball® Salt for Pickling & Preserving, divided
- 2 cups (500 mL) water
- 2½ to 3 lb. (1.25 to 1.5 kg) cabbage
- 2 (4-oz./125-mL) Ball® jars

--- ★ ---

Tricks of the Trade

Read the directions on Fermentation (pages 20-21) for important and safe guidelines. Remember to keep your fermenting food beneath its brine during the entire fermentation process.

1. Combine 2 tsp. (10 mL) salt and water in a 1-pt. (500-mL) jar, stirring until salt dissolves; cover with lid; set brine aside and reserve for later use.

2. Remove and discard outer leaves of cabbage, reserving 2 to 4 leaves that are in good condition. Wash cabbage and reserved leaves under cold running water. Set reserved leaves aside. Cut remaining cabbage into quarters, and remove cores. Finely shred quarters, and place in a large bowl. Gradually sprinkle remaining 1½ Tbsp. salt over cabbage, massaging and squeezing salt into cabbage with thoroughly clean hands until liquid is released. Cover bowl and let stand 1 hour.

3. Mix cabbage with thoroughly clean hands for several more minutes. Divide cabbage evenly between 2 (1-qt./1-L) jars, pressing down firmly with a wooden spoon. Place 1 or 2 reserved cabbage leaves on top of shredded cabbage in each jar, pushing down and tucking leaf in to cover shredded cabbage.

4. Fill 2 clean 4-oz. (125-mL) Ball® jars with reserved brine and set on top of cabbage leaves inside each 1-qt. (1-L) jar to weight down cabbage. Place each jar on a plate in a dark, cool (65°F/18°C to 75°F/24°C) place. Cover jars with a clean dish towel, and let stand 24 to 36 hours.

5. If brine does not cover cabbage after 36 hours, add a small amount of reserved brine to cover. Return brine-filled weights to jars, and let sauerkraut stand, covered with towel, 2 weeks, checking daily to ensure cabbage remains submerged in brine, and skimming white film from top of brine and around weight as necessary.

6. After 2 weeks, cabbage will be translucent and perhaps slightly yellow in color. Check flavor for a fresh mild tang, and, if desired, remove weights, wipe jar rims, and cover jars with lids. Store in refrigerator.

7. If a stronger, more traditional, sour flavor is desired, return weights to jars to keep cabbage submerged; cover and continue to let stand in a dark, cool (65°F/18°C to 75°F/24°C) place for 1 to 3 more weeks or until desired flavor develops. Remove weights; wipe jar rims, and cover jars with lids. Store in refrigerator up to 6 months.

ASIAN PEAR KIMCHI

MAKES ABOUT 2 (1-QT./1-L) JARS

Firm, crisp, and plenty juicy, Asian pears, or apple pears, make a sturdy base for kimchi because they don't get mushy during the fermentation process. Asian pears have the ability to mingle happily when combined with sweet, salty, and spicy flavors.

4 tsp. (20 mL) Ball® Salt for Pickling & Preserving, divided

2 cups (500 mL) water

4 unpeeled Asian pears (about 1¾ lb./875 g), quartered and cored

4 garlic cloves, peeled

½ cup (125 mL) Korean chili flakes

¼ cup (60 mL) water

¼ cup (60 mL) sugar

2 Tbsp. (30 mL) white miso

1 (1-inch/2.5-cm) piece fresh ginger, peeled and grated

2 bunches green onions, roots removed, green and white parts thinly sliced

2 (1-qt./1-L) canning jars

2 (4-oz./125-mL) Ball® jars

★

Tricks of the Trade

Fermenting lids may be used for weights instead of the 4-oz. (60-mL) canning jars. Follow manufacturer's directions for use.

1. Combine 2 tsp. (10 mL) salt and water in a 1-pt. (500-mL) jar, stirring until salt dissolves; cover with lid; set brine aside and reserve for later use.

2. Cut pear quarters crosswise into thin slices, and place in a bowl. Sprinkle pear slices with remaining 2 tsp. (10 mL) salt; toss well. Cover and let stand 1 to 2 hours.

3. With processor on, gradually drop garlic cloves through food chute; process until minced. Add chili flakes and next 4 ingredients. Process until a paste forms, scraping sides as necessary. Stir paste and green onions into pear slices.

4. Divide pear mixture evenly between 2 (1-qt./1-L) jars, pouring any remaining brine from bottom of bowl evenly over pear mixture in both jars. (Jars will not be full, but brine should cover pear mixture by ½ inch (1 cm.) If brine does not cover pear mixture adequately, cover jars and let stand 3 hours. If liquid still does not cover pear mixture by ½ inch (1 cm), add reserved brine until pear mixture is covered.

5. Fill 2 clean 4-oz. (125-mL) Ball® jars with additional reserved brine, and set 1 jar on top of pear mixture inside each 1-qt. (1-L) jar to weight down pear mixture. Place each jar on a plate in a dark, cool (65°F/18°C to 75°F/24°C) place. Cover jars with a clean dish towel, and let stand 24 hours.

6. After 24 hours, check to ensure pear mixture remains submerged in brine, and skim white film from top of brine and around weights, if necessary. Taste kimchi, and if it has reached desired flavor, remove weights. Wipe jars and refrigerate. If kimchi has not reached desired flavor, return weights to jars to keep kimchi submerged. Cover and continue to let stand in a dark, cool (65°F/18°C to 75°F/24°C) place for another day, or up to 1 week, until desired flavor develops.

7. Once desired flavor is reached, remove weights; wipe jar rims, and cover jars with plastic lids. Store in refrigerator up to 1 month.

KIMCHI

MAKES ABOUT 2 (1-QT./1-L) JARS

- 2 tsp. (10 mL), plus ¼ cup (60 mL), Ball® Salt for Pickling & Preserving
- 2 cups (500 mL) water
- 2 medium napa cabbages (about 2 lb./1 kg each)
- 6 garlic cloves, peeled
- 1 cup (250 mL) dried Korean chili flakes
- ⅓ cup (75 mL) grated fresh ginger
- 2 Tbsp. (30 mL) fish sauce
- 2 Tbsp. (30 mL) lite soy sauce
- 2 bunches green onions, root removed, green and white parts thinly sliced
- 2 to 3 unpeeled carrots, well-scrubbed and grated
- 2 (1-qt./1-L) canning jars
- 2 (4-oz./125-mL) canning jars

--- ★ ---

Tricks of the Trade

Korean chili flakes can be found at Asian specialty food stores. Using the flakes instead of premade paste allows you to control the amount you want and to mix in your own flavors.

1. Combine 2 tsp. (10mL) salt and water in a 1-pt. (500-mL) jar, stirring until salt dissolves; set brine aside and reserve for later use. Wash cabbage under cold running water. Reserve 2 cabbage leaves that are in good condition; set aside. Cut remaining cabbage into quarters; core. Cut quarters into 2½-inch (6-cm)-wide ribbons. Place cabbage in large bowl and sprinkle with remaining ¼ cup (60 mL) salt, massaging and squeezing salt into cabbage until liquid is released. Cover bowl, and let stand 1 to 2 hours.

2. With processor running, process garlic until minced. Add chili flakes and next 3 ingredients. Process until a paste forms; add to cabbage mixture. Add green onions and grated carrot to cabbage mixture. Divide cabbage mixture evenly between 2 (1-qt./1-L) jars, pressing down firmly with a wooden spoon and pouring any remaining brine from bottom of bowl evenly over cabbage mixture in both jars. (Brine should cover cabbage mixture by ½-inch (1-cm.) If brine does not cover cabbage mixture adequately, cover jars, and let stand 4 hours. If liquid still does not cover cabbage mixture by ½ inch (1 cm), add reserved brine until cabbage is covered.

3. Place 1 reserved cabbage leaf on top of cabbage mixture in each jar, pushing down and tucking in leaf to cover mixture. Fill 2 clean 4-oz. (125-mL) Ball® jars with water, and set 1 jar on top of cabbage mixture inside each 1-qt. (1-L) jar to weigh down cabbage mixture. Place each jar on a plate in a dark, cool (65°F/18°C to 75°F/24°C) place. Cover jars with a clean dish towel, and let stand 24 hours.

4. Check jars daily to ensure cabbage mixture remains submerged in brine; skim white film that forms. Return weights to jars to keep kimchi submerged; cover and continue to let stand in a dark, cool (65°F/18°C to 75°F/24°C) place, checking daily.

5. After 4 days, check flavor. If kimchi has reached desired flavor, remove weights, wipe jar rims, and refrigerate. If kimchi has not reached desired flavor, return weights to jars to keep kimchi submerged. Cover and continue to let stand in a dark, cool (65°F/18°C to 75°F/24°C) place for another day, or up to 2 weeks. Once desired flavor is reached, remove weights; wipe jar rims, and cover jars with lids. Store in refrigerator up to 6 months.

GINGER BUG

MAKES ABOUT 1 (1-QT./1-L) JAR

A fizzy fermented beverage bursting with sweet ginger flavor, this recipe is easy to make and can be used on its own or mixed with mineral water for ginger soda, or try it with a splash of bourbon on ice for a gingery aperitif.

⅓ cup (75 mL) sugar, divided

⅓ cup (75 mL) grated unpeeled fresh organic ginger*, divided

1 (1-qt./1-L) canning jar

3½ cups (875 mL) non-chlorinated water or spring water**

1. Combine 2 Tbsp. (30 mL) each sugar and ginger in a 1-qt. (1-L) canning jar. Add nonchlorinated water, stirring to dissolve sugar. Cover jar with a clean cloth, and secure with a rubber band or kitchen string. Let stand at room temperature for 3 days, adding 1 tsp. (5 mL) each sugar and grated ginger each day, stirring to dissolve sugar and replacing cloth after each addition.

2. On the fourth day, remove cloth. Center lid on jar; apply band, and adjust loosely. Let stand 4 more days or until mixture is very bubbly, adding sugar and ginger daily as above. (The warmer the room temperature, the sooner bubbles will form.) Chill thoroughly. Store in refrigerator and use within 2 weeks. Strain before using.

*Use only organic ginger in this recipe. Non-organic ginger has been irradiated and does not carry the natural yeasts and bacteria essential for fermentation.

**Chlorine may be removed from tap water by allowing water to stand, uncovered, at room temperature overnight. If your tap water is chlorinated, you can fill your jar and let it rest, uncovered, overnight. Chlorine is a gas and will release from the water.

WORCESTERSHIRE SAUCE

MAKES ABOUT 3 (½-PT./250-ML) OR 6 (4-OZ./125-ML) JARS

Tangy, earthy, spicy, rich, and full of umami—what else could you want? Toss this kitchen staple with grilled shrimp bathed in melted butter, slather on steak or chicken, or douse on potato salad or egg salad. Make a double batch to share with family and friends. Don't let the long ingredient list deter you. This one is worth the effort.

¼ cup (60 mL) dark raisins

¼ cup (60 mL) boiling water

½ cup (125 mL) unsulphured molasses

¼ cup (60 mL) jarred tamarind paste

1 (10-oz./284-g) onion, quartered

1 (½-inch/1-cm) piece peeled fresh ginger, chopped

1 garlic clove, crushed

2 cups (500 mL) white vinegar (5% acidity), divided

2 cardamom pods

2 Tbsp. (30 mL) Ball® Salt for Pickling & Preserving

2 Tbsp. (30 mL) dark brown sugar

1 Tbsp. (15 mL) dried crushed red pepper

1 Tbsp. (15 mL) dry mustard

1 tsp. (5 mL) garlic powder

1 tsp. (5 mL) whole cloves

1 tsp. (5 mL) black peppercorns

1 tsp. (5 mL) anchovy paste

½ tsp. (2 mL) ground cinnamon

1 (1-qt./1-L) canning jar

1. Combine raisins and boiling water in a small bowl. Let stand 15 minutes or until raisins are softened. Drain.

2. Process raisins, molasses, next 4 ingredients, and 1 cup (250 mL) vinegar in a blender or food processor until smooth.

3. Remove seeds from cardamom pods; discard pods. Pour raisin mixture into a medium saucepan; add cardamom seeds, salt, next 8 ingredients, and remaining 1 cup (250 mL) vinegar. Bring to a boil, stirring constantly. Remove from heat; cool.

4. Pour mixture into a 1-qt. (1-L) canning jar. Cover with a plastic lid. Store in a dark, cool (65°F/18°C to 75°F/24°C) place for 2 to 4 weeks, depending upon desired strength, checking once a week.

5. Pour mixture through a fine wire-mesh sieve into a 1-qt. (1-L) glass measuring cup; discard solids. Pour into clean glass jars; cover with plastic lids. Store in refrigerator 1 year.

KOMBUCHA

MAKES ABOUT 2½ QT. (2½-L)

This lightly effervescent drink is made from fermenting tea with bacteria and SCOBY cultures.

SCOBY PREPARATION

- 4 cups (1 L) boiling water
- 4 regular-size black tea bags, paper tags removed
- 1 (½-gal./2-L) canning jar
- ½ cup (125 mL) sugar
- 2 cups (500 mL) cold water
- 1 cup (250 mL) commercial raw organic kombucha, containing some sediment, if possible*

BREWED KOMBUCHA TEA

- 4 cups (1 L) boiling water
- 6 to 8 regular-size black tea bags, paper tags removed
- 1 (½-gal./2-L) canning jar
- 1 cup sugar
- 6 cups (1.5 L) cold water
- 2 cups (500 mL) brewed kombucha (reserved from SCOBY preparation or a previous batch of tea)

GINGER-HONEY FLAVORING
(optional)

- 2 Tbsp. (30 mL) grated peeled fresh ginger
- 3 to 6 Tbsp. (45 to 90 mL) honey

TURMERIC-HONEY FLAVORING
(optional)

- 2 Tbsp. (30 mL) grated peeled fresh turmeric
- 3 to 6 Tbsp. (45 to 90 mL) honey

1. Prepare SCOBY: Pour boiling water over tea bags in a pre-warmed (or pre-heated) (½-gal./2-L) canning jar; cover and steep at least 30 minutes, but no longer than 1 hour. Remove tea bags. Add sugar, stirring until dissolved. Stir in 2 cups cold water to reduce temperature of tea. Let stand until a thermometer registers 75°F (24°C).

2. Stir in 1 cup (250 mL) commercial kombucha. Cover with a clean cotton cloth or coffee filter; secure with a rubber band. Place jar in a dark, cool (65°F/18°C to 75°F/24°C) place. Let stand, undisturbed, 3 to 5 weeks or until a creamy, tan pancake-shaped SCOBY forms.

3. Carefully remove SCOBY, and place it in a clean bowl. Remove 2 cups (500 mL) kombucha tea; pour over SCOBY. (Discard remaining kombucha tea used for growing the SCOBY.) Use reserved SCOBY and the 2 cups kombucha tea to immediately brew a new batch of kombucha tea (see Note).

4. Prepare Brewed Kombucha Tea (First Ferment): Pour boiling water over tea bags in a pre-warmed (or pre-heated) (½-gal./2-L) canning jar; cover and steep at least 30 minutes, but no longer than 1 hour. Remove tea bags. Add sugar, stirring until dissolved. Stir in 6 cups cold water to reduce temperature of tea. Let stand until a thermometer registers 75°F (24°C). Stir in 2 cups (500 mL) brewed kombucha (reserved from SCOBY preparation or a previous batch of kombucha tea). Carefully add SCOBY.

5. Cover with a clean cotton cloth or coffee filter; secure with a rubber band. Place jar in a dark, cool (65°F/18°C to 75°F/24°C) place. Let stand, undisturbed, 7 to 10 days (First Ferment) or until desired flavor develops. Flavor depends on personal preference and strength of the SCOBY (see Note).

6. Decant and flavor the tea (Second Ferment): Remove and store SCOBY as described above. Pour remaining kombucha tea into bottles or jars (see tip at right) large enough to accommodate 1 qt. (1 L) kombucha, plus room for the addition of a flavoring, if using. If desired, flavor each 1 qt. (1-L) of kombucha tea with your choice of flavoring ingredients.

BERRY FLAVORING (optional)

- ½ cup fresh or frozen berries
- 3 to 6 Tbsp. (45 to 90 mL) honey or sugar

CINNAMON-SPICE FLAVORING (optional)

- ½ (3-inch/7.5-cm) cinnamon stick
- ½ tsp. whole allspice
- 1 whole clove
- 3 to 6 Tbsp. (45 to 90 mL) maple syrup

7. Cover jar with a plastic lid. Let stand, undisturbed, in a dark, cool (65°F/18°C to 75°F/24°C) place 1 to 2 more days, or until bubbly (the Second Ferment). Store in refrigerator up to 1 month.

8. To serve: Carefully remove lid, slowly releasing gas. Pour unflavored kombucha tea into glasses. Pour flavored kombucha tea through a wire-mesh strainer into glasses, discarding solids.

*We tested with GT's Enlightened™ Original Organic Raw Kombucha to prepare the SCOBY.

NOTE: The first "mother" SCOBY will become stronger and more active each time it is used to prepare a new batch of kombucha tea, in which a new "baby" SCOBY will also grow. (Baby SCOBYs may be discarded or given to friends.) When the "mother" SCOBY matures and is sufficiently strong, it will be thicker and able to complete the First Ferment much quicker than in previous batches.

STORAGE: You will need to brew several batches of kombucha tea to strengthen the "mother" SCOBY before attempting long-term storage. To store a strong, mature SCOBY, place it, covered with freshly brewed sweetened tea, in a clean 1-qt. (1-L) jar in a dark refrigerator. Cover jar with a tight-fitting plastic lid. (Do not use a metal lid.) As long as a SCOBY has a sugar source from fresh sweet tea, it may be stored indefinitely in refrigerator. Loosen lid from time-to-time to release any built up fermentation pressure.

HARISSA

MAKES ABOUT 1 (1-PT./500 ML) JAR

Harissa is a bracing blend of hot chiles, garlic, cumin, coriander, and olive oil. Fiery-hot and intense, it traces its roots to Tunisia in North Africa where it's the traditional accompaniment with couscous but also finds its way into soups and stews.

2	tsp. (10 mL) cumin seeds
2	tsp. (10 mL) coriander seeds
1	tsp. (5 mL) caraway seeds
½	lb. (250 g) fresh hot red chile peppers (such as New Mexican, cayenne, or a combination), seeded and coarsely chopped
2	Tbsp. (30 mL) sugar
1	tsp. (5 mL) dried mint
5	large garlic cloves, crushed
2½	tsp. (12 mL) Ball® Salt for Pickling & Preserving, divided
	Olive oil
3	Tbsp. (45 mL) water

1. Heat first 3 ingredients in a small nonstick skillet over medium-low heat, stirring often, until toasted and fragrant. Remove skillet from heat; cool seeds slightly. Process seeds in a spice grinder, blender, or with a mortar and pestle until finely ground.

2. Process ground seeds, chiles, next 3 ingredients, and 2 tsp. (10 mL) salt until smooth. Spoon harissa into a clean 1-pt. (500-mL) jar, pressing with a spoon to remove air bubbles. Cover harissa with a ½-inch (1-cm) layer of olive oil; cover with lid and store in refrigerator.

3. For deeper flavor, stir together water and remaining ½ tsp. (2 mL) salt; pour salt mixture over harissa in jar. Do not stir. Cover jar loosely with a plastic lid. Let stand, at room temperature, 2 days. Adjust lid to fingertip-tight. Chill. Store in refrigerator up to 6 months.

4. Cover harissa completely with a thin layer of olive oil after each use.

★

Tricks of the Trade

One pound dried chile peppers may be substituted for the fresh chiles. Soak dried chiles in a bowl in boiling water to cover 20 minutes; drain, discarding soaking liquid. Seed chiles and tear into large pieces. Process in blender with seed mixture as directed, and proceed with recipe.

TEPACHE (FERMENTED PINEAPPLE DRINK)

MAKES ABOUT 2 (1-QT./1-L) OR 1 (½-GAL./2-L) JAR

Visit Mexico in this drink! Tepache is traditionally made with the rind and core of pineapple along with piloncillo and spices. Enjoy tepache straight up or poured over ice, but it shines brightest as a cocktail mixer.

1 cup (250 mL) sugar

1 (½-gal./2-L) canning jar

6 cups (1.5 L) non-chlorinated water or spring water, divided

1 (3-inch/7.5-cm) cinnamon stick (optional)

2 whole cloves (optional)

1 very ripe pineapple

Cheesecloth

1. Place sugar in a ½-gal. (2-L) jar. Add 1 qt. (1-L) non-chlorinated water, stirring until sugar dissolves. Add cinnamon and cloves, if desired.

2. Scrub pineapple; rinse with cold water. Using a sharp nonserrated knife, cut off a thin slice from top and bottom of pineapple, removing leaves and creating a flat surface on each end.

3. Position pineapple upright on cutting board. Thinly slice downward around pineapple to remove rough skin, being careful not to waste fruit. Add skin to sugar mixture in jar.

4. Cut pineapple lengthwise into quarters. Cut core away from each quarter; add pieces of core to jar, reserving fruit for another use. Add remaining 2 cups (500 mL) water or until jar is filled to within 1 inch (2.5 cm) of the top.

5. Cover jar with a clean cloth, and secure with a rubber band or kitchen string. Let stand at room temperature 12 to 24 hours or until mixture is bubbly, scraping off any white foam that develops. If no bubbling at top of mixture occurs after 24 hours, center lid on jars. Apply bands, and adjust loosely. Let stand 12 more hours.

6. Pour mixture through a fine wire-mesh strainer lined with 3 layers of moist cheesecloth into a clean ½-gal. (2-L) jar or 2 (2-qt./2-L) jars. Center lids on jars. Apply bands, and adjust loosely. Chill thoroughly and store in refrigerator up to 2 weeks. Keep covered tightly to keep bubbly.

7. To serve, pour over ice in tall glasses and dilute with desired amount of water or mineral water.

STUFFED CABBAGE ROLLS

MAKES 6 TO 8 SERVINGS

Humble cabbage's versatility and sweetness shines when stuffed with a savory meat filling and nestled in a rich tomato-and-sauerkraut broth.

---

2   large heads cabbage

1   lb. (450 g) lean ground beef

1   lb. (450 g) ground pork

½   cup (125 mL) uncooked long-grain rice

2   tsp. (10 mL) salt

1   tsp. (5 mL) ground black pepper

2   garlic cloves, minced

¼   lb. (125 g) bacon, chopped

1   small onion, finely chopped

3   Tbsp. (45 mL) all-purpose flour

6   to 8 cups (1.5 to 2 L) tomato juice

2   cups (500 mL) water

1   qt. (1 L) Sauerkraut (page 252)

1. Remove and discard the 2 outermost leaves of each cabbage. Using a paring knife, cut through stems of outside leaves to, but not through, the core. Place cabbages in a steaming basket, and steam over simmering water for 2 to 3 minutes or until next set of outer leaves are softened enough to be removed easily.

2. Pierce the core of a cabbage with a carving fork. Using the fork to hold cabbage, remove as many intact leaves as possible; reserve leaves. Cut through stems of remaining leaves as before. Return cabbage to steamer basket. Repeat procedure with each cabbage as many times as necessary until you have removed 12 intact leaves from each. Remove cabbage heads from steamer; cool completely, and shred. Set shredded cabbage aside.

3. Combine beef and next 5 ingredients in a medium bowl.

4. Trim thick stems of the 24 cabbage leaves to a thickness even with the rest of each leaf. Place a cabbage leaf, inner side up, on a work surface. With stem end toward you, spoon 2 Tbsp. (30 mL) meat mixture in center of leaf close to the near edge. Fold in sides over filling, and roll up burrito-style; secure with a wooden pick. Place roll, seam side down, on a rimmed baking sheet. Repeat procedure until all 24 leaves are filled. Chill rolls until ready to cook.

5. Cook bacon and onion in a large Dutch oven over medium heat until golden brown. Stir in flour; cook, stirring constantly, until flour begins to brown slightly. Gradually stir in tomato juice; cook over medium heat, stirring constantly, until mixture is thickened and bubbly. Stir in water, Sauerkraut, and reserved shredded cabbage.

6. Nestle cabbage rolls into sauerkraut mixture until almost covered. Cover and bring to a boil; reduce heat, and simmer 1 hour or until cabbage is tender and filling is done.

FIERY FERMENTED HOT SAUCE

MAKES ABOUT 1 (1-QT./1-L) JAR

This sauce serves as a starter base for three classic hot sauce variations.

- ³/₄ lb. (350 g) habanero peppers
- 1 lb. (450 g) red bell peppers
- ¹/₄ cup (60 mL) water
- 2 tsp. (10 mL) sea salt or kosher salt
- 1 (1-qt./1-L) canning jar
- 1 (4-oz./125 mL) canning jar
- Cheesecloth
- 1 cup (250 mL) white vinegar (5% acidity)

★

Peak of Freshness
Harvest hot peppers once they've reached their peak color, or choose peppers from the market that are firm and one solid color.

---

1. Cut habanero peppers and bell peppers in half; remove stems and seeds. Cut peppers into uniform pieces. Process peppers, water, and salt in a food processor until peppers are finely minced. Transfer to a 1-qt. (1-L) canning jar. (Pepper mixture should come up to the shoulder of the jar.)

2. Set a 4-oz. (125-mL) jar on top of pepper mixture inside jar to weight down pepper mixture. (The small jar will keep the peppers submerged in the liquid that will form in the pepper mixture within 1 to 2 days.) Cover jar with cheesecloth, and secure with a rubber band. Place jar on a plate in a dark, cool (65°F/18°C to 75°F/24°C) place. Check jar periodically; skim and discard any white foam (harmless Kahm yeast) from top of mixture, and clean any overflow from jars and plate. Ensure that pepper pieces are submerged, and re-cover with clean cheesecloth.

3. Let pepper mixture stand for 3 weeks or until all active bubbling stops. Check mixture daily; skim foam, clean jars, and replace cheesecloth as necessary.

4. Once fermentation is complete (bubbling stops), remove small jar; skim off any remaining yeast, and stir in vinegar.

5. Store in refrigerator up to 1 year.

SRIRACHA-STYLE HOT SAUCE: Add 6 peeled garlic cloves and 3 Tbsp. (45 mL) sugar while processing peppers.

YUCATAN HOT SAUCE: Omit vinegar, and stir in 1 cup (250 mL) fresh lime juice, ¹/₂ cup (125 mL) chopped fresh cilantro, and 2 garlic cloves, minced, after fermentation stops.

ASIAN HOT SAUCE: Omit white vinegar. Stir in 1 cup (250 mL) rice wine vinegar, 1 Tbsp. (15 mL) grated fresh ginger, and 2 garlic cloves, minced, after fermentation stops.

YOGURT

MAKES ABOUT 2 QT. (2 L)

Homemade yogurt is simply the best! An easy and delicious cultured food that can be prepped before bed and eaten, still warm, with berries and granola in the morning.

2   qt. (2 L) whole milk

6   Tbsp. (90 mL) plain yogurt with active live cultures

2   (1-qt./1-L) canning jars

1. Rinse a 4-qt. (4-L) saucepan with water. Pour in milk; bring to 180°F (90°C), stirring constantly to prevent scorching. Remove from heat and cool to 110°F (43°C).

2. Place 3 Tbsp. (45 mL) yogurt in each canning jar. Remove protein film from top of milk. Gradually pour 110°F (43°C) milk evenly into jars, stirring to blend yogurt into milk. Wipe jar rim. Center lid on jar. Apply band, and adjust loosely.

3. Incubate 6 to 8 hours at a constant temperature of about 110°F (43°C). Do not disturb during incubation.

4. After 6 hours, tighten lids and tip jars slightly to see if yogurt is firm. If not, incubate 1 more hour and check again. As soon as yogurt begins to set, chill at least 6 hours before serving. Store in refrigerator up to 3 weeks.

NOTE: Yogurt needs a warm place (100° to 110°F/38° to 43°C) to culture in for 6 to 8 hours; the cooler the temperature the longer the culture will take, up to 12 hours. Using a cooler with a heating pad fitted into it and set on warm is an ideal way to maintain the proper environment. Alternately, placing the jars in an oven that has an inside light turned on is a sufficient alternative; the light can heat the oven between (90° to 100°F/32° to 38°C).

WHOLE GRAIN THYME MUSTARD

MAKES ABOUT 3 (1/2-PT./250-ML) JARS

A simple recipe for a grainy, thyme-infused mustard makes a perfect complement for good roasts and grilled steaks. Or puree a spoonful into a vinaigrette.

- 2 cups (500 mL) water
- 1 cup (250 mL) mustard seeds (a combination of brown and yellow seeds)
- 1½ Tbsp. (22 mL) salt
- ¼ cup (60 mL) dry mustard
- 2 tsp. (10 mL) honey or sugar
- 1½ tsp. (7.5 mL) sea salt
- ½ tsp. (2 mL) garlic powder
- ¼ cup (60 mL) unfiltered apple cider vinegar (5% acidity)
- 1 Tbsp. (15 mL) fresh thyme leaves

★

Tricks of the Trade

Though this mustard is ready to use in less than a week, the sharp tang of mustard seed mellows to a lovely subtle creamy taste over the course of a couple of months.

1. Combine first 3 ingredients in a bowl. Cover and let stand 2 to 4 hours.

2. Drain mustard seeds in a wire-mesh strainer, lined with a coffee filter or cheesecloth, discarding liquid.

3. Pulse seeds in a food processor until crushed. Add dry mustard and next 3 ingredients. Pulse until blended. Add vinegar; pulse just until blended.

4. Transfer mustard mixture to a medium glass or nonmetallic bowl; stir in thyme. Cover with plastic wrap and let stand at room temperature up to 3 days or until slightly bubbly, stirring daily.

5. Spoon mustard into clean ½-pt. (250-mL) jars. Remove air bubbles. Wipe jar rim. Center lid on jar. Apply band, and adjust to fingertip-tight. Chill for 4 weeks before serving. Store in refrigerator up to 1 year.

PRESERVED LEMONS

MAKES ABOUT 1 (1-QT./1-L) JAR

Popular in Middle Eastern cuisines, preserved lemons are brined or pickled in a mixture of salt and their own juices. Once preserved, the slivered rind will add huge flavor to your recipes.

8 to 10 small unblemished organic lemons, scrubbed under hot water and divided

5 tsp. (25 mL) Ball® Salt for Pickling & Preserving

1 (1-qt./1-L) canning jar

Flavoring herbs: 1 bay leaf, fresh thyme sprig, 1 tsp. (5 mL) black peppercorns, 1 tsp. (5 mL) dried crushed Aleppo pepper

1. Remove stems from lemons. Place 1 lemon, stem end down, on a cutting board; cut from top to bottom to, but not through, stem end, quartering lemon, but leaving bottom intact. Spread lemon quarters apart, and rub flesh with 1 tsp. (5 mL) salt. Close lemon, and place in jar, pressing with a wooden spoon to release juice. If desired, add 1, or more, flavoring herbs.

2. Repeat procedure with as many of remaining lemons as can be tightly packed into jar, leaving 1-inch (2.5-cm) headspace. Squeeze juice from remaining lemons, discarding seeds; add juice to jar, pressing lemons down until completely submerged. Cover top of jar with plastic wrap. Center lid on jars. Apply bands, and adjust loosely. Let stand, at room temperature, for 3 days, adding additional lemon juice as necessary to keep lemons submerged.

3. After 3 days, place in refrigerator and let ferment for 1 month before using. Store lemons in refrigerator up to 1 year.

Chapter 3

PRESSURE CANNING

Imagine your pantry shelves stocked with hearty soups, chili, bone broths, even BBQ pulled pork all made with fresh ingredients and ready to use for dinner with friends or a quick weeknight meal. Pressure canning has been the favored process for safely preserving low-acid vegetables and meats since the early 20th century. We've come a long way since then and now have the technology to test and develop even more varieties of safe, creative, and delicious recipes that have perfect texture and mouthwatering seasoning. With the recipes in this chapter, you'll see for yourself that pressure canning has moved into the 21st century.

STEP-BY-STEP FRESH PRESERVING OF LOW-ACID FOODS THROUGH PRESSURE CANNING

Getting started: Visually examine jars for defects. Fill a large saucepan or stockpot halfway with water. Place jars in water to warm. (Filling jars with water from the saucepan will prevent flotation.) Bring almost to a simmer over medium heat. Keeping jars hot until ready for use is important as it will prevent jar breakage due to an abrupt change in temperature (also known as thermal shock). You may also use a dishwasher to wash and heat jars.

YOU WILL NEED:

- Tested preserving recipe

- Fresh vegetables, meat, poultry, or seafood, and other quality ingredients

- Pressure canner (at least 16-qt. capacity)

- Glass preserving jars with lids and bands (always start with new lids)

- Common kitchen utensils, such as a wooden spoon, ladle, timer, kitchen towel, and rubber spatula.

- Jar Funnel

- Jar Lifter

- Bubble Remover & Headspace Measuring Tool

STEP 1: Prepare pressure canner. Fill canner with 2 to 3 inches of water. Place over medium-high heat. Bring to a simmer. Keep water at a simmer until jars are filled and placed in canner. Follow manufacturer's instructions for usage.

STEP 2: Fill hot jars one at a time with fresh vegetables, meat, poultry, or seafood, and other quality ingredients. Cover with simmering water or broth.

STEP 3: Measure headspace of jar with designated tool, leaving 1-inch (2.5-cm) headspace for low-acid food.

STEP 4: Remove air bubbles by sliding a bubble remover or rubber spatula between the jar and food to release trapped air and ensure proper headspace during processing. Repeat around jar 2 or 3 times.

STEP 5: Clean rim and threads of jar using a clean, damp cloth to remove any food residue. Adjust hot lid on jar allowing sealing compound to come in contact with the jar rim. Apply band and adjust until fit is fingertip-tight.

STEP 6: Place filled jar in canner. Repeat until recipe is used or canner is full. Check that water level is about 2 to 3 inches high or height recommended in manufacturer's manual.

STEP 7: Lock canner lid in place. Adjust heat to medium-high. Once there is a steady stream of steam through vent pipe for 10 minutes, place counter weight or weighted gauge on vent; bring to pressure indicated in recipe and then set timer and process for time indicated in recipe. Monitor to ensure pressure does not fluctuate.

STEP 8: Turn off heat after processing period is completed. Let the canner cool naturally. Do not remove the gauge. Let canner stand undisturbed until pressure returns to zero naturally. Wait 5 minutes. Remove gauge and unlock lid, tilting away from yourself. Wait 10 more minutes to allow jars to begin to cool.

STEP 9: Remove jars from canner and set upright on a towel to prevent jar breakage that can occur from temperature differences. Leave jars undisturbed for 12 to 24 hours. Bands should not be retightened as this may interfere with the sealing process.

STEP 10: Check lids for seals. Lids should not flex up and down when center is pressed. Remove bands. Gently, try to lift lids off with your fingertips. If the lid is concave and cannot be removed with your fingertips, the jar is vacuum sealed. Clean jars and lids. Label and store in a cool, dry, dark place up to 1 year.

Simple One-Jar Meals

Divide ingredient amounts between 2 (1-qt./1-L) or 4 (1-pt./500-mL) jars.

These easy raw pack recipes are an innovative way to create delicious ready-to-eat meals for your pantry all year long. Raw ingredients and seasonings are combined, packed in the jar, and covered with hot broth; all of the cooking takes place right in the jar! **NOTE: To ensure proper pressure and temperature is achieved for safe processing, you must process at least 2 quart or 4 pint jars in the pressure canner at one time.**

STEP 1: Prepare pressure canner and jars. Keep jars warm until ready to fill.

STEP 2: Combine prepared ingredients and dry seasonings in a large bowl. **Amounts listed are for 2 (1-qt./1-L) or 4 (1-pt./500-mL) jars.**

STEP 3: Filling one jar at a time, pack ingredients and remaining liquid seasonings tightly in hot jar, leaving 1-inch (2.5-cm) headspace. Ladle hot broth over ingredients, leaving 1-inch (2.5-cm) headspace (you may have room for only a few tablespoons of broth). Remove air bubbles and apply band to fingertip-tight. Place jar in pressure canner containing 2 inches of simmering water; repeat until all jars are filled.

STEP 4: Place lid on canner and turn to locked position. Adjust heat to medium-high. Vent steam for 10 minutes. Place the counter weight or weighted gauge on vent; bring pressure to 10 pounds (psi) for a weighted-gauge canner or 11 pounds (psi) for a dial-gauge canner. Process for time indicated in chart below. Turn off heat; cool canner to zero pressure. After 5 minutes, remove lid. Let jars cool 10 minutes. Remove from canner.

SERVING SUGGESTION	INGREDIENTS PER 2 (1-QT.) OR 4 (1-PT.) JARS	SEASONINGS PER 2 (1-QT.) OR 4 (1-PT.) JARS	HOT BROTH	PROCESSING TIME
Chicken Chili Verde **To Serve:** Transfer contents of jar to saucepan and simmer over medium heat for 10 minutes, stirring frequently. Serve over hot cooked rice.	2 lb. (1 kg) boneless chicken, cut into 2-inch (5-cm) chunks 1 cup (250 mL) canned white beans, drained and rinsed 1 cup (250 mL) sliced green onions 1 cup (250 mL) Roasted Salsa Verde (page 167)	2 tsp. (10 mL) salt 2 garlic cloves, sliced 4 Tbsp. (60 mL) sliced pickled jalapeños 4 Tbsp. (60 mL) chopped fresh cilantro	Chicken Broth	Quart: (1 liter) 1 hour, 30 minutes Pint: (500 mL) 1 hour, 15 minutes
Chicken Curry **To Serve:** Transfer contents of jar to saucepan and simmer over medium heat for 10 minutes, stirring frequently. Serve over hot cooked rice.	2 lb. (1 kg) boneless chicken, cut into 2-inch (5-cm) chunks 1 cup (250 mL) finely chopped onion 1 cup (250 mL) finely chopped tomatoes 1 cup (250 mL) peeled and diced potatoes ½ cup (125 mL) raisins	2 tsp. (10 mL) salt 4 Tbsp. (60 mL) chopped fresh cilantro 4 Tbsp. (60 mL) tomato paste 1 tsp. (5 mL) curry powder 1 tsp. (5 mL) garam masala	Chicken Broth	Quart: (1 liter) 1 hour, 30 minutes Pint: (500 mL) 1 hour, 15 minutes

SERVING SUGGESTION	INGREDIENTS *PER 2 (1-QT.) OR 4 (1-PT.) JARS*	SEASONINGS *PER 2 (1-QT.) OR 4 (1-PT.) JARS*	HOT BROTH	PROCESSING TIME
Chicken & Gravy Dinner in a Jar **To Serve:** Transfer contents of quart (liter) jar to saucepan and whisk in 2 Tbsp. (30 mL) flour until well combined; 1 Tbsp. (15 mL) for pint jar/500-mL jar. Simmer over medium heat for 10 minutes, stirring often.	2 lb. (1 kg) boneless chicken, cut into 2-inch (5-cm) chunks 1 cup (250 mL) finely chopped celery 1 cup (250 mL) finely chopped onions 1 cup (250 mL) peeled and diced potatoes	2 tsp. (10 mL) salt 1 tsp. (5 mL) ground black pepper 2 tsp. (10 mL) poultry seasoning 4 Tbsp. (60 mL) dry white wine	Chicken Broth	Quart: (1 liter) 1 hour, 30 minutes Pint: (500 mL) 1 hour, 15 minutes
Pot Roast in a Jar **To Serve:** Transfer contents of quart (liter) jar to saucepan and whisk in 2 Tbsp. (30 mL) flour until well combined; 1 Tbsp. (15 mL) for pint jar/500-mL jar. Simmer over medium heat for 10 minutes, stirring often.	2 lb. (1 kg) boneless beef chuck, trimmed and cut into 2-inch (5-cm) chunks 1 cup (250 mL) peeled and diced potatoes 1 cup (250 mL) diced onions ½ cup (125 mL) diced celery 1 cup (250 mL) sliced carrots	2 tsp. (10 mL) salt 1 tsp. (5 mL) ground black pepper 2 bay leaves 2 garlic cloves, sliced 2 tsp. (10 mL) dried thyme 1 cup (250 mL) dry red wine	Beef Broth	Quart: (1 liter) 1 hour, 30 minutes Pint: (500 mL) 1 hour, 15 minutes
Beef Stroganoff **To Serve:** Transfer contents of quart (liter) jar to saucepan and whisk in 2 Tbsp. (30 mL) flour until well combined; 1 Tbsp. (15 mL) for pint jar/500-mL jar. Simmer over medium heat for 10 minutes, stirring often. Remove from heat, and stir in a large spoonful of sour cream.	2 lb. (1 kg) boneless beef chuck, trimmed and cut into 2-inch (5-cm) chunks 1 cup (250 mL) sliced mushrooms 1 cup (250 mL) chopped onion 4 Tbsp. (60 mL) tomato paste	2 tsp. (10 mL) salt 1 tsp. (5 mL) ground black pepper 4 Tbsp. (60 mL) Worcestershire sauce 2 tsp. (10 mL) dried thyme 2 tsp. (10 mL) dried parsley 2 garlic cloves, sliced	Beef Broth	Quart: (1 liter) 1 hour, 30 minutes Pint: (500 mL) 1 hour, 15 minutes
Shredded Chipotle Beef for Tacos **To Serve:** Drain contents of jar and shred meat (reserve broth). Sauté a sliced onion in oil until soft; add beef and ½ cup (125 mL) broth; simmer 10 minutes. Serve in warmed tortillas with taco toppings.	2 lb. (1 kg) beef brisket, trimmed and cut into 2-inch (5-cm) chunks 2 cups (500 mL) sliced onions	2 tsp. (10 mL) salt 2 tsp. (10 mL) dried oregano 8 garlic cloves, sliced ½ cup (125 mL) chopped fresh cilantro 2 chipotle chili peppers in adobo, finely chopped	Beef Broth	Quart: (1 liter) 1 hour, 30 minutes Pint: (500 mL) 1 hour, 15 minutes

Simple One-Jar Vegetables

Divide ingredient amounts between 2 (1-qt./1-L) or 4 (1-pt./500-mL) jars.

These simple raw pack recipes are an innovative way to create delicious ready-to-eat vegetables for your pantry all year long. Raw ingredients and seasonings are combined, packed in the jar, and covered with hot broth; all of the cooking takes place right in the jar! **NOTE: To ensure proper pressure and temperature is achieved for safe processing, you must process at least 2 quart or 4 pint jars in the pressure canner at one time.**

STEP 1: Prepare pressure canner and jars. Keep jars warm until ready to fill.

STEP 2: Combine prepared ingredients and dry seasonings in a large bowl. **Amounts listed are for 2 (1-qt./1-L) or 4 (1-pt./500-mL) jars.**

STEP 3: Filling one jar at a time, pack ingredients and remaining liquid seasonings tightly in layers in hot jar, leaving 1-inch (2.5-cm) headspace. Ladle hot broth over ingredients, leaving 1-inch (2.5-cm) headspace (you may only have room for a few tablespoons of broth). Remove air bubbles and

apply band to fingertip-tight. Place jar in pressure canner and repeat until all jars are filled.

STEP 4: Place lid on canner and turn to locked position. Adjust heat to medium-high. Vent steam for 10 minutes. Place the counter weight or weighted gauge on vent; bring pressure to 10 pounds (psi) for a weighted-gauge canner or 11 pounds (psi) for a dial-gauge canner. Process for time indicated in chart below. Turn off heat; cool canner to zero pressure. After 5 minutes, remove lid. Let jars cool 10 minutes. Remove from canner.

SERVING SUGGESTION	INGREDIENTS PER 2 (1-QT.) OR 4 (1-PT.) JARS	SEASONINGS PER 2 (1-QT.) OR 4 (1-PT.) JARS	HOT BROTH	PROCESSING TIME
Curried Carrots **To Serve:** Transfer contents of jar to saucepan and simmer over medium heat for 10 minutes; drain. Garnish with a dollop of Greek yogurt. To make *Curried Carrot Soup,* puree contents of jar and simmer over medium heat for 10 minutes.	2¼ lb. (1.25 kg) carrots: Wash and peel; cut into slices, or leave whole.	2 tsp. (10 mL) salt 4 Tbsp. (60 mL) chopped fresh cilantro ½ tsp. (2 mL) curry powder	Chicken or Vegetable Broth	Quart: (1 liter) 30 minutes Pint: (500 mL) 25 minutes
Herbed Carrots **To Serve:** Transfer contents of jar to saucepan and simmer over medium heat for 10 minutes; drain.	2¼ lb. (1.25 kg) carrots: Wash and peel; cut into slices, or leave whole.	2 tsp. (10 mL) salt 1 tsp. (5 mL) dried rosemary 1 tsp. (5 mL) dried thyme 1 tsp. (5 mL) lemon zest (optional)	Chicken or Vegetable Broth	Quart: (1 liter) 30 minutes Pint: (500 mL) 25 minutes

SERVING SUGGESTION	INGREDIENTS PER 2 (1-QT.) OR 4 (1-PT.) JARS	SEASONINGS PER 2 (1-QT.) OR 4 (1-PT.) JARS	HOT BROTH	PROCESSING TIME
Honey-Ginger Carrots **To Serve:** Transfer contents of jar to saucepan and simmer over medium heat for 10 minutes; drain and serve.	2¼ lb. (1.25 kg) carrots: Wash and peel; cut into slices, dice, or leave whole.	2 tsp. (10 mL) salt 1 tsp. (5 mL) ground ginger ½ cup (120 mL) orange juice 4 Tbsp. (60 mL) soy sauce 4 Tbsp. (60 mL) honey	Chicken or Vegetable Broth	Quart: (1 liter) 30 minutes Pint: (500 mL) 25 minutes
Mexican Corn **To Serve:** Transfer contents of jar to saucepan and simmer over medium heat for 10 minutes; drain and serve. Also makes a great base for quick weeknight chili. Brown 1 lb. (450 g) ground beef or turkey, stir in 1 pt. (500 mL) Mexican Corn (drained) and 1 can black beans.	3 cups (750 mL) corn kernels 1 cup (250 mL) finely chopped onions 1 cup (125 mL) finely chopped bell pepper	2 tsp. (10 mL) salt 2 tsp. (10 mL) dried oregano 2 tsp. (10 mL) cumin or ground chipotle chile powder	Chicken or Vegetable Broth	Quart: (1 liter) 1 hour, 25 minutes Pint: (500 mL) 55 minutes
Succotash **To Serve:** Transfer contents of jar to saucepan and simmer over medium heat for 10 minutes; drain. Garnish with crumbled crisp-cooked bacon.	4 cups (1 L) corn kernels 2 cups (500 mL) baby lima beans 1 cup (250 mL) diced red bell pepper 1 cup (250 mL) diced onions	2 tsp. (10 mL) salt 1 tsp. (5 mL) ground black pepper	Chicken or Vegetable Broth	Quart: (1 liter) 1 hour, 25 minutes Pint: (500 mL) 55 minutes
Lemon-Garlic Green Beans **To Serve:** Transfer contents of jar to saucepan and simmer over medium heat for 10 minutes; drain.	2 lb. (1 kg) green, snap, or wax beans: Wash, trim, and remove strings; cut into 2-inch (5-cm) pieces.	2 tsp. (10 mL) salt 1 tsp. (5 mL) ground black pepper 4 garlic cloves, crushed 1 tsp. (5 mL) lemon zest 4 Tbsp. (60 mL) lemon juice	Chicken or Vegetable Broth	Quart: (1 liter) 25 minutes Pint: (500 mL) 20 minutes

SERVING SUGGESTION	INGREDIENTS PER 2 (1-QT.) OR 4 (1-PT.) JARS	SEASONINGS PER 2 (1-QT.) OR 4 (1-PT.) JARS	HOT BROTH	PROCESSING TIME
Balsamic Beans **To Serve:** Transfer contents of jar to saucepan and simmer over medium heat for 10 minutes; drain.	2 lb. (1 kg) green, snap, or wax beans: Wash, trim, and remove strings; cut into 2-inch (5-cm) pieces. 1 cup (250 mL) thinly sliced red onion	2 tsp. (10 mL) salt 1 tsp. (5 mL) ground black pepper 4 Tbsp. (60 mL) balsamic syrup	Chicken or Vegetable Broth	Quart: (1 liter) 30 minutes Pint: (500 mL) 25 minutes
Green Beans and Mushrooms **To Serve:** Transfer contents of jar to saucepan and simmer over medium heat for 10 minutes; drain.	1½ lb. (750 g) green, snap, or wax beans: Wash, trim, and remove strings; cut into 2-inch (5-cm) pieces. 1 cup (250 mL) fresh mushrooms, sliced	2 tsp. (10 mL) salt 1 tsp. (5 mL) ground black pepper 1 tsp. (5 mL) dried thyme	Chicken or Vegetable or Beef Broth	Quart: (1 liter) 30 minutes Pint: (500 mL) 25 minutes
Herbed Potatoes **To Serve:** Transfer contents of jar to saucepan and simmer over medium heat for 10 minutes; drain. Stir in some melted butter and milk, and mash for super quick smashed potatoes.	2½ lb. (1.25 kg) white potatoes: Peel; rinse. Halve or quarter. If desired, leave potatoes less than 2 inches (5 cm) in diameter whole.	2 tsp. (10 mL) salt 1 tsp. (5 mL) ground black pepper 1 tsp. (5 mL) dried rosemary 1 tsp. (5 mL) dried thyme	Chicken or Vegetable Broth	Quart: (1 liter) 40 minutes Pint: (500 mL) 35 minutes
Chipotle Potatoes **To Serve:** Transfer contents of jar to saucepan and simmer over medium heat for 10 minutes; drain.	2½ lb. (1.25 kg) white potatoes: Peel; rinse. Halve or quarter. If desired, leave potatoes less than 2 inches (5 cm) in diameter whole.	2 tsp. (10 mL) salt 2 tsp. (10 mL) ground chipotle chile powder ½ cup (125 mL) chopped fresh cilantro 4 tsp. (20 mL) minced garlic	Chicken or Vegetable or Beef Broth	Quart: (1 liter) 40 minutes Pint: (500 mL) 35 minutes
Mediterranean Potatoes **To Serve:** Transfer contents of jar to saucepan and simmer over medium heat for 10 minutes; drain. To make Home Fries, drain potatoes; heat oil in a skillet and saute until potatoes are brown and crispy.	2½ lb. (1.25 kg) white potatoes: Peel; rinse. Halve or quarter. If desired, leave potatoes less than 2 inches (5 cm) in diameter whole. 1 cup (250 mL) diced onion 1 cup (250 mL) diced bell pepper	2 tsp. (10 mL) salt 1 tsp. (10 mL) ground black pepper 2 tsp. (5 mL) dried oregano or dried rosemary 2 tsp. (10 mL) lemon zest	Chicken or Vegetable or Beef Broth	Quart: (1 liter) 40 minutes Pint: (500 mL) 35 minutes

AZTEC CHICKEN SOUP

MAKES ABOUT 6 (1-PT./500-ML) OR 3 (1-QT./1-L) JARS

Rev up this broth-based soup with a hit of Fiery Fermented Hot Sauce (page 264) to taste. Ladle the hot soup into large shallow bowls over a bed of crushed tortilla chips. Top with shredded cheese and chopped fresh cilantro. Serve with a squeeze of lime for added zing.

1 large poblano pepper

1 to 2 jalapeño peppers

6 fresh tomatillos, husks removed

1½ cups (375 mL) chopped white onion (1 large onion)

1 tsp. (5 mL) ground cumin

2 Tbsp. (30 mL) olive oil

4 ears fresh corn

3 garlic cloves, minced

4 cups (1 L) chicken stock or Chicken Bone Broth (page 288)

⅔ cup (150 mL) fresh lime juice (about 7 limes)

1½ tsp. (7 mL) salt

1 tsp. (5 mL) ground black pepper

1½ lb. (750 g) skinned and boned chicken thighs or breasts, cut into 1-inch (2.5-cm) chunks

1. Preheat oven to 425°F (220°C). Arrange first 3 ingredients on a large rimmed baking sheet lined with aluminum foil. Bake at 425°F (220°C) for 25 minutes or until vegetables are soft and skins are beginning to blister, turning peppers every 5 minutes. Remove vegetables from oven; transfer peppers to a small bowl. Cover bowl with plastic wrap, and let stand 20 minutes. Let tomatillos stand on baking sheet until cool enough to handle. Coarsely chop tomatillos, and place in a medium bowl.

2. After peppers have stood for 20 minutes, peel, seed, and chop; add to tomatillos.

3. Sauté onion and cumin in hot olive oil in a 6-qt. (6-L) stainless steel or enameled Dutch oven over medium-high heat 12 minutes or until onion is softened.

4. Cut tips of corn kernels into a large bowl; scrape milk and remaining pulp from cobs. Add corn and garlic to onion in Dutch oven; cook, stirring constantly, 5 minutes. Stir in chopped peppers, chopped tomatillos, chicken stock, and next 3 ingredients. Bring to a boil; reduce heat, and simmer, uncovered, 5 minutes, stirring often. Stir in chicken. Bring to a boil over high heat; boil 5 minutes. Remove from heat.

5. Ladle hot soup into a hot jar, leaving 1-inch (2.5-cm) headspace. Remove air bubbles. Wipe jar rim. Center lid on jar. Apply band, and adjust to fingertip-tight. Place jar on rack in a pressure canner containing 2 inches (5 cm) of simmering water (180°F/90°C). Repeat until all jars are filled.

6. Place lid on canner, and turn to locked position. Adjust heat to medium-high. Vent steam for 10 minutes. Place the counter weight or weighted gauge on vent; bring pressure to 10 pounds (psi) for a weighted-gauge canner or 11 pounds (psi) for a dial-gauge canner.

7. Process 1-pt. (500-mL) jars for 1 hour and 15 minutes or 1-qt. (1-L) jars for 1 hour and 30 minutes. Turn off heat; cool canner to zero pressure. Let stand 5 more minutes before removing lid.

8. Cool jars in canner 10 minutes. Remove jars and cool.

END-OF-SUMMER PASTA SAUCE

MAKES ABOUT 8 (1-PT./500-ML) OR 4 (1-QT./1-L) JARS

A hearty variety of summer's bounty enveloped in a wine-and-herb-spiked tomato sauce creates an outstanding new pressure canning recipe sure to become part of your canning traditions.

3½ lb. tomatoes, cored and coarsely chopped

1 (1-lb./450-g) eggplant, cut into 1-inch (2.5-cm) cubes (5 cups/1.25 L)

4 thyme sprigs

2 bay leaves

6 Tbsp. (90 mL) olive oil, divided

2 tsp. (10 mL) salt

1½ cups (375 mL) chopped onion

2 large carrots, sliced

2 large bell peppers, chopped

2 cups (500 mL) Pinot Grigio or other dry white wine

2 cups (500 mL) cauliflower florets

2 cups (500 mL) coarsely chopped fresh green beans

½ cup (125 mL) loosely packed basil leaves, chopped

1 cup (250 mL) fresh corn kernels (about 2 ears)

1 tsp. (5 mL) ground black pepper

1. Preheat oven to 375°F (190°C). Place first 4 ingredients in a large bowl; drizzle with 3 Tbsp. (45 mL) olive oil, sprinkle with salt, and toss well. Spread vegetable mixture in a large roasting pan lined with aluminum foil. Bake at 375°F (190°C) for 35 minutes or until vegetables are very tender and lightly browned.

2. While vegetable mixture bakes, heat remaining 3 Tbsp. (45 mL) oil in a 6-qt. (6-L) stainless steel or enameled Dutch oven over medium heat. Add onion and next 2 ingredients; cook 15 minutes or until onion is tender and carrot and bell pepper are crisp-tender. Add wine, and cook 5 minutes, stirring to loosen brown bits from bottom of Dutch oven.

3. Remove and discard thyme sprigs and bay leaves. Press tomato mixture through a food mill to remove seeds and skins. Discard seeds and skins. Stir tomato puree into onion mixture. Add cauliflower and remaining ingredients. Bring to a boil; reduce heat, and simmer, uncovered, 5 minutes, stirring occasionally.

4. Ladle hot sauce into a hot jar, leaving 1-inch (2.5-cm) headspace. Remove air bubbles. Wipe jar rim. Center lid on jar. Apply band, and adjust to fingertip-tight. Place jar on rack in a pressure canner containing 2 inches (5 cm) of simmering water (180°F/90°C). Repeat until all jars are filled.

5. Place lid on canner, and turn to locked position. Adjust heat to medium-high. Vent steam for 10 minutes. Place the counter weight or weighted gauge on vent; bring pressure to 10 pounds (psi) for a weighted-gauge canner or 11 pounds (psi) for a dial-gauge canner.

6. Process 1-pt. (500-mL) jars for 1 hour and 15 minutes or 1-qt. (1-L) jars for 1 hour and 30 minutes. Turn off heat; cool canner to zero pressure. Let stand 5 more minutes before removing lid.

7. Cool jars in canner 10 minutes. Remove jars and cool.

HEARTY CHICKEN STEW

MAKES ABOUT 6 (1-PT./500-ML) JARS

Chicken and vegetables simmer in a rich stock base and white wine, perfect for a soup-and-sandwich lunch or as the star in chicken pot pie.

3 Tbsp. (45 mL) butter

1½ cups (375 mL) diced onion (about 2 medium)

½ cup (125 mL) diced fresh mushrooms

1½ cups (375 mL) diced carrot (about 3 medium)

1 cup (250 mL) diced Yukon gold potatoes

½ cup (125 mL) diced celery

5 cups (1.25 L) chicken stock or Chicken Bone Broth (page 288)*

1 cup (250 mL) dry white wine

1 tsp. (5 mL) dried thyme

1 tsp. (5 mL) salt

½ tsp. (2 mL) ground black pepper

1 bay leaf

3 cups (750 mL) 1-inch (2.5-cm) cubed skinned and boned raw chicken

½ cup (125 mL) frozen baby sweet peas, thawed

1 Tbsp. (15 mL) bottled lemon juice

1. Melt butter in a large stainless steel or enameled Dutch oven over medium heat. Add onion and mushrooms; sauté 3 minutes or until mushrooms are lightly browned. Add carrot and next 2 ingredients; sauté 2 minutes. Stir in stock and next 5 ingredients. Bring to a boil; reduce heat to medium, and cook, uncovered, 10 minutes or until vegetables are tender, stirring occasionally. Remove from heat.

2. Stir in chicken, peas, and lemon juice. Remove and discard bay leaf.

3. Ladle hot stew into a hot jar, leaving 1-inch (2.5-cm) headspace. Remove air bubbles. Wipe jar rim. Center lid on jar. Apply band, and adjust to fingertip-tight. Place jar on rack in a pressure canner containing 2 inches (5 cm) of simmering water (180°F/90°C). Repeat until all jars are filled.

4. Place lid on canner, and turn to locked position. Adjust heat to medium-high. Vent steam for 10 minutes. Place the counter weight or weighted gauge on vent; bring pressure to 10 pounds (psi) for a weighted-gauge canner or 11 pounds (psi) for a dial-gauge canner.

5. Process 1-pt. (500-mL) jars for 1 hour and 15 minutes. Turn off heat; cool canner to zero pressure. Let stand 5 more minutes before removing lid. Cool jars in canner 10 minutes. Remove jars and cool.

*Commercial canned chicken broth may be substituted.

CHICKEN POT PIE FOR 2: Preheat oven to 400°F (200°C). Strain broth from 1 (1-pt./500-mL) jar Hearty Chicken Stew, reserving broth. Melt 2 Tbsp. (30 mL) butter in a deep 9-inch ovenproof skillet over medium heat; stir in 2 Tbsp. (30 mL) all-purpose flour. Cook, stirring constantly, until golden. Gradually add reserved broth, stirring constantly, until thickened and smooth. Stir in strained chicken mixture. Remove from heat. Place ½ (14.1-oz./399-g) refrigerated piecrust or ½ recipe Flaky Piecrust (page 315), thawed, over filling; carefully tuck edges under and crimp with a fork. Cut slits in top of pie for steam to escape. Bake at 400°F (200°C) for 20 minutes or until crust is golden and filling is bubbly.

THAI COCONUT-SQUASH SOUP

MAKES ABOUT 6 (1-PT./500-ML) OR 3 (1-QT./1-L) JARS

A variation on Tom Kha Gai soup, this version gets its heft from winter squash instead of chicken. Lemongrass, ginger, coconut milk, and cilantro give it its Thai accent.

SOUP

- 2 qt. (2 L) chicken or vegetable broth
- ½ tsp. (2 mL) ground red pepper
- 3 garlic cloves, minced
- 2 fresh Thai chiles, seeded and minced
- 1 lemongrass stalk, quartered
- 1 (2-inch/5-cm) piece peeled fresh ginger, grated
- 1½ lb. (750 g) butternut, acorn, kabocha, or other orange-fleshed winter squash, peeled and cut into ½-inch (1-cm) cubes (about 5 cups/1.25 L)
- 2 Tbsp. (30 mL) sugar
- 2 tsp. (10 mL) salt
- 1 tsp. (5 mL) lime zest
- 2 Tbsp. (30 mL) fresh lime juice
- 4 shallots, chopped
- 1 red bell pepper, chopped

SERVE WITH
(For each 1-pt./500-mL jar)

- ½ cup (250 mL) coconut milk
- 2 Tbsp. (30 mL) red onion slivers
- 1 Tbsp. (15 mL) chopped fresh cilantro

Lime wedges

1. For Soup: Bring broth to a boil in a 6-qt (6-L) stainless steel or enameled Dutch oven. Stir in ground red pepper and next 4 ingredients; cover, reduce heat, and simmer 20 minutes, stirring occasionally. Remove lemongrass. Add squash and next 6 ingredients. Return to a boil; reduce heat, and simmer, uncovered, 5 minutes, stirring occasionally.

2. Ladle hot soup into a hot jar, leaving 1-inch (2.5-cm) headspace. Remove air bubbles. Wipe jar rim. Center lid on jar. Apply band, and adjust to fingertip-tight. Place jar on rack in a pressure canner containing 2 inches (5 cm) of simmering water (180°F/90°C). Repeat until all jars are filled.

3. Place lid on canner, and turn to locked position. Adjust heat to medium-high. Vent steam for 10 minutes. Place the counter weight or weighted gauge on vent; bring pressure to 10 pounds (psi) for a weighted-gauge canner or 11 pounds (psi) for a dial-gauge canner.

4. Process 1-pt. (500-mL) jars for 1 hour and 15 minutes or 1-qt. (1-L) jars for 1 hour and 30 minutes. Turn off heat; cool canner to zero pressure. Let stand 5 more minutes before removing lid.

5. Cool jars in canner 10 minutes. Remove jars and cool.

6. To serve, pour contents of a 1-pt. (500-mL) or 1-qt. (1-L) jar into a medium stainless steel or enameled saucepan. Bring to a boil over high heat. For each 1-pt. (500-mL) jar, stir in ½ cup (250 mL) coconut milk, 2 Tbsp. (30 mL) red onion slivers, and 1 Tbsp. (15 mL) chopped fresh cilantro. Bring to a simmer; cook 1 to 2 minutes or until thoroughly heated. (If reheating a 1-qt. (1-L) jar of soup, double the amounts of coconut milk, red onion slivers, and cilantro.) Serve with lime wedges.

ROASTED TOMATO SOUP

MAKES ABOUT 6 (1-PT/500-ML) OR 3 (1-QT./1-L) JARS

Bring a burst of flavor and color to a comfort food classic. Serve up the sunny flavor of tomato soup laced with basil alongside a hearty whole-grain grilled cheese sandwich oozing with Swiss cheese.

---

8 lb. (4 kg) plum tomatoes, cored and halved crosswise

5 tsp. (25 mL) salt, divided

2 tsp. (10 mL) ground black pepper, divided

1 Tbsp. (15 mL) olive oil

2 cups (500 mL) chopped onion

4 garlic cloves, minced

1 cup (250 mL) dry white wine

4 cups (1 L) chicken or vegetable stock

1 cup (250 mL) tightly packed basil leaves

1. Preheat oven to 375°F (190°C). Remove seeds from tomatoes. Arrange tomatoes, cut side up, on large rimmed baking sheets. Sprinkle with 1 Tbsp. (15 mL) salt and 1 tsp. (5 mL) pepper. Bake at 375°F (190°C) for 45 minutes or until tomatoes are very soft; cool, peel, and coarsely chop.

2. Heat olive oil in a 6-qt. (6-L) stainless steel or enameled Dutch oven over medium heat. Add onion, garlic, remaining 2 tsp. (10 mL) salt, and remaining 1 tsp. (5 mL) pepper; cover and cook 8 to 10 minutes or until very tender, but not brown, stirring occasionally.

3. Add wine, and cook, uncovered, 10 minutes or until wine evaporates, stirring often. Stir in tomatoes, stock, and basil. Cook 20 minutes or until thoroughly heated, stirring occasionally. Remove from heat and cool slightly. Process in a blender, in batches, until smooth; pour each batch into a large bowl.

4. Return tomato mixture to Dutch oven; bring to a simmer. Ladle hot soup into a hot jar, leaving 1-inch (2.5-cm) headspace. Remove air bubbles. Wipe jar rim. Center lid on jar. Apply band, and adjust to fingertip-tight. Place jar on rack in a pressure canner containing 2 inches (5 cm) of simmering water (180°F/90°C). Repeat until all jars are filled.

5. Place lid on canner, and turn to locked position. Adjust heat to medium-high. Vent steam for 10 minutes. Place the counter weight or weighted gauge on vent; bring pressure to 10 pounds (psi) for a weighted-gauge canner or 11 pounds (psi) for a dial-gauge canner.

6. Process 1-pt. (500-mL) jars for 50 minutes or 1-qt. (1-L) jars for 60 minutes. Turn off heat; cool canner to zero pressure. Let stand 5 more minutes before removing lid.

7. Cool jars in canner 10 minutes. Remove jars and cool.

CHICKEN BONE BROTH

MAKES ABOUT 4 (1-PT./500-ML) OR 2 (1-QT./1-L) JARS

Using leftover roasted whole chicken or chicken parts is one of the best ways to make stock. The addition of fresh chicken wings increases the flavor and natural mineral content. For bone broth, follow the directions below.

Carcass (including skin from 1 (4- to 5-lb./2- to 2.25-kg) roast chicken, broken into large pieces

2 qt. (2 L) water

1 Tbsp. (15 mL) salt

1 Tbsp. (15 mL) unfiltered apple cider vinegar (5% acidity)

2 large carrots, coarsely chopped

2 bay leaves

1 large onion, coarsely chopped

1. Preheat oven to 225°F (107°C). Combine all ingredients in a large stainless steel or enameled Dutch oven. Bake, covered, at 225°F (107°C) for 7 hours.

2. Reduce oven temperature to 180°F (90°C), and bake 7 more hours. Remove bones from broth. Pour broth through a fine wire-mesh strainer into a 2-qt. (2-L) glass measure or large bowl; discard solids. Skim fat, and add water, if necessary, until broth measures 2 qt. (2 L). Wash Dutch oven. Return broth to Dutch oven; bring to a simmer.

3. Ladle hot broth into a hot jar, leaving 1-inch (2.5-cm) headspace. Remove air bubbles. Wipe jar rim. Center lid on jar. Apply band, and adjust to fingertip-tight. Place jar on rack in a pressure canner containing 2 inches (5 cm) of simmering water (180°F/90°C). Repeat until all jars are filled.

4. Place lid on canner, and turn to locked position. Adjust heat to medium-high. Vent steam for 10 minutes. Place the counter weight or weighted gauge on vent; bring pressure to 10 pounds (psi) for a weighted-gauge canner or 11 pounds (psi) for a dial-gauge canner.

5. Process 1-pt. (500-mL) jars for 20 minutes or 1-qt. (1-L) jars for 25 minutes. Turn off heat; cool canner to zero pressure. Let stand 5 more minutes before removing lid.

6. Cool jars in canner 10 minutes. Remove jars and cool.

BEEF BONE BROTH

MAKES ABOUT 4 (1-PT./500-ML) OR 2 (1-QT./1-L) JARS

Meaty beef bones form the foundation and contribute abundant gelatin in broth. Gelatin, a protein thickener, comes from the breakdown of connective tissue in meat and bones as they simmer in liquid (water) along with aromatic vegetables and herbs. The addition of apple cider vinegar helps to draw out the natural gelatin from the meat.

---

4 lb. (2 kg) meaty beef bones

2 qt. (2 L) water

2 Tbsp. (30 mL) unfiltered apple cider vinegar (5% acidity)

2 tsp. (10 mL) salt

3 garlic cloves, crushed

2 bay leaves

1 large onion, quartered

——————— ★ ———————

Tricks of the Trade

Save beef bones from steaks and roasts by placing them in the freezer in zip-top plastic freezer bags. Once you have about 4 lb. (2 kg), skip the roasting step in the broth recipe.

1. Preheat oven to 400°F (200°C). Place beef bones in a large roasting pan. Bake at 400°F (200°C) for 30 minutes. Remove bones from oven. Reduce oven temperature to 225°F (107°C). Add bones and pan drippings to a large stainless steel or enameled Dutch oven. Stir in water and remaining ingredients. Cover and bake at 225°F (107°C) for 8 hours.

2. Reduce oven temperature to 180°F (90°C), and bake 8 more hours. Remove bones from broth. Pour broth through a fine wire-mesh strainer into a 2-qt. (2-L) glass measure or large bowl; discard solids. Skim fat, and add water, if necessary, until broth measures 2 qt. (2 L). Place broth in a large Dutch oven; bring to a simmer.

3. Ladle hot broth into a hot jar, leaving 1-inch (2.5-cm) headspace. Remove air bubbles. Wipe jar rim. Center lid on jar. Apply band, and adjust to fingertip-tight. Place jar on rack in a pressure canner containing 2 inches (5 cm) of simmering water (180°F/90°C). Repeat until all jars are filled.

4. Place lid on canner, and turn to locked position. Adjust heat to medium-high. Vent steam for 10 minutes. Place the counter weight or weighted gauge on vent; bring pressure to 10 pounds (psi) for a weighted-gauge canner or 11 pounds (psi) for a dial-gauge canner.

5. Process 1-pt. (500-mL) jars for 20 minutes or 1-qt. (1-L) jars for 25 minutes. Turn off heat; cool canner to zero pressure. Let stand 5 more minutes before removing lid.

6. Cool jars in canner 10 minutes. Remove jars and cool.

FRENCH ONION SOUP

MAKES ABOUT 8 (1-PT./500-ML) OR 4 (1-QT./1-L) JARS

Generous amounts of onions simmered in a gently seasoned white wine and beef broth—c'est merveilleux.

1 Tbsp. (15 mL) butter

4 lb. (2 kg) onions, thinly sliced

1 Tbsp. (15 mL) salt

1 tsp. (5 mL) ground black pepper

1 tsp. (5 mL) dried thyme

3 cups (750 mL) dry white wine, divided

3 qt. (3 L) Beef Bone Broth (page 289), or commercial canned chicken, beef, or vegetable stock

---
★

Perfect Pairing

To enjoy your French Onion Soup fresh from your pantry, open a jar and transfer it to a small saucepan. Bring to a simmer for 10 minutes to heat through. Broil sliced baguette smothered in Swiss and Gruyère cheese and sprinkle with fresh thyme leaves.

1. Melt butter in an 8-qt. (8-L) stainless steel or enameled Dutch oven over medium-low heat. Stir in onion, next 3 ingredients, and 2 cups (500 mL) white wine. Cover and cook 1 hour or until onion is very tender, stirring occasionally.

2. Uncover and cook, stirring constantly, until onion is caramel colored. Add remaining 1 cup (250 mL) wine, and cook 2 minutes, stirring to loosen browned bits from bottom of Dutch oven. Stir in broth. Bring to a boil; reduce heat, and simmer, uncovered, 15 minutes.

3. Ladle hot soup into a hot jar, leaving 1-inch (2.5-cm) headspace. Remove air bubbles. Wipe jar rim. Center lid on jar. Apply band, and adjust to fingertip-tight. Place jar on rack in a pressure canner containing 2 inches (5 cm) of simmering water (180°F/90°C). Repeat until all jars are filled.

4. Place lid on canner, and turn to locked position. Adjust heat to medium-high. Vent steam for 10 minutes. Place the counter weight or weighted gauge on vent; bring pressure to 10 pounds (psi) for a weighted-gauge canner or 11 pounds (psi) for a dial-gauge canner.

5. Process 1-pt. (500-mL) jars for 60 minutes or 1-qt. (1-L) jars for 1 hour and 15 minutes. Turn off heat; cool canner to zero pressure. Let stand 5 more minutes before removing lid.

6. Cool jars in canner 10 minutes. Remove jars and cool.

BEEF CHIPOTLE CHILI

MAKES ABOUT 9 (1-PT./500-ML) JARS

This hearty thick beef and bean chili rich with enticing spices will be your new go-to recipe and a truly perfect one to stockpile.

3 cups (750 mL) dried black or pinto beans

6 cups (1.5 L) water

4 lb. (2 kg) beef stew meat

1 Tbsp. (15 mL) salt

2 tsp. (10 mL) ground black pepper

¼ cup (60 mL) olive oil

2 cups (500 mL) chopped onion

1 cup (250 mL) chopped red or green bell pepper

6 cups (1.5 L) canned, diced tomatoes

⅓ cup (75 mL) finely chopped canned chipotle peppers in adobo sauce

¼ cup (60 mL) fresh lime juice (about 3 large limes)

★

Perfect Pairing

Enjoy this chili alone with fixings or use it to top nachos and chili dogs, fold into tacos, or layer under baked macaroni and cheese for a truly decadent meal.

1. Rinse and sort beans according to package directions. Place beans in a large saucepan. Cover with water 2 inches above beans; let soak 12 hours.

2. Drain beans, discarding soaking water. Return beans to pan; add 6 cups water. Bring to a boil; reduce heat, cover, and simmer 40 minutes or just until tender. Drain.

3. Trim all fat from beef, and cut into ½-inch (1-cm) cubes. Sprinkle beef with salt and pepper. Brown beef, in batches, in hot olive oil in a 6-qt. (6-L) stainless steel or enameled Dutch oven over medium-high heat. Remove beef from Dutch oven.

4. Add onion and bell pepper to Dutch oven; cook, stirring often, 5 minutes. Return beef and any accumulated juices to Dutch oven; add drained beans, tomatoes, and remaining 2 ingredients. Bring to a boil; reduce heat, and simmer, uncovered, 10 minutes or until slightly thickened.

5. Ladle hot chili into a hot jar, leaving 1-inch (2.5-cm) headspace. Remove air bubbles. Wipe jar rim. Center lid on jar. Apply band, and adjust to fingertip-tight. Place jar on rack in a pressure canner containing 2 inches (5 cm) of simmering water (180°F/90°C). Repeat until all jars are filled.

6. Place lid on canner, and turn to locked position. Adjust heat to medium-high. Vent steam for 10 minutes. Place the counter weight or weighted gauge on vent; bring pressure to 10 pounds (psi) for a weighted-gauge canner or 11 pounds (psi) for a dial-gauge canner.

7. Process 1-pt. (500-mL) jars for 1 hour and 15 minutes. Turn off heat; cool canner to zero pressure. Let stand 5 more minutes before removing lid. Cool jars in canner 10 minutes. Remove jars and cool.

ENCHILADA SAUCE

MAKES ABOUT 8 (1-PT./500-ML) JARS

This enchilada sauce is sweet with caramelized onions and just spicy enough to be a versatile pantry staple. The amount of New Mexican chiles may seem daunting, but they are easy to work with and make the flavorful base of the recipe.

- 12 dried New Mexican chile peppers
- 2 cups (500 mL) boiling water
- 4 garlic cloves, minced
- 1 Tbsp. (15 mL) olive oil
- 5 cups (1.25 L) coarsely chopped onion (about 4 large onions)
- 6 cups (1.5 L) canned, diced tomatoes
- ¼ cup (60 mL) firmly packed dark brown sugar (optional)
- 2 Tbsp. (30 mL) chili powder
- 2 tsp. (10 mL) salt
- 2 tsp. (10 mL) ground cumin
- 1 tsp. (5 mL) ground red pepper

★

Perfect Pairing
Use this as a braising sauce for chicken or pork, add it to cooking beans, or drizzle it on fish tacos, fajitas, and huevos rancheros.

1. Rinse any dirt from dried chiles, and pat dry with a paper towel. Toast peppers on a very hot griddle, or in a skillet, 8 to 10 seconds on each side or just until beginning to puff and blister. (Do not allow peppers to burn or they will become bitter.) When cool enough to handle, remove and discard stems and seeds from chiles; tear into large pieces and place in a medium bowl. Cover with boiling water. Let stand 20 minutes or until softened. Drain, reserving 1 cup (250 mL) soaking liquid.

2. Sauté garlic in hot oil in a 6-qt. (6-L) stainless steel or enameled Dutch oven over medium-high heat 30 seconds. Stir in onion. Cover and cook, stirring often, 10 minutes or until onion is tender. Uncover and cook, stirring often, 5 to 10 minutes or until onions are caramel colored. Stir in tomatoes, next 5 ingredients, softened chiles, and reserved soaking liquid. Remove from heat.

3. Process tomato mixture, in batches, in a blender until smooth. Return pureed mixture to Dutch oven. Bring to a boil; reduce heat, and simmer, uncovered, stirring often, 25 minutes or until sauce is thick and darkens in color. (As sauce thickens, partially cover Dutch oven to avoid splatters.)

4. Ladle hot enchilada sauce into a hot jar, leaving 1-inch (2.5-cm) headspace. Remove air bubbles. Wipe jar rim. Center lid on jar. Apply band, and adjust to fingertip-tight. Place jar on rack in a pressure canner containing 2 inches (5 cm) of simmering water (180°F/90°C). Repeat until all jars are filled.

5. Place lid on canner, and turn to locked position. Adjust heat to medium-high. Vent steam for 10 minutes. Place the counter weight or weighted gauge on vent; bring pressure to 10 pounds (psi) for a weighted-gauge canner or 11 pounds (psi) for a dial-gauge canner.

6. Process 1-pt. (500-mL) jars for 50 minutes. Turn off heat; cool canner to zero pressure. Let stand 5 more minutes before removing lid. Cool jars in canner 10 minutes. Remove jars and cool.

BEEFY BOLOGNESE SAUCE

MAKES ABOUT 6 (1-PT./500-ML) OR 3 (1-QT./1-L) JARS

Laden with beef and vegetables simmered in a robust wine-and-balsamic-infused tomato sauce, our version of this classic Italian dish will have you reinstating Sunday family suppers of hearty pasta and big salads.

- 5 lb. (2.5 kg) lean ground beef
- 3 cups (750 mL) diced onion
- 1 cup (250 mL) diced carrot
- 1 cup (250 mL) diced celery
- 1 Tbsp. (15 mL) dried oregano
- 1 Tbsp. (15 mL) dried basil
- 6 garlic cloves, thinly sliced
- 1½ cups (375 mL) Roasted Tomato Paste (page 206)*
- 1 cup (250 mL) dry red wine
- ¼ (60 mL) cup balsamic vinegar (6% acidity)
- 3 qt. (3 L) canned diced tomatoes, undrained

★

Tricks of the Trade

As with all of our pressure-canned recipes, this Bolognese sauce was specifically designed and tested for pressure canning. If the temptation to experiment with recipes overcomes you, then please FREEZE them in freezer-safe containers rather than pressure canning them.

---

1. Brown beef, in batches, in a 6-qt. (6-L) Dutch oven over medium-high heat, stirring until meat crumbles and is no longer pink; drain and set aside.

2. Add onion and next 5 ingredients to stainless steel or enameled Dutch oven; cook over medium heat 8 to 10 minutes or until tender, stirring occasionally. Stir in tomato paste; cook, stirring constantly, until tomato paste is reduced and beginning to turn brown and stick to Dutch oven. Add wine and vinegar, stirring to loosen browned bits from bottom of Dutch oven.

3. Return beef to Dutch oven, and stir in tomatoes. Bring to a boil; reduce heat, and simmer, uncovered, 15 minutes or until thickened, stirring occasionally.

4. Ladle hot sauce into a hot jar, leaving 1-inch (2.5-cm) headspace. Remove air bubbles. Wipe jar rim. Center lid on jar. Apply band, and adjust to fingertip-tight. Place jar on rack in a pressure canner containing 2 inches (5 cm) of simmering water (180°F/90°C). Repeat until all jars are filled.

5. Place lid on canner, and turn to locked position. Adjust heat to medium-high. Vent steam for 10 minutes. Place the counter weight or weighted gauge on vent; bring pressure to 10 pounds (psi) for a weighted-gauge canner or 11 pounds (psi) for a dial-gauge canner.

6. Process 1-pt. (500-mL) jars for 1 hour or 1-qt. (1-L) jars for 1 hour and 15 minutes. Turn off heat; cool canner to zero pressure. Let stand 5 more minutes before removing lid. Cool jars in canner 10 minutes. Remove jars and cool.

*Commercial canned tomato paste may be substituted.

ROAST PORK IN SPICY BROTH

MAKES ABOUT 6 (1-PT./500-ML) OR 3 (1-QT./1-L) JARS

This moist pork recipe will convert you to the joys of pressure-canned meats. A rich, mildly spicy broth is the perfect pairing for lean roast pork.

3 lb. (1.5 kg) boneless pork shoulder (Boston butt), trimmed and cut into 1½-inch (4-cm) cubes

4 tsp. (20 mL) salt, divided

½ tsp. (2 mL) ground black pepper

1 Tbsp. (15 mL) canola oil

2 qt. (2 L) Chicken Bone Broth (page 288)

1 (8-oz./250-g) onion, halved vertically and cut crosswise into thin slices

2 Tbsp. (30 mL) dried crushed red pepper

1½ Tbsp. (22 mL) dried oregano

3 garlic cloves, minced

★

Perfect Pairing
Use this as a soup, ladled hot into bowls and sprinkled with cilantro and slivered red onions; top with a dollop of sour cream.

1. Preheat oven to 425°F (220°C). Sprinkle pork with 1 tsp. (5 mL) salt and black pepper; drizzle with oil and toss to coat. Arrange pork cubes in a single layer on an aluminum foil–lined rimmed baking sheet. Bake at 425°F (220°C) for 30 minutes or until pork is beginning to brown.

2. Meanwhile, bring broth, next 4 ingredients, and remaining 1 Tbsp. (15 mL) salt to a boil in a 4-qt. (4-L) stainless steel or enameled Dutch oven; cover, reduce heat, and simmer 5 minutes.

3. Fill 1 hot jar half full with pork cubes. Ladle broth mixture over pork, leaving 1-inch (2.5-cm) headspace. Remove air bubbles. Wipe jar rim. Center lid on jar. Apply band, and adjust to fingertip-tight. Place jar on rack in a pressure canner containing 2 inches (5 cm) of simmering water (180°F/90°C). Repeat until all jars are filled.

4. Place lid on canner, and turn to locked position. Adjust heat to medium-high. Vent steam for 10 minutes. Place the counter weight or weighted gauge on vent; bring pressure to 10 pounds (psi) for a weighted-gauge canner or 11 pounds (psi) for a dial-gauge canner.

5. Process 1-pt. (500-mL) jars for 1 hour and 15 minutes or 1-qt. (1-L) jars for 1 hour and 30 minutes. Turn off heat; cool canner to zero pressure. Let stand 5 more minutes before removing lid.

6. Cool jars in canner 10 minutes. Remove jars and cool.

PORK CARNITAS TACOS

MAKES 4 SERVINGS

With canned spicy pork, Lime-Pickled Radishes, and Chipotle Tomatillo Salsa in your pantry, you've got the ultimate gratifying taco experience.

1 (1-pt./250-mL) jar Roast Pork in Spicy Broth (page 297)

Chopped fresh cilantro

Lime wedges

8 (6-inch/15-cm) corn or flour tortillas, warmed

Toppings: crumbled queso fresco or feta cheese, finely diced white onion, Chipotle Tomatillo Salsa (page 171), Lime-Pickled Radishes (page 244)

1. Preheat oven to 375°F (190°C). Pour Roast Pork in Spicy Broth into a medium stainless steel or enameled saucepan. Bring to a boil; reduce heat, and simmer, uncovered, 10 minutes.

2. Pour pork mixture through a wire-mesh strainer into a bowl, reserving broth. Return pork to saucepan; shred pork with 2 forks. Transfer pork to an aluminum foil–lined baking sheet.

3. Bake at 375°F (190°C) for 20 minutes or until edges of pork begin to become crisp. Arrange pork on a serving platter; moisten, if desired, with some of reserved broth and top with cilantro and lime wedges. Serve pork in tortillas with desired toppings.

BBQ PULLED PORK

MAKES ABOUT 6 (1-PT./500-ML) OR 3 (1-QT./1-L) JARS

Roast pork simmered in a simple brown sugar BBQ sauce until it practically melts apart is the base for this revolutionary and truly useful pressure-canned recipe.

1½ cups (375 mL) chopped onion (about 1 large)

1½ cups (375 mL) ketchup

½ cup (125 mL) firmly packed light brown sugar

¼ cup (60 mL) apple cider vinegar (5% acidity)

2 Tbsp. (30 mL) Worcestershire Sauce (page 257)

2 Tbsp. (30 mL) brown mustard

2 Tbsp. (30 mL) honey

3 garlic cloves, minced

1 (4- to 5-lb./2- to 2.25-kg) boneless pork shoulder roast (Boston butt), cut into large chunks

---
★

Tricks of the Trade

Empty contents of desired number of jars into a saucepan or Dutch oven. Bring to a boil; reduce heat, and simmer 15 minutes. Remove from heat; shred pork using 2 forks. Spoon onto toasted buns or into warmed tortillas.

1. Stir together all ingredients, except pork, in a 6-qt. (6-L) stainless steel or enameled Dutch oven until blended. Add pork, turning to coat. Bring to a boil; reduce heat, and simmer 5 minutes.

2. Ladle hot pork mixture into a hot jar, leaving 1-inch (2.5-cm) headspace. Remove air bubbles. Wipe jar rim. Center lid on jar. Apply band, and adjust to fingertip-tight. Place jar on rack in a pressure canner containing 2 inches (5 cm) of simmering water (180°F/90°C). Repeat until all jars are filled.

3. Place lid on canner, and turn to locked position. Adjust heat to medium-high. Vent steam for 10 minutes. Place the counter weight or weighted gauge on vent; bring pressure to 10 pounds (psi) for a weighted-gauge canner or 11 pounds (psi) for a dial-gauge canner.

4. Process 1-pt. (500-mL) jars for 1 hour and 15 minutes or 1-qt. (1-L) jars for 1 hour and 30 minutes. Turn off heat; cool canner to zero pressure. Let stand 5 more minutes before removing lid. Cool jars in canner 10 minutes. Remove jars and cool.

Chapter 4

FREEZING

Freezing just-ripe foods captures flavors at their best and allows you to preserve the pick of the crop in any size batch. Here we cover the basics of freezing fruits and vegetables to create an assortment of recipes, such as pie fillings, quick jams, pickles, and more. Just imagine fresh Peach-Raspberry Pie in the middle of a blustery winter, quick pickles that stay super crisp and brightly colored, and a harvest of herb-based sauces at the ready when grilling or roasting—any time of the year.

Guidelines for Freezing Vegetables

VEGETABLE	SELECTION	PREPARATION	BLANCHING TIME	PACKAGING
Asparagus	Choose tender, thin spears with tightly formed heads.	Trim off woody portion of spears.	1½ to 3 minutes	Pack in plastic freezer jars, bags, or containers; seal, label, and freeze.
Beans (Green or Yellow Wax)	Choose firm, tender beans.	Trim ends, and cut beans into 3- to 4-inch (7.5- to 10-cm) pieces.	3 minutes	Pack in plastic freezer jars, bags, or containers; seal, label, and freeze.
Beets (whole)	Choose deep-colored with smooth skin.	Wash thoroughly; trim stems to 1 inch (2.5 cm).	1 hour, or until tender	Pack in plastic freezer jars, bags, or containers; seal, label, and freeze.
Broccoli or Cauliflower	Choose young stalks with thin skins and firm heads.	Trim off leaves and woody portion of stalks. Separate heads into 1-inch (2.5-cm) florets. Immerse in brine (1 cup/250 mL salt to 1 gal./4-L water) for 30 minutes. Rinse; drain.	3 to 4 minutes	Pack in plastic freezer jars, bags, or containers; seal, label, and freeze.
Brussels sprouts	Choose dark-green, compact heads.	Remove discolored leaves; cut off stem ends. Halve, if desired. Sort by size.	3 to 5 minutes according to size	Pack in plastic freezer jars, bags, or containers; seal, label, and freeze.
Carrots	Choose young, tender medium-length carrots.	Remove leafy tops. Wash; peel. Wash again; dice or quarter. (Freeze small carrots whole.)	Cut carrots—3 minutes Whole carrots—5 minutes	Pack in plastic freezer jars, bags, or containers; seal, label, and freeze.
Corn (on the cob)	Choose very fresh ears with tender, juicy kernels.	Remove husks; trim ends, and remove silk.	Blanch according to diameter: 1½ inches (4 cm)—6 minutes 2 inches (5 cm)—8 minutes Larger—10 minutes	Wrap ears individually in moisture-free film heavy-duty plastic wrap, and pack in plastic freezer bags; seal, label, and freeze.
Corn (whole-kernel)	Choose very fresh ears with tender, juicy kernels.	Remove husks; trim ends, and remove silk.	Steam ears 5 to 6 minutes, according to size. Cool; drain. Cut kernels from cobs.	Pack in plastic freezer jars, bags, or containers; seal, label, and freeze.
Corn (cream-style)	Choose very fresh ears with tender, juicy kernels.	Remove husks; trim ends, and remove silk.	Blanch as for whole-kernel corn. Cool; drain. Cut off tips of kernels; scrape milk and pulp from cobs.	Pack in plastic freezer jars, bags, or containers; seal, label, and freeze.
Greens	Choose young, tender green leaves.	Wash thoroughly. Remove coarse stems.	Blanch 2 minutes, stirring to separate leaves. Drain; cool.	Pack into plastic freezer jars or containers, leaving ½-inch (1-cm) headspace.

Guidelines for Freezing Vegetables

VEGETABLE	SELECTION	PREPARATION	BLANCHING TIME	PACKAGING
Okra	Choose tender pods.	Wash. Sort according to sizes larger or smaller than 4 inches (10 cm). Remove stems, but do not open seed cells.	Small pods—3 minutes Large pods—5 minutes	Pack in plastic freezer jars, bags, or containers; seal, label, and freeze.
Parsnips, Turnips, or Rutabagas	Choose firm, unblemished roots.	Remove leafy tops. Wash and drain. Peel and cut in half lengthwise; slice crosswise, or dice.	3 minutes	Pack in plastic freezer jars, bags, or containers; seal, label, and freeze.
Potatoes (White or Yukon gold)	Choose smooth-skinned potatoes.	Scrub, rinse, and peel. Keep small potatoes whole; cut large potatoes as desired.	3 to 5 minutes, depending upon size	Pack in plastic freezer jars, bags, or containers, leaving $1/2$-inch (1-cm) headspace; seal, label, and freeze.
Potatoes (Sweet)	Choose potatoes that have been allowed to cure at least one week, with smooth skin.	Scrub, rinse, and drain. Sort according to size.	Blanch or bake (350°F/180°C) whole until almost tender, depending upon size. Cool, peel, and slice or mash. (Stir in 2 Tbsp. (30 mL) lemon juice per quart (1-L) to prevent browning.)	Pack in plastic freezer jars, bags, or containers, leaving $1/2$-inch (1-cm) headspace.
Pumpkin	Choose mature cooking pumpkins with uniform color and a stem that breaks easily from the vine.	Wash; drain. Cut in half; remove seeds and membranes. Cut into sections.	Steam or bake until soft. Scoop out pulp. Puree using a food processor or food mill. If desired, stir in 1 part sugar to 6 parts puree. Cool.	Pack puree into plastic freezer jars, leaving $1/2$-inch (1-cm) headspace; seal, label, and freeze.
Peas (Green or Garden)	Choose pods filled with young tender peas that have not become starchy.	Wash peas; shell. Wash again.	2 minutes	Pack in plastic freezer jars, bags, or containers; seal, label, and freeze.
Peas (Snow or Sugar Snap)	Choose firm, unblemished pods.	Wash and drain.	2 minutes	Pack in plastic freezer jars, bags, or containers; seal, label, and freeze.
Summer squash (Zucchini, Yellow, or Pattypan)	Choose young squash with tender, unblemished skin.	Wash and drain. Cut squash crosswise into slices.	3 minutes	Pack in plastic freezer jars, bags, or containers; seal, label, and freeze.
Winter Squash (Acorn, Butternut, or Spaghetti)	Choose firm, fully mature squash with hard rinds.	Cut in half; remove seeds and membranes. If desired, cut into slices.	Steam or bake just until tender. Scoop out pulp. Puree pulp using a food processor or food mill.	Pack in plastic freezer jars, bags, or containers; seal, label, and freeze.

Guidelines for Freezing Fruits

FRUIT	SELECTION	PREPARATION	PACKAGING
Apples	Choose firm, crisp fruit.	Wash, peel, and core. Cut into ¼-inch (.5-cm) slices. Treat with Ball® Fruit-Fresh® Produce Protector to prevent darkening.	**Syrup Pack:** Use heavy syrup (page 112). Add 1 tsp. Ball® Fruit-Fresh® Produce Protector to each 1 cup (250 mL) syrup. Pack apple slices into plastic freezer jars or containers. Cover with syrup, leaving ½-inch (1-cm) headspace; seal, label, and freeze. **Pie Apples:** Place apple slices in boiling water 2 minutes; cool in ice water. Drain. Pack slices into plastic freezer jars or containers; seal, label, and freeze.
Berries (Blackberries, Mulberries, Red or Black Raspberries)	Choose firm, fully ripe berries, discarding soft, under-ripe or imperfect berries.	Remove stems. Wash in cold water; drain. Dry in a single layer on paper towels.	**Sugar Pack:** Mix 1 part sugar with 4 parts berries. Pack into plastic freezer jars or containers; seal, label, and freeze. **Syrup Pack:** Use heavy syrup (page 112). Place drained berries into plastic freezer jars or containers, shaking gently to pack berries. Cover with syrup, leaving ½-inch (1-cm) headspace; seal, label, and freeze.
Berries (Blueberries, Huckleberries, Elderberries, or Gooseberries)	Choose firm, fully ripe berries, discarding soft, under-ripe or imperfect berries.	Remove stems. Wash in cold water; drain. Dry in a single layer on paper towels.	**Dry Pack (Unsweetened):** Spread berries on rimmed baking sheets; freeze. Quickly pack frozen berries into plastic freezer jars, bags, or containers; seal, label, and return to freezer. **Sugar Pack:** Mix 1 qt. (1-L) berries with ⅔ cup (150 mL) sugar. Pack into plastic freezer jars or containers; seal, label, and freeze.
Cherries (Tart, Red)	Choose tender-skinned, bright red fruit.	Wash in cold water; drain. Remove stems and pits.	**Sugar Pack:** Mix 1 part sugar with 4 parts cherries. Pack into plastic freezer jars or plastic containers; seal, label, and freeze. **Syrup Pack:** Use heavy syrup (page 112). Pack drained cherries into plastic freezer jars or containers, shaking gently to pack berries. Cover with syrup, leaving ½-inch (1-cm) headspace; seal, label, and freeze.

Guidelines for Freezing Fruits

FRUIT	SELECTION	PREPARATION	PACKAGING
Cherries (Dark, Sweet)	Choose tender-skinned, fully ripe, dark-red fruit.	Wash in cold water; drain. Remove stems and pits.	**Syrup Pack:** Use heavy syrup (page 112). Place drained cherries into plastic freezer jars or containers, shaking gently to pack fruit. Cover with syrup, leaving 1/2-inch (1-cm) headspace; seal, label, and freeze.
Figs	Choose fully ripe fruit.	Wash in cold water; drain. Dry in a single layer on paper towels. Cut off stems.	**Dry Pack (Unsweetened):** Spread figs on rimmed baking sheets; freeze. Quickly pack frozen figs into plastic freezer jars, bags, or containers; seal, label, and return to freezer. **Sugar Pack:** Leave figs whole or cut in half. Mix 1 part sugar with 4 parts figs. Pack into plastic freezer jars or containers; seal, label, and freeze. **Syrup Pack:** Use heavy syrup (page 112). Pack whole or halved into plastic freezer jars or containers. Ladle syrup over figs, leaving 1/2-inch (1-cm) headspace; seal, label, and freeze.
Grapefruit or Oranges	Choose firm, heavy fruit.	Wash, peel, and section, discarding membranes and seeds.	**Syrup Pack:** Use medium syrup (page 112). Pack into plastic freezer jars or containers. Ladle syrup over fruit, leaving 1/2-inch (1-cm) headspace; seal, label, and freeze.
Grapes (Red, Green, Purple)	Choose firm, ripe, sweet fruit. Cut seeded grapes in half; remove seeds. Leave seedless grapes whole.	Wash in cold water; drain. Remove stems.	**Syrup Pack:** Use medium syrup (page 112). Pack into plastic freezer jars or containers. Ladle syrup over fruit, leaving 1/2-inch (1-cm) headspace; seal, label, and freeze. **Juice:** Prepare and heat grapes as for puree. Strain through a damp jelly bag or several layers of cheesecloth. Sweeten juice to taste with sugar. Cool. Ladle juice into plastic freezer jars or containers, leaving 1/2-inch (1-cm) headspace; seal, label, and freeze.
Melons	Choose firm, fully ripe melons.	Cut in half; remove seeds. Cut into wedges, and peel; cut into 3/4-inch (2-cm) cubes, slices, or balls.	Pack in plastic freezer jars or containers; seal, label, and freeze. Serve partially thawed.

BLUEBERRY-RASPBERRY FREEZER JAM

MAKES ABOUT 5 (½-PT./250-ML) JARS

Another reason to hoard berries when they're in season! This jam is fresh, simple, and delightful come midwinter, and perfect for thumbprint cookies!

3½ **cups (875 mL) fresh blueberries**

2¾ **cups (675 mL) fresh raspberries**

1¾ **cups (425 mL) sugar**

1 **Tbsp. (15 mL) lemon zest**

2 **Tbsp. (30 mL) fresh lemon juice**

5 **Tbsp. (75 mL) Ball® RealFruit™ Instant Pectin**

★

Simple Switch

If you're lucky enough to find a windfall of black raspberries, substitute them for all the berries in this recipe. Freezing the jam will keep that fresh flavor locked in.

1. Pulse blueberries in a food processor 3 times or until crushed to measure 2 cups (500 mL), stopping to scrape down sides.

2. Place raspberries in a large glass or nonmetallic bowl; mash with a potato masher until crushed. Add blueberries, sugar, and next 2 ingredients, stirring well. Let stand 15 minutes.

3. Gradually stir in pectin; stir 3 minutes. Let stand 30 minutes.

4. Spoon mixture into jars, leaving ½-inch (1-cm) headspace. Center lid on jars. Apply bands, and adjust loosely. Place jars in freezer. Once jam is frozen, adjust bands to fingertip-tight. Store in freezer up to 1 year. Thaw in refrigerator. Refrigerate after thawing, and use within 3 weeks.

GRANNY SMITH FREEZER JAM

MAKES ABOUT 4 (½-PT./250-ML) JARS

A speedy way to preserve tart Granny Smith apples, this no-cook method takes the work out of jam.

5 cups (1.25 L) coarsely chopped, unpeeled Granny Smith apples

1 cup (250 mL) sugar

½ cup (125 mL) pasteurized apple juice

1 tsp. (5 mL) lemon juice

4 Tbsp. (60 mL) Ball® RealFruit™ Instant Pectin

★

Peak of Freshness

Preserving apples is best done in late summer and fall when apples are seasonally fresh and can be bought direct from a local farm or farmers' market. Apples out of season are actually cold stored from last year and lose their nutrients and pectins over the storage process.

1. Pulse half of chopped apple in a food processor until finely chopped, stopping to scrape down sides as needed. Place in a medium glass or nonmetallic bowl. Repeat procedure with remaining half of apple. Stir in sugar and juices; let stand 15 minutes.

2. Gradually stir in pectin; stir 3 minutes. Let stand 5 minutes.

3. Spoon into jars, leaving ½-inch (1-cm) headspace. Center lid on jars. Apply bands, and adjust loosely. Once jam is frozen, adjust bands to fingertip-tight. Store in freezer up to 1 year. Thaw in refrigerator. Refrigerate after thawing, and use within 3 weeks.

PEACH-PLUM FREEZER JAM

MAKES ABOUT 5 (1/2-PT./250-ML) JARS

This is the ultimate summer jam. Stock up when stone fruit is in season!

- 1 lb. (450 g) red plums (about 4 large), pitted and quartered
- 1½ cups (375 mL) diced peeled peaches (2 large)
- 3 cups (750 mL) sugar
- 2 Tbsp. (30 mL) bottled lemon juice
- ¾ cup (175 mL) water
- 6 Tbsp. (90 mL) Ball® Classic Pectin*

★

Tricks of the Trade

Though freezer jam is not water bath canned, it's still a good idea to remove air bubbles from each jar before sealing and freezing.

1. Pulse plum quarters in a food processor until minced. Measure 2 cups (500 mL) minced plums, and place in a large glass or nonmetallic bowl. Stir in peaches, sugar, and lemon juice.

2. Combine water and pectin in a small stainless steel or enameled saucepan. Bring to a boil. Boil 1 minute. Add pectin mixture to fruit mixture, stirring gently for 3 minutes. Cool completely (about 1 hour).

3. Spoon jam into jars, leaving ½-inch (1-cm) headspace. Center lid on jars. Apply bands, and adjust loosely. Once jam is frozen, adjust bands to fingertip-tight. Store in freezer up to 1 year. Thaw in refrigerator. Refrigerate after thawing, and use within 3 weeks.

*Ball® RealFruit™ Instant Pectin may be substituted.

STRAWBERRY-BLUEBERRY FREEZER JAM

MAKES ABOUT 6 (½-PT./250-ML) JARS

This simple berry jam tastes incredibly fresh, even in the middle of January!

4	cups (1 L) fresh blueberries
4	cups (1 L) halved fresh strawberries
1½	cups (375 mL) sugar
5	Tbsp. (60 mL) Ball® Real-Fruit™ Instant Pectin

★

Perfect Pairing
Thaw jam and fold into whipped cream to top an angel food or layer cake for a dessert reminiscent of summer.

1. Pulse blueberries in a food processor until finely chopped, stopping to scrape down sides as needed. Place in a medium bowl. Pulse strawberries in food processor until finely chopped, stopping to scrape down sides as needed. Add to blueberries in bowl. Stir in sugar; let stand 15 minutes.

2. Gradually stir in pectin; stir 3 minutes. Let stand 5 minutes.

3. Spoon into jars, leaving ½-inch (1-cm) headspace. Center lid on jars. Apply bands, and adjust loosely. Once jam is frozen, adjust bands to fingertip-tight. Store in freezer up to 1 year. Thaw in refrigerator. Refrigerate after thawing, and use within 3 weeks.

PUMPKIN-GINGER BUTTER

MAKES ABOUT 6 (½-PT./250-ML) JARS

The ever-enticing pumpkin really shines in this creamy, spiced butter.

---

1 (3-lb./1.5-kg) pie pumpkin, peeled, seeded, and cubed (about 8 cups/2 L)

1 cup (250 mL) apple juice

2 Tbsp. (30 mL) minced fresh ginger

2 cups (500 mL) firmly packed light brown sugar

2 Tbsp. (30 mL) fresh lemon juice

½ tsp. (2 mL) ground cinnamon

⅛ tsp. (.5 mL) ground cloves

1. Bring first 3 ingredients to a boil in a 4-qt. (4-L) stainless steel or enameled Dutch oven; cover, reduce heat, and simmer 30 minutes or until pumpkin is very soft.

2. Process pumpkin mixture, in 2 batches, in a blender until smooth, pouring each batch into a bowl. Return pumpkin mixture to Dutch oven. Stir in brown sugar and next 3 ingredients. Cook, partially covered, over medium-low heat 20 minutes or until mixture thickens and holds its shape on a spoon, stirring often.

3. Spoon pumpkin mixture into hot jars, leaving ½-inch (1-cm) headspace. Center lid on jars. Apply bands, and adjust loosely. Cool jars completely on a wire rack. Place jars in freezer. Once pumpkin butter is frozen, adjust bands to fingertip-tight. Store in freezer up to 8 months. Thaw in refrigerator. Refrigerate after thawing, and use within 3 weeks.

STRAWBERRY-RHUBARB PIE FILLING

MAKES ABOUT 4 (1-PT./500-ML) JARS

Make this filling at the peak of rhubarb and strawberry season for that juicy ripe flavor year-round.

1½   cups (375 mL) sugar

½   cup (125 mL) cornstarch

⅛   tsp. (.5 mL) ground cinnamon

1   cup (250 mL) water

2   Tbsp. (30 mL) bottled lemon juice

5   cups (1.25 L) ½-inch (1-cm) diced rhubarb (about 1¾ lb./800 g)

5   cups (1.25 L) strawberries, hulled

2   Tbsp. (30 mL) orange liqueur (optional)

1. Whisk together sugar, cornstarch, and cinnamon in a 4-qt. (4-L) stainless steel or enameled saucepan until blended. Gradually whisk in water and lemon juice until smooth. Bring to a boil, stirring constantly over medium heat. Cook 1 minute or until mixture thickens. Add fruit; return to a boil, stirring constantly. Boil 1 minute. Stir in orange liqueur, if desired.

2. Ladle hot pie filling evenly into jars, leaving ½-inch (1-cm) headspace. Center lid on jars. Apply bands, and adjust loosely. Let jars stand 2 hours on a wire rack or until cool. Place jars in freezer. Once pie filling is frozen, adjust bands to fingertip-tight. Store in freezer 1 year. Thaw in refrigerator. Refrigerate after thawing, and use within 3 weeks.

CLASSIC STRAWBERRY-RHUBARB HAND PIES: Roll out Flaky Piecrust (below) on a floured surface to ¼-inch thickness. Cut into rectangles or circles (with a cookie cutter), spoon in filling, and seal with another rectangle or circle. Use a beaten egg white to seal the edges and to gloss over the tops. Prick tops with a fork, and bake at 375°F (190°C) for 25 minutes.

FLAKY PIECRUST

MAKES 2 (9-INCH/23-CM) PIECRUSTS

It's a great idea to make several recipes at one time and have them in the freezer for a fast dessert!

2½   cups (625 mL) all-purpose flour

½   tsp. (2 mL) salt

½   cup (125 mL) cold unsalted butter

½   cup (125 mL) cold shortening

⅓   to ½ cup (75 mL to 125 mL) cold water

1. Combine first 4 ingredients in a bowl with a pastry blender until crumbly.

2. Sprinkle cold water, 1 Tbsp. (15 mL) at a time, over surface of mixture in bowl; stir with a fork just until dry ingredients are moistened. Shape dough into a ball. Divide dough in half. Shape each half into a disk, and wrap in plastic wrap; place in a large zip-top plastic freezer bag. Seal bag and freeze up to 3 months.

PEACH-RASPBERRY PIE FILLING

MAKES ABOUT 4 (1-PT./500-ML) JARS

Have this favorite summertime combination at the ready for when you're craving a fresh pie midwinter.

---

5 cups (1.25 L) fresh raspberries

Parchment paper

Ice water

1 lemon

5 firm, ripe peaches (about 2.25 lb./1 kg)

1½ cups (375 mL) sugar

½ cup (125 mL) cornstarch

⅛ tsp. (.5 mL) ground cinnamon

1 cup (250 mL) water

2 Tbsp. (30 mL) brandy

1. Spread raspberries in a single layer on a large rimmed baking sheet lined with parchment paper; freeze.

2. Bring a large pot of water to a boil. Fill a large bowl two-thirds full of ice water. Cut lemon in half, and squeeze juice into ice water. Place peaches in a wire basket, lower into boiling water, and blanch 60 seconds. Place immediately in lemon water. When cool enough to handle, peel peaches, cut in half, and remove pits. Cut peach halves into slices; return to lemon juice mixture. Drain.

3. Whisk together sugar, cornstarch, and cinnamon in a 4-qt. (4-L) stainless steel or enameled saucepan until blended. Gradually whisk in 1 cup water until smooth. Cook, whisking constantly, over medium heat 1 minute or until thickened. Remove from heat; whisk in brandy. Gently fold in peach slices and raspberries.

4. Spoon pie filling evenly into jars, leaving 1-inch (2.5-cm) headspace. Center lid on jars. Apply bands, and adjust loosely. Let jars stand on a wire rack 2 hours or until cool. Place jars in freezer. Once pie filling is frozen, adjust bands to fingertip-tight. Store in freezer 1 year. Thaw in refrigerator. Refrigerate after thawing, and use within 3 weeks.

PEACH MELBA SLAB PIE

MAKES 12 SERVINGS

This rustic pie uses our Flaky Piecrust recipe (page 315) and Peach-Raspberry Pie Filling, making it super quick to put together and producing a beautiful rectangular top-crusted pie.

PIECRUST

- 3 cups (750 mL) all-purpose flour
- ½ tsp. (2 mL) salt
- 9 Tbsp. (135 mL) butter
- 9 Tbsp. (135 mL) shortening
- ½ cup to 10 Tbsp. (125 to 150 mL) cold water

FILLING

- 1 (1-qt./1-L) jar Peach-Raspberry Pie Filling (page 316), thawed

TART LEMON GLAZE
(optional)

- ⅓ cup (75 mL) powdered sugar
- 2 tsp. (10 mL) fresh lemon juice or milk

---- ★ ----

Perfect Pairing
Dish this summer delight into a bowl and top with vanilla ice cream.

---

1. Prepare Piecrust: Combine first 4 ingredients in a bowl with a pastry blender until crumbly.

2. Sprinkle cold water, 1 Tbsp. (15 mL) at a time, over surface of mixture in bowl; stir with a fork just until dry ingredients are moistened. Shape dough into a ball. Divide dough in half. Shape each half into a disk, and wrap in plastic wrap; chill 1 hour.

3. Preheat oven to 425°F (220°C). Roll half of dough into a 13- x 9-inch (33- x 23-cm) rectangle on a floured surface. Fit pastry into a 12- x 8-inch (30- x 20-cm) rimmed baking sheet. Moisten edges with water. Spoon Filling into pastry.

4. Roll remaining half of dough into a 13- x 9-inch (33- x 23-cm) rectangle; place on top of filling. Fold edges under, sealing to bottom crust, and crimp with a fork. Cut 8 slits in top of pie for steam to escape.

5. Bake at 425°F (220°C) for 20 minutes. Reduce oven temperature to 375°F (190°C), and bake 35 to 40 minutes or until filling is bubbly and crust is golden brown. Cool completely in pan on a wire rack.

6. If desired, prepare Tart Lemon Glaze: Stir together powdered sugar and lemon juice in a small bowl until smooth. Drizzle over pie. Serve with scoops of vanilla ice cream.

CARAMEL SAUCE

MAKES ABOUT 4 (½-PT./250-ML) JARS

Heavy cream cooked down to golden goodness with a big pat of butter makes this caramel sauce the real deal. You might have to hide the jars!

2½ cups (635 mL) sugar

2 cups (500 mL) heavy cream

¾ cup (175 mL) light corn syrup

5 Tbsp. (75 mL) unsalted butter

Pinch of kosher salt

2 tsp. (10 mL) vanilla extract

1. Combine all ingredients, except vanilla, in a 4-qt. (4-L) stainless steel or enameled Dutch oven.

2. Cook, stirring constantly, over medium-low heat until sugar dissolves. Bring to a simmer, brushing down any sugar crystals on sides of pan with a pastry brush dipped in hot water. Attach a candy thermometer to side of pan. Cook until thermometer registers 220°F (104°C), stirring occasionally. Remove from heat and stir in vanilla.

3. Pour sauce into a hot jar, leaving ½-inch (1-cm) headspace. Wipe jar rim. Center lid on jar. Apply band, and adjust to fingertip-tight. Repeat until all jars are filled. Let jars cool completely on a wire rack. Store in refrigerator for 2 weeks, or freeze for 1 year.

BANANA-CARAMEL BREAD PUDDING

MAKES 8 TO 10 SERVINGS

This heavenly bread pudding is laden with a lush banana-and-caramel custard. Bake it whole, or use a muffin pan to portion into individual servings; cut baking time to 25 to 30 minutes.

Butter

3 large eggs

2 cups (500 mL) milk

1 cup (250 mL) Caramel Sauce, warmed

½ cup firmly packed light brown sugar

4 very ripe bananas, mashed

Pinch of ground nutmeg

8 cups (2 L) day-old firm white bread cubes

Ground cinnamon

¼ cup (60 mL) chopped walnuts (optional)

1. Preheat oven to 350°F (180°C). Butter a 9-inch (2.5-L) square baking dish.

2. Whisk eggs in a large bowl. Whisk in milk and next 4 ingredients until blended. Add bread cubes, stirring to coat; let stand 10 minutes or until most of liquid is absorbed.

3. Pour bread mixture into prepared dish. Sprinkle lightly with cinnamon, and, if desired, sprinkle with walnuts.

4. Bake at 350°F (180°C) for 40 to 45 minutes or until lightly browned and set in center. Cool in dish on a wire rack.

ORANGE-PINEAPPLE FREEZER PRESERVES

MAKES ABOUT 4 (½-PT./250 ML) JARS

Take a tropical twist with this chunky and quick no-cook preserve starring fresh oranges and crushed pineapple.

2½   cups (625 mL) chopped orange sections (about 6 medium oranges)

1½   cups (375 mL) sugar

2   Tbsp. (30 mL) lemon juice

1   (8-oz./250-g) can crushed pineapple in juice, undrained

4   Tbsp. (60 mL) Ball® Real-Fruit™ Instant Pectin

⭑

Perfect Pairing
For a wholesome breakfast treat, layer the preserves with plain yogurt and your favorite granola.

1. Stir together first 4 ingredients in a medium glass or nonmetallic bowl. Let stand 15 minutes.

2. Gradually stir in pectin; stir 3 minutes. Let stand 30 minutes.

3. Spoon into jars, leaving ½-inch (1-cm) headspace. Center lid on jars. Apply bands, and adjust loosely. Once preserves are frozen, adjust bands to fingertip-tight. Store in freezer up to 1 year. Thaw in refrigerator. Refrigerate after thawing, and use within 3 weeks

LIME-MINT FREEZER PICKLES

MAKES ABOUT 6 (½-PT./250-ML) JARS

Crunchy pickling cucumbers are marinated overnight with lime and sugar in this incredible, intensely flavored pickle.

2½ lb. (1.25 kg) 3- to 5-inch (7.6- to 13-cm) pickling cucumbers, thinly sliced

4 Tbsp. (60 mL) Ball® Salt for Pickling & Preserving

2 large limes

1½ cups (375 mL) sugar

1 cup (250 mL) chopped red bell pepper

¾ cup (175 mL) white vinegar (5% acidity)

½ cup (125 mL) thinly sliced small sweet onion (separated into rings)

¼ cup (60 mL) finely chopped fresh mint

2 garlic cloves, minced

1. Toss together sliced cucumber slices and salt in a large glass or nonmetallic bowl. Cover and let stand 3 hours; drain and return to bowl.

2. Zest limes and squeeze juice to measure 1 Tbsp. (15 mL) zest and ¼ cup (60 mL) juice, respectively.

3. Add lime zest, lime juice, sugar, and remaining ingredients to cucumber slices; stir well. Cover and chill 8 hours.

4. Drain cucumber mixture, reserving liquid. Pack cucumbers into jars, leaving 1-inch (2.5-cm) headspace. Pour reserved liquid over cucumber mixture, leaving ½-inch (1-cm) headspace. Center lid on jars. Apply bands, and adjust loosely. Once pickles are frozen, adjust bands to fingertip-tight. Store in freezer 6 months. Thaw in refrigerator. Refrigerate after thawing, and use within 3 weeks.

★

Simple Switch

For a Mexican twist, use chopped cilantro and minced garlic in place of mint.

PEPPERY TEXAS FREEZER PICKLES

MAKES ABOUT 7 (1/2-PT./250-ML) JARS

These quick and easy south-of-the-border pickles can be spicy hot or not, depending on the chiles you use.

2 lb. (1 kg) 3- to 5-inch (7.5- to 12.5-cm) pickling cucumbers, cut into 1/4-inch (.5-cm)-thick slices

1 large (9-oz./275-g) sweet onion, halved and thinly sliced

1 cup (250 mL) fresh cilantro, coarsely chopped

6 small dried red chile peppers, coarsely broken

4 garlic cloves, thinly sliced

3 cups (750 mL) white vinegar (5% acidity)

1 cup (250 mL) water

1/3 cup (75 mL) sugar

2 Tbsp. (30 mL) Ball® Salt for Pickling & Preserving

1 Tbsp. (15 mL) pickling spice

1. Place first 5 ingredients in a large glass or other nonmetallic bowl.

2. Combine vinegar and next 4 ingredients in a 2-qt. (2-L) glass measuring cup. Microwave at HIGH 3 minutes or until hot, stirring until sugar dissolves.

3. Pour hot mixture over cucumber mixture. Stir well; cover and chill 48 hours.

4. Drain cucumber mixture, reserving liquid. Pack cucumbers into jars, leaving 1/2-inch (1-cm) headspace. Pour liquid over cucumber mixture, leaving 1/2-inch (1-cm) headspace. Center lid on jars. Apply bands, and adjust loosely. Once pickles are frozen, adjust bands to fingertip-tight. Store in freezer 6 months. Thaw in refrigerator. Refrigerate after thawing, and use within 3 weeks.

SPICY TEXAS CHILI BASE

MAKES ABOUT 2 (1-PT./500-ML) JARS

Rich with a tantalizing mix of four different chiles, this spicy sauce base is a necessity for quick weeknight meals.

- 2 oz. (60 g) ancho chiles
- 1 oz. (30 g) guajillo chiles
- ½ oz. (15 g) chile de árbol
- 4 cups (1 L) boiling water
- 4 canned chipotle peppers in adobo sauce
- 2 cups (500 mL) finely chopped onion (about 2 onions)
- 2 Tbsp. (30 mL) vegetable oil
- 1 garlic clove, coarsely chopped
- 2 tsp. (10 mL) salt
- 1 tsp. (5 mL) ground cumin
- ½ tsp. (2 mL) ground coriander
- 1 bay leaf
- 1 cup (250 mL) beef broth
- 1 cup (250 mL) diced tomatoes, undrained

★

Perfect Pairing
Not only for chili fixings, jazz up stews, ladle over beef before roasting, or braise chicken with this incredible sauce.

---

1. Rinse any dirt from first 3 ingredients, and pat dry with a paper towel. Toast peppers on a very hot griddle, or in a skillet, 8 to 10 seconds on each side or just until beginning to puff and blister. (Do not allow peppers to burn or they will become bitter.) When cool enough to handle, remove and discard stems and seeds from chiles; tear into large pieces and place in a large bowl. Cover with boiling water. Let stand 30 minutes or until softened. Drain, reserving soaking liquid.

2. Process drained chiles and chipotle peppers in a food processor until very smooth, gradually adding reserved soaking liquid until mixture is the consistency of thick mayonnaise.

3. Sauté onion in hot oil in a 12-inch (30-cm) skillet over medium-high heat 7 to 10 minutes or until tender. Add garlic; sauté 30 seconds. Stir in salt and next 3 ingredients. Add broth, tomatoes, and pureed chiles. Bring to a simmer; cook 20 minutes or until slightly thickened, stirring occasionally. Remove from heat. Remove and discard bay leaf.

4. Spoon hot chile mixture into hot jars, leaving ½-inch (1-cm) headspace. Center lid on jars. Apply bands, and adjust loosely. Cool jars completely on a wire rack. Place jars in freezer. Once chili mixture is frozen, adjust bands to fingertip-tight. Store in freezer 6 months. Thaw in refrigerator. Refrigerate after thawing, and use within 3 weeks.

CHILI CON CARNE

MAKES 6 TO 8 SERVINGS

This hearty, thick beef-and-bean chili laced with enticing spices will be your new go-to recipe. Top with sour cream, shredded cheese, cilantro, and red onions.

2½ lb. (1.25 kg) beef chuck, ground for chili or cut into ½-inch (1-cm) cubes

3 Tbsp. (45 mL) vegetable oil

1 tsp. (5 mL) salt

½ tsp. (2 mL) freshly ground black pepper

1 (1-pt./500-mL) jar Spicy Texas Chili Base (page 326), thawed

½ cup (125 mL) water

1 (15-oz./470-g) can black beans, undrained (optional)

Garnishes: hot cooked brown or white rice, shredded Cheddar or Monterey Jack cheese, sliced onion, sour cream

1. Brown beef, in batches, in hot oil in a large skillet over medium-high heat, stirring often, 5 to 7 minutes or until meat crumbles and is no longer pink; transfer to a bowl using a slotted spoon. Drain excess fat from skillet. Return beef to skillet. Sprinkle with salt and pepper.

2. Add Spicy Texas Chili Base and water, stirring to loosen browned bits from bottom of skillet. Bring to a simmer over medium-low heat; cook, partially covered, 1 to 1½ hours or until beef is tender if using cubes (browned if using ground), stirring occasionally.

3. Add beans and simmer 15 more minutes, if desired. Serve with desired accompaniments.

LEMON CURD

MAKES 2 (½-PT./250-ML) JARS

Lemon curd is a most exquisite taste, buttery and intense with bright, sharp flavor. Keep a few jars on hand for impromptu desserts.

---

2   lb. (1 kg) lemons (about 6 lemons)

½   cup (125 mL) butter, softened

2   cups (500 mL) sugar

4   large eggs

★

Simple Switch
Swap limes for lemons to make Lime Curd.

---

1. Grate zest and squeeze juice from lemons to measure 2 Tbsp. (30 mL) and 1 cup (250 mL), respectively.

2. Beat butter and sugar at medium speed with an electric mixer until blended. Add eggs, 1 at a time, beating just until blended after each addition. Gradually add lemon juice to butter mixture, beating at low speed just until blended after each addition; stir in zest. (Mixture will look curdled.) Transfer to a heavy 4-qt. (4-L) stainless steel or enameled saucepan.

3. Cook over medium-low heat, whisking constantly, 14 to 16 minutes. Spoon into clean jars, leaving ½-inch (1-cm) headspace.

4. Place small pieces of heavy-duty plastic wrap directly on warm curd (to prevent a film from forming). Center lid on jars. Apply bands, and adjust loosely. Cool completely (about 1 hour).

5. Remove plastic wrap. Place jars in freezer. Once lemon curd is frozen, adjust bands to fingertip-tight. Store in freezer up to 1 year. Thaw in refrigerator. Refrigerate after thawing, and use within 3 weeks.

MINT-CILANTRO CHUTNEY

MAKES ABOUT 2 (¹/₂-PT./250-ML) JARS

Get your papadum or naan bread ready; this traditional Indian chutney is the perfect dipping sauce!

- 1 garlic clove, peeled
- 2 long green Asian chile peppers or cayenne peppers
- 2 cups (500 mL) loosely packed fresh mint leaves
- 2 cups (500 mL) loosely packed fresh cilantro leaves and tender stems
- ¼ cup (60 mL) bottled lemon juice
- 1 Tbsp. (15 mL) minced fresh ginger
- 1 tsp. (5 mL) salt
- 1 medium tomato, peeled, cored, and quartered

★

Tricks of the Trade

Make in bulk and freeze in ice trays. Once frozen, store the chutney cubes in a zip-top plastic freezer bag in the freezer for an ultimately convenient condiment.

---

1. With food processor running, drop garlic through food chute; process until minced.

2. Cut chiles into equal pieces, and add to garlic in food processor. Add mint leaves, next 4 ingredients, and 2 tomato quarters. Process until a smooth paste forms. (If paste is too thick, add remaining half of tomato, 1 quarter at a time, and process to desired consistency—do not add water.)

3. Use immediately, or spoon into jars, leaving 1-inch (2.5-cm) headspace. Center lid on jars. Apply bands, and adjust loosely. Place jars in freezer. Once chutney is frozen, adjust bands to fingertip-tight. Store in freezer up to 1 year. Thaw in refrigerator. Refrigerate after thawing, and use within 3 weeks.

CHIMICHURRI

MAKES ABOUT 4 (4-OZ./125-ML) JARS

Full of herbs and spices, this vinegary sauce hails from Argentina, known for its perfect grilled meats, and is an essential condiment on every table.

- 3 garlic cloves
- 4 cups (1 L) fresh parsley leaves
- 1 cup (250 mL) chopped fresh cilantro
- 1 cup (250 mL) olive oil
- ⅓ cup (75 mL) red wine vinegar
- 1 tsp. (5 mL) lemon zest
- ¼ cup (60 mL) fresh lemon juice (about 2 large lemons)
- ¾ tsp. (3 mL) salt
- ½ tsp. (2 mL) freshly ground black pepper

★

Perfect Pairing
Chimichurri can be used as a quick marinade for meats and fish, as well as a topping. For a vegetarian meal, top grilled or roasted vegetables, then serve over rice or couscous.

1. With processor running, drop garlic through food chute; process until minced. Add parsley and remaining ingredients; process until smooth.

2. Use immediately, or spoon into jars, leaving ½-inch (1-cm) headspace. Center lid on jars. Apply bands, and adjust loosely. Once sauce is frozen, adjust bands to fingertip-tight. Store in freezer 6 months. Thaw in refrigerator. Refrigerate after thawing, and use within 3 weeks.

GAUCHO-STYLE SKIRT STEAK WITH CHIMICHURRI

MAKES 4 SERVINGS

Get your grill going Argentinian style! This skirt steak is infused with complex flavors from our Chimichurri marinade and sauce.

- 1 cup (250 mL) Chimichurri (page 330), divided
- ¼ (60 mL) cup dry red wine
- 1 (1¼-lb./625-g) skirt steak, trimmed
- 2 red or yellow bell peppers, halved and seeded
- 1 large sweet onion, cut into ¾-inch (2-cm)-thick slices

Warm flour tortillas

Crumbled queso fresco

Guacamole

1. Preheat grill to 350°F/180°C (medium-high) heat. Stir together ½ cup (125 mL) Chimichurri and wine in a small bowl. Place steak and bell pepper halves in a large zip-top plastic freezer bag. Pour wine mixture into bag. Seal bag; carefully turn bag to coat steak and vegetables. Carefully add onion to bag, keeping slices intact. Seal bag; carefully turn bag to coat onion slices. Marinate in refrigerator at least 2 hours or overnight.

2. Remove bell pepper and onion from bag; place on grill rack, keeping onion slices intact. Grill, covered with grill lid, 8 minutes or until tender, turning often. Remove vegetables from grill; keep warm.

3. Remove steak from marinade, discarding marinade. Grill steak, covered with grill lid, 8 to 10 minutes on each side or to desired degree of doneness. Let stand 10 minutes.

4. While steak stands, cut bell pepper into strips, and separate onion into rings.

5. Cut steak diagonally across the grain into thin strips. Arrange steak and vegetables on a serving platter. Drizzle with remaining ½ cup (125 mL) Chimichurri. Serve immediately on tortillas with cheese and guacamole.

CHERMOULA

MAKES 1 (1-PT/500-ML) JAR

This spicy North African condiment of cilantro, parsley, lemon, and seasonings is a superb accompaniment to grilled meats, fish, and vegetables.

- 1½ cups (375 mL) packed fresh cilantro leaves and tender stems, coarsely chopped
- ½ cup (125 mL) packed fresh parsley leaves, coarsely chopped
- ½ tsp. (2 mL) lemon zest
- ¼ cup (60 mL) fresh lemon juice (about 2 large lemons)
- 2 tsp. (10 mL) paprika
- 1 tsp. (5 mL) ground cumin
- 1 tsp. (5 mL) salt
- ½ tsp. (2 mL) ground coriander
- ½ tsp. (2 mL) ground red pepper
- ¼ tsp. (1 mL) freshly ground black pepper
- ⅔ cup (150 mL) extra virgin olive oil

1. Process all ingredients, except olive oil, in a food processor until finely chopped. With processor on, gradually add olive oil until mixture forms a thick paste. Add additional salt and black pepper to taste, if desired.

2. Use immediately or spoon into jars, leaving ½-inch (1-cm) headspace. Center lid on jars. Apply bands, and adjust loosely. Once sauce is frozen, adjust bands to fingertip-tight. Store in freezer up to 1 year. Thaw in refrigerator. Refrigerate after thawing, and use within 3 weeks.

TUNA STEAKS WITH MOROCCAN SPICES AND CHERMOULA SAUCE

MAKES 4 SERVINGS

A dry rub of Moroccan spices adds flavor to grilled tuna steaks, which are then topped with our Chermoula sauce for a bright kick of flavor.

- 2 Tbsp. (30 mL) extra virgin olive oil
- 1 tsp. (5 mL) Moroccan Spice Mix
- 4 (6-oz./180-g) tuna fillets
- 1 cup (250 mL) Chermoula (page 332), divided

1. Preheat grill to medium-high (350° to 400°F/180° to 200°C) heat. Combine olive oil and Moroccan Spice Mix. Rub spice mixture over surface of tuna. Let stand 10 minutes.

2. Place tuna on grill rack. Grill, covered with grill lid, 2 to 3 minutes on each side or to desired degree of doneness. Place tuna on a serving platter; drizzle with 2 Tbsp. (30 mL) Chermoula sauce. Serve immediately with remaining sauce.

MOROCCAN SPICE MIX

MAKES ABOUT 4 TBSP. (60 ML)

- 1 Tbsp. (15 mL) ground coriander
- 1 Tbsp. (15 mL) ground Aleppo pepper
- 2 tsp. (10 mL) ground ginger
- 1½ tsp. (7.5 mL) salt
- 1 tsp. (5 mL) ground cardamom
- 1 tsp. (5 mL) ground turmeric

1. Combine all ingredients. Store in a small airtight container in a cool, dry place.

Chapter 5

DEHYDRATING

The art of drying food dates back thousands of years to a time when year-round fresh food was scarce and sun, wind, and salt were the natural means of food preservation. Today, we dehydrate food to create chewy, healthy snacks. Since dehydrating pulls up natural sugars and reserves much of food's nutrients as it removes moisture, we're able to enjoy the flavors of last summer's bumper crops well into cold weather. From fruit leather and jerky to camp-style soups and stews, the recipes included here offer creative ways to preserve fruits, vegetables, and meats for long-term storage and use as well as everyday snacking.

Preparing Fruit for Dehydration

Prepare fruits according to the guidelines in the following chart. Dry fruit in a dehydrator according to manufacturer's instructions. Store dehydrated fruits in Ball® canning jars, plastic storage containers, or vacuum packaging. Label and date.

FRUIT	SELECTION	PREPARATION	DRYING TEMPERATURE	DRYNESS INDICATOR	USAGE IDEAS
Apples	Choose firm, tart fruit.	Wash, peel, and core; cut into ¼-inch (.5-cm) slices or rings. Treat with Ball® Fruit-Fresh®.	130° to 135°F (54° to 57°C)	Pliable and leathery	Applesauce, snacks, baked goods, and recipes using cooked apples
Apricots	Choose firm, ripe fruit with deep-yellow to orange color.	Wash; halve and remove pits.	130° to 135°F (54° to 57°C)	Pliable with no moist pockets	Snacks, sauces, meat dishes, salads, and baked goods
Bananas	Choose large fruit with a few brown spots.	Peel; cut into ¼- to ½-inch (.5- to 1-cm) slices. Treat with Ball® Fruit-Fresh®.	130° to 135°F (54° to 57°C)	Pliable with crisp edges	Snacks, trail mix, baked goods, cereal.
Blueberries or Cranberries	Choose large, firm berries.	Wash and remove stems. Blanch for 30 seconds or until skins pop.	130° to 135°F (54° to 57°C)	Leathery	Baked goods
Cherries (Dark, sweet, or tart red)	Choose firm fruit with unblemished skin.	Wash; halve and remove pits.	165°F (74°C)	Leathery and slightly sticky	Snacks, baked goods, and savory sauces
Citrus peel	Choose firm oranges, lemons, or limes.	Wash well to remove wax, dirt, and pesticides. Cut thin strips of rind from fruit with vegetable peeler, avoiding white pith.	135°F (57°C)	Crisp	All-purpose seasoning
Coconut	Choose heavy fresh coconuts.	Crack outer shell with hammer; remove coconut flesh. Grate or cut into very thin slices.	135°F (57°C)	Crisp	Baked goods, candies, snacks, trail mix, cereal

Preparing Fruit for Dehydration

Prepare fruits according to the guidelines in the following chart. Dry fruit in a dehydrator according to manufacturer's instructions. Store dehydrated fruits in Ball® canning jars, plastic storage containers, or vacuum packaging. Label and date.

FRUIT	SELECTION	PREPARATION	DRYING TEMPERATURE	DRYNESS INDICATOR	USAGE IDEAS
Grapes	Choose firm seedless varieties.	Wash; remove stems. Blanch for 30 to 60 seconds or until skins pop.	130° to 135°F (54° to 57°C)	Pliable with no moist pockets	Snacks, baked goods
Nectarines	Choose firm, plump fruit with bright orange and red patches.	Wash; halve and remove pits. Cut into ¼- to ½-inch (.5- to 1-cm) slices. Treat with Ball® Fruit-Fresh®.	130° to 135°F (54° to 57°C)	Pliable with no moist pockets	Snacks, baked goods
Peaches (Clingstone or Freestone)	Choose firm fruit with unblemished skin.	Peel and remove pits. Cut into ½-inch (.5-cm) slices. Treat with Ball® Fruit-Fresh®.	130° to 135°F (54° to 57°C)	Pliable with no moist pockets	Snacks, baked goods
Pears	Choose firm, ripe fruit.	Wash, peel, and core. Cut into ½-inch (1-cm) slices or rings. Pretreat with Ball® Fruit-Fresh.	130° to 135°F (54° to 57°C)	Leathery with no moist pockets	Snacks, baked goods
Pineapples	Choose firm, ripe fruit with golden peel.	Wash, peel, and core; cut into ½-inch (1-cm) slices.	130° to 135°F (54° to 57°C)	Leathery, but not sticky	Granola, snacks, baked goods
Plums	Choose firm, ripe fruit.	Wash; halve and remove pits.	130° to 135°F (54° to 57°C)	Pliable with no moist pockets	Snacks, baked goods
Prune Plums	Choose firm, ripe fruit.	Wash; halve and remove pits.	130° to 135°F (54° to 57°C)	Pliable with no moist pockets	Baked goods, stuffing, snacks, and salads
Strawberries	Choose ripe, red fruit with no blemishes.	Wash; remove hulls. Halve or cut into ½-inch (1-cm) slices.	130° to 135°F (54° to 57°C)	Pliable to almost crisp	Snacks, baked goods, salads, and cereals

Preparing Veggies for Dehydration

Blanching is a crucial step in preparing vegetables for successful dehydration. The guidelines in the following chart will ensure that your produce is preserved safely. Store dehydrated vegetables in Ball® canning jars, plastic storage containers, or vacuum packaging. Label and date.

VEGETABLE	SELECTION	PREPARATION	STEAM TIME (MINUTES)	DRYING TEMP.	DRYNESS INDICATOR	USAGE IDEAS
Asparagus	Choose tender, thin spears with tightly formed heads.	Trim off woody portion of spears. Cut into 1-inch (2.5-cm) pieces.	3 to 4	125°F (52°C)	Brittle	Soups, stews, casseroles
Beans (Green or Yellow Wax)	Choose firm, tender beans.	Trim ends, and cut beans diagonally into 1-inch (2.5-cm) pieces.	4 to 6	125°F (52°C)	Brittle	Soups, stews, casseroles
Beets (Whole)	Choose deep-colored beets with smooth skin.	Wash. Peel and trim off stems and root ends. Cut into ¼-inch (.5-cm) slices.	30	125°F (52°C)	Leathery	Soups
Broccoli	Choose young stalks with thin skins and firm heads.	Wash. Peel, trim, and quarter stalks to no more than ½-inch (1-cm) thickness.	6 to 8	125°F (52°C)	Brittle	Soups, stews, casseroles, and recipes using cooked broccoli
Carrots	Choose young, tender medium-length carrots.	Peel; shred or cut into ¼-inch (.5-cm) slices.	3 to 4 (shreds) 4 to 6 (slices)	125°F (52°C)	Brittle and tough	Soups, stews, casseroles, and recipes using cooked carrots
Cauliflower	Choose clean, white, firm heads.	Wash. Cut into ¼-inch (.5-cm) slices.	4 to 6	125°F (52°C)	Brittle	Soups, stews, casseroles, and recipes using cooked cauliflower
Celery	Choose green, crisp ribs.	Wash. Trim and cut into ¼-inch (.5-cm) slices.	4 to 6	125°F (52°C)	Crisp and hard	Soups, stews, casseroles, and recipes using cooked celery
Corn	Choose very fresh ears with tender, juicy kernels.	Remove husks and silk. Steam cobs; cut kernels from cob after steaming.	5 to 8	125°F (52°C)	Hard	Soups, stews, casseroles, and recipes using cooked corn

Preparing Veggies for Dehydration

Blanching is a crucial step in preparing vegetables for successful dehydration. The guidelines in the following chart will ensure that your produce is preserved safely. Store dehydrated vegetables in Ball® canning jars, plastic storage containers, or vacuum packaging. Label and date.

VEGETABLE	SELECTION	PREPARATION	STEAM TIME (MINUTES)	DRYING TEMP.	DRYNESS INDICATOR	USAGE IDEAS
Eggplant	Choose small, firm eggplants with deep color.	Wash. Trim and cut into ¼-inch (.5-cm) slices.	4 to 5	125°F (52°C)	Brittle	Casseroles, sauces, and recipes using cooked eggplant
Greens (Kale, Chard, Spinach, Beet, etc.)	Choose young, tender leaves.	Wash; drain and spin dry. Remove stems.	3 to 5	125°F (52°C)	Brittle	Soups, stews, casseroles, and creamed dishes
Herbs	Choose fresh, tender leaves and stems.	Wash; drain and spin dry.	None	125°F (52°C)	Brittle	All-purpose seasoning
Mushrooms	Choose small mushrooms with tightly closed caps.	Wash; remove stems, and cut into ¼-inch (.5-cm) slices.	4 to 6	125°F (52°C)	Brittle	Recipes using cooked mushrooms
Okra	Choose firm, unblemished pods.	Wash. Trim ends, and cut into ¼-inch (.5-cm) slices.	4 to 6	125°F (52°C)	Leathery	Stews and soups
Onions	Choose firm onions.	Peel; dice or cut into ¼-inch (.5-cm) slices.	None	125°F (52°C)	Crisp	Recipes using onions, or as seasoning
Peas	Choose plump, medium-size peas.	Shell peas. Wash and drain well.	3	125°F (52°C)	Brittle	Soups, stews, and any recipe using peas
Peppers (Hot)	Choose firm, unblemished peppers.	Wash. Cut into ¼-inch (.5-cm) slices.	None	125°F (52°C)	Brittle	As seasoning

Preparing Veggies for Dehydration

Blanching is a crucial step in preparing vegetables for successful dehydration. The guidelines in the following chart will ensure that your produce is preserved safely. Store dehydrated vegetables in Ball® canning jars, plastic storage containers, or vacuum packaging. Label and date.

VEGETABLE	SELECTION	PREPARATION	STEAM TIME (MINUTES)	DRYING TEMP.	DRYNESS INDICATOR	USAGE IDEAS
Peppers (Bell)	Choose firm, crisp, unblemished peppers.	Wash. Halve and remove seeds and stems. Cut into ¼-inch (.5-cm)-wide strips.	None	125°F (52°C)	Brittle	Recipes using cooked peppers
Popcorn	Choose full ears with well-formed kernels.	Leave kernels on cob until dry. Shell corn from cobs.	None	130°F (54°C)	Shriveled; pop when heated	Snacks
Potatoes (Sweet)	Choose firm potatoes with deep-orange flesh.	Wash; peel, dice, or cut into ¼-inch (.5-cm) slices.	3	125°F (52°C)	Brittle	Pies, breads, casseroles
Potatoes (White)	Choose firm potatoes of any variety.	Wash; peel, dice, or cut into ¼-inch (.5-cm) slices. Rinse to remove starch after steaming.	5 to 6	125°F (52°C)	Crisp	Soups, casseroles, and recipes using potatoes
Pumpkin or Winter Squash	Choose firm, fully mature vegetables with hard rinds.	Wash; peel, remove seeds and membranes. Cut into thin strips. Steam until tender.	2 to 3	125°F (52°C)	Brittle	Pies, casseroles, breads, pastries, pasta
Summer Squash (Zucchini, Yellow, or Pattypan)	Choose young squash with tender, unblemished skin.	Wash; grate, or cut into ¼-inch (.5-cm) slices.	None	125°F (52°C)	Hard and brittle	Soups, casseroles, and recipes using summer squash
Tomatoes	Choose paste-type varieties.	Wash; peel, if desired. Cut into ¼-inch (.5-cm) slices.	None	125°F (52°C)	Crisp	Sauces, paste, ketchup, and recipes using tomatoes
Turnips	Choose firm, unblemished turnips.	Wash; remove tops, and peel. Cut into ¼- to ½-inch (.5- to 1-cm) slices.	3 to 5	125°F (52°C)	Brittle	Soups, casseroles, and snack chips

SMOKY CORN CHOWDER

MAKES 4 SERVINGS

Bacon and wine add depth of flavor and smokiness. Welcome to the fancy side of the campground.

- ⅓ cup (75 mL) diced Smoked Maple-Juniper Bacon (page 352)
- 1½ cups (375 mL) dried corn
- 1 cup (250 mL) dried potatoes
- ¼ cup (60 mL) dried onions
- ¼ cup (60 mL) dried celery
- ¼ cup (60 mL) dried carrot
- 1 tsp. (5 mL) garlic powder
- 1 tsp. (5 mL) dried parsley
- 1½ tsp. (2 mL) salt
- ½ tsp. (2 mL) ground black pepper
- 1 bay leaf
- 8 cups (2 L) chicken broth, vegetable broth, or water
- ½ cup (125 mL) white wine or beer

1. Cook bacon in a 4-qt. (4-L) stainless steel or enameled saucepan over medium-high heat until crisp; remove bacon, and drain on paper towels, reserving 2 Tbsp. (30 mL) drippings in pan.

2. Add corn and next 9 ingredients, stirring until vegetables are coated with bacon drippings. Stir in broth and wine. Bring to a boil; cover, reduce heat, and simmer 45 minutes or until vegetables are very tender. Remove from heat and cool slightly. Remove and discard bay leaf.

3. Process chowder, in batches, in a blender until smooth. Stir in bacon. Return chowder to saucepan. Bring to a simmer; cook 1 to 2 minutes or until thoroughly heated.

★

Simple Switch

Use ½ cup diced Tasso "Ham" (page 355) in place of bacon for a super spicy kick.

VEGETABLE CURRY STEW

MAKES 2 SERVINGS

Another quick meal made out of dehydrated, fresh, local vegetables, turning this into a thick-and-chunky curry. Adding coconut milk at the end gives the perfect finishing touch. If you like curry more intensely flavored, up the quantity to 1 Tbsp. (15 mL). Increasing the coconut milk at the end will give you a thinner stew, great for serving over rice.

- 4 cups (1 L) water or vegetable broth
- ¾ cup (175 mL) dehydrated cauliflower pieces
- ½ cup (125 mL) dehydrated sliced okra
- ⅓ cup (75 mL) dehydrated carrot slices or cubes
- ⅓ cup (75 mL) dehydrated chopped onion
- ⅓ cup (75 mL) dehydrated zucchini slices or cubes
- ¼ cup (60 mL) dehydrated tomato slices
- 2 Tbsp. (30 mL) dried sweet peas
- 1 tsp. (5 mL) salt
- 1 tsp. (5 mL) curry powder
- ½ tsp. (2 mL) dried minced garlic
- ½ cup (125 mL) coconut milk

1. Bring all ingredients, except coconut milk, to a boil in a 4-qt. (4-L) stainless steel or enameled saucepan. Cover, reduce heat, and simmer 45 minutes or until vegetables are completely hydrated and very tender.

2. Stir in coconut milk. Cook 1 to 2 minutes or until thoroughly heated.

HOMEMADE JERKY

MAKES ABOUT ½ LB.

You can make jerky from a variety of red meats, poultry, or game. It can easily be made safely in a dehydrator or your home oven. Drying times will depend on the thickness of strips and the initial moisture content of meat, but typical drying times are between five to seven hours.

JERKY

3 lb. (1.5 kg) lean red meat (such as flank or round steak, trimmed) or poultry breasts partially frozen

MAPLE TERIYAKI MARINADE
(USE FOR RED MEAT)

½ cup (125 mL) pineapple juice

¼ cup (60 mL) lite soy sauce

¼ cup (60 mL) maple syrup

2 Tbsp. (30 mL) grated fresh ginger

1 tsp. (5 mL) dried crushed red pepper

1 tsp. (5 mL) black pepper

1 tsp. (5 mL) salt

¼ tsp. (1 mL) ground cinnamon

4 garlic cloves, minced

MEXICAN CHIPOTLE MARINADE
(USE FOR RED MEAT OR POULTRY)

¼ cup (60 mL) toasted cumin seeds

3 chipotles in adobo sauce

4 garlic cloves, minced

2 tsp. (10 mL) kosher salt

½ cup (124 mL) lime juice

⅓ cup (75 mL) firmly packed dark brown sugar

1. Prepare Jerky: Cut meat or poultry across the grain into ⅛- to ¼-inch (3-mm- to .5-cm)-thick slices.

2. Prepare desired marinade: Process all ingredients in a blender until smooth. Pour marinade into a large shallow dish. Add desired meat or poultry slices, turning to coat. Cover and chill red meat up to 48 hours or poultry up to 24 hours. Drain well, discarding marinade.

3. Dry meat or poultry slices in a dehydrator according to manufacturer's directions, or preheat oven to lowest temperature (165° to 180°F/75° to 90°C).

4. Place marinated meat or poultry in a single layer on wire racks set in rimmed baking sheets. Place in oven with door partially open. Dry at (165° to 180°F/75° to 90°C) for 5 to 7 hours or until jerky is dry, but still pliable, with no visible moisture, alternating baking sheets on oven racks several times for even drying. Cool completely.

5. Store jerky in an airtight container or zip-top plastic freezer bag in refrigerator up to 1 month or in freezer up to 6 months.

FRUIT LEATHER »

MAKES ABOUT 4 (10- X 8-INCH/25- X 20-CM) SHEETS

Fresh fruit pureed and sweetened, then dried, makes a quick, portable treat to have on hand. These go-to, take-along wraps are handy for lunchboxes, as snacks after school, and as a pick-me-up at the office.

1 lb. (450 g) ripe fruit (such as strawberries, blueberries, peeled and pitted peaches, pitted plums, or peeled and cored pineapple), cut into uniform chunks

2 to 4 Tbsp. (30 mL to 60 mL) honey, agave syrup, or maple syrup

1 tsp. (5 mL) lemon juice

1 to 3 Tbsp. (15 mL to 45 mL) water

Parchment paper

1. Process fruit, sweetener, and lemon juice in a food processor or blender until pureed, adding water, 1 Tbsp. at a time, until mixture measures 2 cups.

2. Line dehydrator trays or mats with heavy-duty plastic wrap. Spread fruit puree into a ⅛-inch (3-mm)-thick layer with ¼-inch (.5-cm)-thick edges. (Edges will dry more quickly than center.) Dry according to manufacturer's instructions at 135°F (57°C) for 2 to 5 hours or until leather is soft and pliable, but will not stick to fingers. Cool.

3. Carefully peel fruit leather from plastic wrap; place on parchment paper. Roll up paper and leather together, and cut into strips. Store rolls, at room temperature, in an airtight container up to 2 months.

PINA COLADA FRUIT LEATHER

Soft ripe fruit to slightly overripe fruit is just fine for making fruit leather. Frozen fruit works well too, so if you have a bumper crop, go ahead and freeze what you have on hand for leather all year long.

3 cups (750 mL) cubed pineapple (fresh, canned, or frozen, thawed)

1 cup (250 mL) sweetened flaked coconut, lightly toasted

1 Tbsp. (15 mL) agave syrup or honey

1 Tbsp. (15 mL) coconut milk

1. Process all ingredients in a blender or food processor until pureed, adding water, if necessary, to measure 2 cups. Proceed with Fruit Leather recipe as directed.

Chapter 6

CURING AND SMOKING

If you've ever swooned over a house-cured and smoked bacon and wished you could make it yourself, this chapter is for you. Preserving meat and fish by curing and smoking is a technique as old as dehydrating, and it's fairly easy once you've gathered the right supplies and equipment. Cured Gravlax and Canadian Bacon, for example, are easily within even a beginner's culinary reach and are actually the best recipes to try first. Such delicacies as Smoked Maple-Juniper Bacon and Tasso "Ham" can be smoked or simply finished in a low oven. Generally, the spices and herbs you use can be pretty flexible, according to your tastes; however, the salts and sugars are not as they add to the overall cure of the meats and fish. Learning the fine craft of curing and smoking will reward you with a tremendously gratifying DIY knowledge, along with some truly fine eating.

STEP-BY-STEP CURING AND SMOKING

Getting started: Read through recipe before beginning. Wash a food-grade plastic container large enough to hold the meat for curing; set aside. Measure all cure ingredients into a small bowl and combine thoroughly. Start with a large workspace, free of clutter. This will eliminate the off-chance of liquid from meat splattering and make cleanup easier. Finish by smoking it or follow our oven directions.*

YOU WILL NEED:

- Tested recipe from chapter on Curing and Smoking

- Large food-grade plastic container or extra-large resealable plastic bags

- Large cooling rack and baking sheet

- Paper towels

- Sharp knife

- Smoker* (See instructions at right for oven finishing if you do not have a smoker.)

- Freezer bags for storage

STEP 1: Rub the trimmed pork belly completely with seasoning cure.

STEP 2: Place the belly skin side down in a large container that allows the meat to lay flat (or into doubled resealable plastic bags); scoop any remaining cure over the meat, rubbing it in.

350 CANNING AND PRESERVING

STEP 3: Flip the pork belly once a day, for 7 days, rubbing the cure in each time.

STEP 4: Keep the bacon submerged in the brine. The bacon will begin to release liquid as the salts draw moisture from the meat.

STEP 5: Remove the belly from the brine and rinse completely under cold water after 7 days.

STEP 6: Dry the bacon with paper towels, then place fat side down on a rack set over a baking sheet. Let it air-dry uncovered in the refrigerator overnight.

STEP 7: Smoke the belly meat side down at 180° to 200°F (356° to 392°C), allowing the fat to drip down and flavor the meat. The bacon is finished when internal temperature is 145°F (63°C), usually 2 to 3 hours.*

STEP 8: Slice off the skin, leaving the fat layer attached to the bacon once fully smoked. Let the bacon cool, then cut it into usable sections. Store in zip-top plastic freezer bags in the freezer for up to 6 months.

*If you don't have access to a wood smoker you can still cure and finish recipes using your oven. While this method will not add that wonderful smoked flavor, it will release some of the fat off the meat and raise the internal temperature for safe storage. Preheat oven to 200°F (392°C). Place meat fat side up on cooking rack set into a baking sheet. Place in center of oven. Slow-roast until internal temperature reaches 145°F (63°C). Let cool completely before storing.

SMOKED MAPLE-JUNIPER BACON

MAKES ABOUT 3½ LB. (1.75 KG)

Pork belly, with its sliver of a fat cap anchoring ribbons of silky white fat and pretty pink meat, is prized for its texture and taste. If this sounds familiar, it should. Pork belly is uncured bacon, and today it's a darling among pork fans. This DIY version brings home the flavor.

- ¾ cup (175 mL) dark maple syrup
- ½ cup (125 mL) kosher salt
- ½ cup (125 mL) firmly packed dark brown sugar
- 2 Tbsp. (30 mL) juniper berries, crushed
- 1 Tbsp. (15 mL) freshly ground black pepper
- 1½ tsp. (7 mL) pink curing salt
- 1 (5-lb./2.25-kg) pork belly, skin on

1. Combine all ingredients, except pork belly, in a bowl. Rub meat and fat surfaces of pork belly with syrup mixture. Place pork belly, skin side down, in a large food-grade plastic container. Cover with lid. Let cure for 7 days in refrigerator, rubbing syrup mixture over entire surface and turning pork belly over twice each day.

2. Thoroughly rinse pork belly under cold running water. Pat dry with several layers of paper towels. Place on a rack set in a shallow roasting pan. Chill, uncovered, overnight.

3. Smoke in a smoker according to manufacturer's instructions 2 to 3 hours or until a meat thermometer inserted in center registers 150°F (66°C). Let bacon stand until cool enough to handle. Using a sharp knife, trim skin from bacon, leaving fat layer on bacon and reserving skin for another use.

4. Cut bacon into desired portions. Wrap bacon tightly in plastic wrap and place in zip-top plastic freezer bags. Store in freezer for 4 to 6 months.

BROWN SUGAR–CURED CANADIAN BACON

MAKES ABOUT 3 LB. (1.5 KG)

Everyone will think you're a kitchen magician with this simple pork roast that's transformed into delicious lean bacon. Soaked in a brown sugar-salt brine, it's versatile enough to serve for breakfast, on sandwiches, or in soups and salads. Be sure to use a lean pork loin roast with minimal fat for best results.

- 1 (3- to 4-lb./1.5- to 2-kg) boneless center-cut pork loin roast
- 3 qt. (3 L) water
- 1½ cups (375 mL) firmly packed dark brown sugar
- ¾ cup (175 mL) kosher salt
- ¼ cup (60 mL) dried sage leaves, crumbled
- 2 Tbsp. (30 mL) dried thyme
- 3½ tsp. (18 mL) pink curing salt
- 1 Tbsp. (15 mL) dried crushed red pepper
- 1 Tbsp. (15 mL) garlic powder

1. Trim excess fat from pork. Combine water and next 7 ingredients in a large food-grade plastic container with a tight-fitting lid, stirring to dissolve salts and sugar. Add pork; cover tightly with lid. Chill 72 hours, turning twice each day.

2. Remove pork from brine, discarding brine. Pat dry with paper towels. Place pork on a rack set in a roasting pan. Chill, uncovered, 8 hours.

3. Smoke in a smoker according to manufacturer's instructions 2 to 3 hours or until a meat thermometer inserted in center registers 145°F (63°C). Cool completely. Wrap bacon tightly in plastic wrap and place in zip-top plastic freezer bags. Store in refrigerator up to 3 weeks, or freeze for 4 to 6 months. Thaw in refrigerator and cut into thin slices just before serving. If desired, bacon may be sliced and vacuum sealed before storing in refrigerator or freezer.

TASSO "HAM"

MAKES ABOUT 4½ LB. (2 KG)

Tasso is a spicy Cajun smoked ham traditionally used in recipes such as gumbo and jambalaya and works well in most recipes calling for ham or bacon. It's often made of the fatty muscular parts of the hog so it's not technically "ham." Seasonings in this recipe are based on a 5 lb. pork shoulder. If using a smaller cut, reduce the salt cure and seasonings.

---

1 (5-lb./2.25-kg) boneless pork shoulder roast (Boston butt)

2 cups (500 mL) kosher salt

½ cup (125 mL) firmly packed light brown sugar

¼ cup (60 mL) ground red pepper

3 Tbsp. (45 mL) smoked paprika

3 Tbsp. (45 mL) garlic powder

3 Tbsp. (45 mL) freshly ground black pepper

1 Tbsp. (15 mL) ground cumin

1. Trim excess fat from pork. Cut pork across the grain into 5 (1-lb./450-g) pieces. Combine salt and brown sugar; rub over surface of pork pieces. Place each piece in a large zip-top plastic freezer bag; seal bags. Place bags on a baking pan, and chill 6 hours.

2. Rinse pork under cool running water, and pat dry with paper towels. Place pork on a rack set in a roasting pan; let stand at room temperature 1 hour.

3. Prepare smoker according to manufacturer's instructions. Combine red pepper and remaining ingredients. Rub seasoning mixture over surface of pork pieces. Smoke pork 1 hour to 1 hour and 30 minutes or until a meat thermometer inserted in center registers 150°F (66°C). Cool completely.

4. Wrap pork in plastic wrap, and place in a large zip-top plastic freezer bag. Seal bag, and store in refrigerator up to 3 weeks or in freezer up to 6 months. Thaw in refrigerator before using.

PANCETTA

MAKES ABOUT 5 LB. (2.25 KG)

Pancetta is an Italian pork belly cured, like fresh bacon, but instead of being smoked, it is seasoned and rolled into a log that is secured and hung to dry for several weeks. Once cured it can then be used like bacon, but it has a very different and complex flavor.

- 2 Tbsp. (30 mL) juniper berries, crushed
- 4 bay leaves, crushed
- ¼ cup (60 mL) firmly packed dark brown sugar
- 3 Tbsp. (45 mL) kosher salt
- 2 Tbsp. (30 mL) pink curing salt
- 2 tsp. (10 mL) garlic powder
- 2 tsp. (10 mL) dried thyme
- 1 tsp. (5 mL) ground nutmeg
- 1 tsp. (5 mL) dried crushed red pepper
- ¼ cup (60 mL) freshly ground black pepper, divided
- 5 lb. pork belly, skin removed and edges trimmed

Kitchen string

Cheesecloth

1. Crush juniper berries and bay leaves with a mortar and pestle; pour into a bowl. Add brown sugar, next 6 ingredients, and 2 Tbsp. (30 mL) black pepper; stir well. Rub mixture over all sides of pork.

2. Place pork, laying flat, in a shallow dish or large zip-top plastic freezer bag; cover or seal and chill 5 to 7 days or until thickest portion is firm, turning and rubbing spices over surface once each day.

3. Rinse pork under cold water; pat dry with paper towels. Place on a wire rack, and let stand, uncovered, until dry.

4. Beginning with 1 long side, tightly roll up pork, jelly-roll fashion, so that there are no air pockets (to prevent mold growth). Tie tightly with butcher's knots using kitchen string. Leave a length of string to create a loop for hanging. Rub remaining 2 Tbsp. (30 mL) pepper over surface of pork. Wrap pork in cheesecloth; secure with string. Hang pork in a humid, food-safe (45° to 60°F/7° to 15°C) place for 1 to 2 weeks or until firm, but slightly supple, checking daily. (If pancetta begins to harden, remove cheesecloth; wrap in plastic wrap and store in refrigerator.)

5. Cut cured pancetta into desired portions. Wrap pancetta tightly in plastic wrap and place in zip-top plastic freezer bags. Store in refrigerator for 2 to 3 weeks or in freezer for 4 to 6 months.

COLD-CURED SALMON

MAKES ABOUT ¾ LB. (350 G)

Gravlax is a Scandinavian name for salt-cured salmon, which is not cooked.

1 (1-lb./450-g) salmon fillet, skin on, about 1-inch (2.5-cm)-thick

¼ cup (60 mL) kosher salt

¼ cup (60 mL) honey

3 Tbsp. (45 ml) gin or vodka

1 tsp. (5 mL) freshly ground black pepper

1. Remove pin bones from salmon; rinse and pat dry with several layers of paper towels. Place salmon on a large piece of plastic wrap.

2. Combine salt and next 3 ingredients in a small bowl, stirring until a paste forms. Rub paste over entire surface of salmon. Wrap salmon in plastic wrap, and place, skin side down, between 2 flat plates. Weight the top with a heavy can. Chill 72 hours or until fish is firm.

3. Unwrap fish; rinse well under cool running water. Pat dry with paper towels. Re-wrap tightly in plastic wrap. Store in refrigerator up to 3 weeks. To serve, cut across the grain into thin slices.

TO SMOKE CURED SALMON: Allow to cure for 2 to 3 days or until fish is firm. Unwrap fish, and place, skin side down, on a rack set in a rimmed baking sheet or roasting pan. Chill 12 hours or until a pellicle (a shiny, shellac-like protein coating necessary to attract smoke without drying out fish) forms. If a pellicle has not formed, chill, uncovered, 12 more hours or until the coating has formed. Smoke salmon in a smoker according to manufacturer's instructions until a meat thermometer inserted in center registers 130°F (55°C). Cool completely. Wrap salmon well in plastic wrap, and store in refrigerator up to 3 weeks.

Home Canning Planning Guide

Seasonal availability is dependent upon growing conditions and location within a region. The actual weight or quantity of produce needed to yield one quart jar is an approximate amount and may vary based on size of produce, recipe preparation, and cooking method.

VEGETABLES	NORTHERN REGION	CENTRAL REGION	SOUTHERN REGION	PURCHASE WEIGHT	UNITS PER POUND	POUNDS PER QUART	PREPARATION	PREPARED YIELD
ASPARAGUS	May–June	April–June	Feb.–May	1 lb	16–20 medium	3–3½	tough ends removed, sliced	3 cups
BEANS, GREEN	July–Sept.	July–Oct.	year-round	1 lb	6 cups	1½–2½	tips removed, sliced	3 cups
BEANS, LIMA	Aug.–Sept.	June–Oct.	year-round	1 lb	3–4 cups	3–5	tips removed, sliced	3 cups
BEETS	July–Nov.	May–Nov.	April–Nov.	1 lb	5–6 medium	2–3½	peeled, diced	2 cups
CABBAGE	July–Nov.	June–Nov.	Jan.–April	1 lb	⅓ head	2½–3	shredded	4–6 cups
CARROTS	July–Nov.	May–Nov.	year-round	1 lb	5–6 medium	2–3	sliced	3 cups
CORN, SWEET	July–Sept.	June–Oct.	April–Nov.	1 lb	2–3 medium ears	3–6	kernels cut from ear	½ cup
CUCUMBERS, PICKLING	July–Sept.	July–Oct.	March–Nov.	1 lb	6–7 medium	1½–2	sliced	3⅓ cups
OKRA	June–Sept.	June–Oct.	May–Oct.	1 lb	50 small	1½–3	x	x
ONIONS	year-round	year-round	year-round	1 lb	3 medium	1½–2	chopped	2½ cups
PEAS, GREEN	June–Sept.	May–Aug.	April–May	1 lb	in shell	2–2¼	shelled	1 cup
PEPPERS, BELL	July–Sept.	July–Oct.	May–Dec.	1 lb	2–3 large	1 lb per pint jar	chopped	1¼ cups
PEPPERS, CHILI	July–Sept.	July–Oct.	May–Dec.	1 lb	15 medium	1 lb per pint jar	x	x
POTATOES, SWEET	Aug.–Nov.	Sept–Oct.	July–Nov.	1 lb	3 medium	2–3	diced	2¼ cups
POTATOES, WHITE	June–Dec.	June–Dec.	year-round	1 lb	3 medium	2	diced	2¼ cups
SQUASH, SUMMER	June–Sept.	June–Oct.	Feb.–Oct.	1 lb	3 medium	2	x	x

FRUITS	NORTHERN REGION	CENTRAL REGION	SOUTHERN REGION	PURCHASE WEIGHT	UNITS PER POUND	POUNDS PER QUART	PREPARATION	PREPARED YIELD
APPLES	June–Dec.	June–Nov.	May–Nov.	1 lb	3–4 medium	2½–3	peeled, cored, sliced	3 cups
APRICOTS	July–Sept.	June–Aug.	May–Aug.	1 lb	8–12 medium	2–2½	pitted, sliced	2–3 cups
BERRIES	July–Oct.	June–Oct.	May–Oct.	6-oz container	3 containers	1½–3	x	x
BLUEBERRIES	July–Aug.	June–July	May–July	6-oz container	3 containers	1½–3	whole	2⅔ cups
CHERRIES	June–Aug.	May–Aug.	May–Aug.	1 lb	3 cups	2–2½	stemmed	3 cups (not pitted) 2 cups (pitted)
FIGS	Market availability	Market availability	June–Oct.	1 lb	12–14 small	2½	stemmed, chopped	2½ cups
GRAPES	Sept.–Oct.	July–Oct.	June–Nov.	1 lb	3 cups	2	stemmed	2½–3 cups
KIWIFRUITS	Market availability	Market availability	Market availability	1 lb	5–6 medium	For jam	x	x
MELONS	Aug.–Oct.	June–Aug.	June–July	3 lb	½ medium	1½–3	peeled, seeded, cubed	6–7 cups
NECTARINES	Market availability	Market availability	April–Oct.	1 lb	3 medium	2–2½	pitted, sliced	2½ cups
PEACHES	July–Sept.	June–Oct.	April–Sept.	1 lb	3–4 medium	2–3	peeled, pitted, sliced	2¼ cups
PEARS	Aug.–Oct.	Aug.–Oct.	April–Nov.	1 lb	3 medium	2–3	peeled, cored, sliced	2¼ cups
PLUMS	Aug.–Oct.	July–Sept.	May–Aug.	1 lb	8–10 medium	1½–2½	pitted, sliced	⅓ cup
RASPBERRIES	Sept.–Nov.	June–Sept.	May–July	6-oz container	3 containers	1½–3	whole	4 cups
RHUBARB	April–July	April–July	April–July	1 lb	4–8 stalks	1½–2	sliced into 1-inch pieces	3 cups
STRAWBERRIES	June–Aug.	May–Sept.	Jan.–Oct.	1 lb	3 cups	2½–3	whole, stemmed	2⅔ cups
TOMATOES	July–Oct.	May–Oct.	Jan.–Dec.	1 lb	3–4 medium	2½–3½	chopped	2 cups

Metric Equivalents

The information in the following charts is provided to help cooks outside the United States successfully use the recipes in this book. All equivalents are approximate.

COOKING/OVEN TEMPERATURES

	Fahrenheit	Celsius	Gas Mark
Freeze Water	32° F	0° C	
Room Temp.	68° F	20° C	
Boil Water	212° F	100° C	
Bake	325° F	160° C	3
	350° F	180° C	4
	375° F	190° C	5
	400° F	200° C	6
	425° F	220° C	7
	450° F	230° C	8
Broil			Grill

LIQUID INGREDIENTS BY VOLUME

¼ tsp	=					1 ml
½ tsp	=					2 ml
1 tsp	=					5 ml
3 tsp	=	1 Tbsp	=	½ fl oz	=	15 ml
2 Tbsp	=	⅛ cup	=	1 fl oz	=	30 ml
4 Tbsp	=	¼ cup	=	2 fl oz	=	60 ml
5⅓ Tbsp	=	⅓ cup	=	3 fl oz	=	80 ml
8 Tbsp	=	½ cup	=	4 fl oz	=	120 ml
10⅔ Tbsp	=	⅔ cup	=	5 fl oz	=	160 ml
12 Tbsp	=	¾ cup	=	6 fl oz	=	180 ml
16 Tbsp	=	1 cup	=	8 fl oz	=	240 ml
1 pt	=	2 cups	=	16 fl oz	=	480 ml
1 qt	=	4 cups	=	32 fl oz	=	960 ml
				33 fl oz	=	1000 ml = 1l

DRY INGREDIENTS BY WEIGHT

(To convert ounces to grams, multiply the number of ounces by 30.)

1 oz	=	¹⁄₁₆ lb	=	30 g
4 oz	=	¼ lb	=	120 g
8 oz	=	½ lb	=	240 g
12 oz	=	¾ lb	=	360 g
16 oz	=	1 lb	=	480 g

LENGTH

(To convert inches to centimeters, multiply the number of inches by 2.5.)

1 in	=					2.5 cm
6 in	=	½ ft	=			15 cm
12 in	=	1 ft	=			30 cm
36 in	=	3 ft	=	1 yd	=	90 cm
40 in	=					100 cm = 1 m

EQUIVALENTS FOR DIFFERENT TYPES OF INGREDIENTS

Standard Cup	Fine Powder (ex. flour)	Grain (ex. rice)	Granular (ex. sugar)	Liquid Solids (ex. butter)	Liquid (ex. milk)
1	140 g	150 g	190 g	200 g	240 ml
¾	105 g	113 g	143 g	150 g	180 ml
⅔	93 g	100 g	125 g	133 g	160 ml
½	70 g	75 g	95 g	100 g	120 ml
⅓	47 g	50 g	63 g	67 g	80 ml
¼	35 g	38 g	48 g	50 g	60 ml
⅛	18 g	19 g	24 g	25 g	30 ml

Index

R

S